A Short Guide to Brain Imaging

A Short Guide to Brain Imaging
The neuroscience of human cognition

Richard E. Passingham
Emeritus Professor of Cognitive Neuroscience,
Oxford University, UK

and

James B. Rowe
Professor of Cognitive Neurology,
Cambridge University, UK

OXFORD
UNIVERSITY PRESS

OXFORD
UNIVERSITY PRESS

Great Clarendon Street, Oxford, OX2 6DP,
United Kingdom

Oxford University Press is a department of the University of Oxford.
It furthers the University's objective of excellence in research, scholarship,
and education by publishing worldwide. Oxford is a registered trade mark of
Oxford University Press in the UK and in certain other countries

Published in the United States of America by Oxford University Press
198 Madison Avenue, New York, NY 10016, United States of America

British Library Cataloguing in Publication Data

Data available

Library of Congress Control Number: 2015937784

ISBN 978–0–19–870913–8

Printed in Great Britain by
Clays Ltd, St Ives plc

To our graduate students and postdocs.

Preface

Psychology is no longer just a matter of IQ tests, reaction times, and question-naires. Most departments of psychology now have access to an MRI scanner, and some now even call themselves departments of cognitive neuroscience. The aim of this book is to show how brain imaging can be used to advance a true neuroscience of human cognition.

It was written with several groups in mind: these include not only those who are starting out in imaging, but also those who have already acquired some expertise. If they are psychologists, they will have been taught how to do behavioral experiments, but may know little neuroanatomy or neurophysiology. If they are neurologists or psychiatrists, they will know their neuroanatomy and neurophysiology, but may not realize that there is an expertise to be acquired on how to carry out experiments on mental phenomena. If they are neurophysiologists, they will know how to record from neurons, but may need to be convinced that it is possible to use the vascular signals from fMRI for physiology.

A short book like this cannot be a substitute for handbooks on the physics, design, and statistical analysis of imaging experiments. We refer the reader to the best of these in the relevant chapters. Each major imaging center has its own materials to tell users how to process the data and interpret the images, and some of them also offer courses on the methods used. We could not hope to cover these issues in the detail needed for a proper understanding of the procedures involved in brain imaging. Nonetheless, since the methods are complex, we point the reader to the most common pitfalls.

The problem is that in some ways imaging has become too easy. The physicist takes care of the acquisition of the images and the MR technician runs the scanning session. The statistical analysis is carried out with a program such as SPM, AFNI or FSL, the activations are displayed using a program such as Freesurfer, and the anatomical areas can be identified using the probability maps from JuBrain. There are even scripts for automating the analysis from start to finish. The danger is that users either do not know, or forget, the basic principles, and are thus not in a position to interpret the results or exert quality control.

Though we call our book a "guide" it is not a technical manual. Instead it was written to convey a message. This is that those who use imaging should recognize that what they are doing is neuroscience. They are studying the brain, not colored pictures. It is only because the activations are shown on a computer screen that it has been possible to take a detached approach. We hope that this book will encourage the reader to look behind these beautiful images to think of the underlying cells and their connections.

We illustrate our message with imaging studies throughout the book. These are chosen to show how imaging can be used as a tool for neuroscience. We are aware that we cite our own studies and those of our colleagues more frequently than would an unbiased authority. We do so, not because we think they are the best studies, but because we know them best.

Style and terminology

When we use the term "brain imaging" without qualification we are referring to functional magnetic resonance imaging (fMRI).

We use the term "activations" when referring to positron emission tomography (PET) and fMRI because the signal is a vascular one rather than an electrical one. We reserve the term "activity" for electrical or magnetic signals.

We often refer to experiments that are carried out on macaque monkeys. Where we use the term "monkeys" alone, it is to macaque monkeys we are referring.

Editors insist that the term "subjects" is demeaning to those who volunteer to take part in psychological experiments. However, the term has the advantage that it can be used when describing both animal and human experiments.

Acknowledgments

We learned our trade together at the Functional Imaging Laboratory in London. This later became the Wellcome Trust Centre for NeuroImaging. It was founded by Richard Frackowiak to whom we and many others owe a great debt.

The first author started out in imaging at the MRC Cyclotron Unit at the Hammersmith Hospital in London. There he carried out studies using Positron Emission Tomography (PET) in collaboration with Richard Frackowiak and David Brooks. A group of us, including Chris Frith, Karl Friston, Ray Dolan, Cathy Price, and Eleanor Maguire then moved to the Functional Imaging Laboratory so as to carry out studies using functional magnetic resonance imaging (fMRI). We are grateful to each of these colleagues not only for collaborations, but also for inspiration.

The second author has since moved to the University of Cambridge Department of Clinical Neurosciences and the MRC Cognition and Brain Sciences Unit, Cambridge, working closely with the Behavioural and Clinical Neuroscience Institute. He is the Professor of Cognitive Neurology, a practicing neurologist as well as a neuroscientist.

Many people have helped us by reading drafts of particular chapters. We thank Richard Frackowiak, Karl Friston, Eleanor Maguire, Matthew Rushworth, Mark D'Esposito, Klaas Stephan, Nick Yeung, Bolton Chau, Andrew Bell, Nick Myers, Tim Behrens, and Heidi Johansen-Berg. Ingrid Johnsrude gave detailed comments on the whole book. We also thank Anita Butterworth for help in preparation of the figures.

We dedicate the book to our graduate students and postdocs, past and present. They are: John Aggleton, Ellemarije Altena, Sara Bengtsson, Pierre Burbaud, Tony Canavan, Johan Carlin, Jim Colebatch, Thomas Cope, Marie-Pierre Deiber, Henrik Ehrsson, Boyd Ghosh, Ian Gilchrist, Timothy Ham, Laura Hughes, Harry Jenkins, Markus Jeuptner, Louise Johns, Mike Krams, Clare Landsall, Hakwan Lau, Julian Macoveanu, David Nesbitt, Phil Nixon, Rosinda Oliveira, Christina Nombela-Otero, Luca Passamonti, Holly Phillips, Charlotte Rae, Narender Ramnani, Timothy Rittman, Matthew Rushworth, Katz Sakai, Saber Sami, Nat Schluter, David Thaler, Alessandro Tomassini, Ivan Toni, Kamen Tsvetanov, Noham Wolpe, Zheng Ye, and Jiaxiang Zhang.

Contents

List of Abbreviations

AFNI	analysis of functional neuroimages	MEG	magneto-encephalography
AIP	anterior inferior parietal	MMN	mismatch negativity
ANOVA	analysis of variance	MR	magnetic resonance
ASL	arterial spin labeling	MRI	magnetic resonance imaging
BA	Brodmann areas	MST	medial superior temporal area
BOLD	blood oxygenation level dependent		
$CMRO^2$	cerebral metabolic rate of oxygen	PET	positron emission tomography
CS	conditioned stimulus	PMv	ventral premotor cortex
CT	computed tomography	PPA	parahippocampal place area
DCM	dynamic causal modeling	PPI	psychophysiological interaction
DLPFC	dorsolateral prefrontal cortex	Pre-SMA	presupplementary motor area
DWI	diffusion weighted imaging	rCBF	regional cerebral blood flow
EEG	electro-encephalography	rTMS	repetitive transcranial magnetic brain stimulation
EPI	echo-planar imaging		
ERP	event-related potentials	SEM	structural equation modeling
FDR	false discovery rate		
FFA	fusiform face area	SMA	supplementary motor area
fMRI	functional magnetic resonance imaging	SPM	statistical parametric mapping
FMRIB	(functional magnetic resonance imaging of the brain) software	SQUIDS	superconducting quantum interference devices
FWHM	full width half maximum	STS	superior temporal sulcus
GLM	general linear model	TMS	transcranial magnetic brain stimulation
JuBrain Standard	brain atlas from Julich		
LIP	lateral intraparietal	UCS	unconditioned stimulus
LOC	lateral occipital complex	VIP	ventral intraparietal cortex

Chapter 1

The background

Abstract

Imaging is one of the major tools for neuroscience but it should be seen against the background of neuroscience in general. The brain can be studied by charting its connections, by recording its activity, or by intervening in its workings. In animals the connections can be demonstrated by tracer techniques, recordings can be taken of the activity of single cells, and lesions can be placed in selective cytoarchitectonic areas. Brain imaging provides methods for studying the human brain. Connections can be inferred using diffusion weighted imaging, activations can be recorded using functional magnetic resonance imaging, and transcranial magnetic brain stimulation can be used to intervene. The development of these methods has provided the means for studying the neural basis of cognitive abilities, including those that are unique to the human brain.

Keywords

brain lesions, Brodmann areas, cytoarchitecture, magnetic resonance imaging, diffusion weighted imaging, transcranial magnetic stimulation.

Introduction

There are three ways to study a system. You can chart its internal connections; you can take measurements while the system is active; and you can intervene in its workings and assess the effects.

Yet, it was only 20 years ago that Crick and Jones (1993) commented that we knew very little indeed about the connections of the human brain. Furthermore, for much of the last century the only measurements that could easily be taken from the active human brain were electro-encephalography (EEG) recordings, and before the invention of desktop computers these were simply sheets of papers to be read by eye. Traditionally, this left psychologists with only two ways of trying to understand the human brain: they could study the behavioral performance of the system when intact or when damaged.

In either case they sought to devise objective tests of perception, cognition, and action. By studying the performance of healthy subjects, psychologists could draw inferences about the transformations that occur from input to output, in other words from stimulus presentation to response. On this basis, computational models can be produced that account for this transformation; there are two such types of model. Symbolic models describe the components, the flow of information, and the rules of the system. Connectionist models describe the input/output transformations that are performed via a layered and interconnected set of units. The first type can be thought of as describing the operation of the overall network and the second as describing the operations that are performed by particular components of the system.

By studying the performance of subjects with brain damage, psychologists could try to draw inferences about the normal workings of the brain. Neuropsychologists test patients with tumors, strokes, or surgical resections. Their deductions rely in particular on noting dissociations. These could be disturbances in long- but not short-term memory, a failure to detect targets in contralateral but not ipsilateral space, or an inability to read words aloud while still having a general idea of the meaning. Observations of this sort allow inferences about memory, attention, and reading that are valid even if we do not know the exact location of the lesion.

But three developments have meant that we no longer need to speculate in the absence of direct information about the brain itself. The first is that computed tomography (CT) and magnetic resonance imaging (MRI) can be used to locate the site of the lesion. The second is that positron emission tomography (PET), functional magnetic resonance imaging (fMRI), EEG with computer analysis, and magneto-encephalography (MEG) can be used to take measurements of the brain at work, whether in healthy subjects or patients. The third is that diffusion weighted imaging (DWI) can be used to chart the general layout of the connections of the human brain. It is the aim of this book to show the reader how these and related methods can be used to establish the neuroscience of human cognition.

The effects of lesions

Before the advent of CT and MRI, the location and extent of the lesions in patients were assessed indirectly either from a surgeon's drawings or from X-rays showing the way in which the ventricles were distorted. The situation was transformed by the invention of tomographic methods. Tomography refers to the procedure by which a three-dimensional volume is reconstructed from a series of two-dimensional slices. For a detailed account of the principles involved in CT and MRI we refer the reader to Huettel et al. (2009). Since MRI has come to dominate human brain imaging research, we provide a brief summary of MRI basics in Box 1.1. Given that it is brief, it is necessarily written in technical language.

Now that it is possible to visualize lesions directly, it is clear that they are rarely discrete. Tumors cause pressure within the skull, or cut across the long-fiber tracts that traverse white matter, and this can disrupt the normal activity of other areas. Strokes deprive the gray matter of its blood supply but the underlying white matter also loses its blood supply. This matters because the white-matter

Box 1.1 MRI

The subject lies in a strong magnetic field, causing a net magnetization of the spins of hydrogen atoms. This magnetization initially aligns with the applied field. An oscillating radiofrequency pulse of the appropriate resonance frequency is then applied briefly to rotate this magnetization. As the magnetization returns to its original orientation, called "relaxation," a radiofrequency signal is emitted whose frequency depends on the magnetic field.

In order to make a 3-D image of the brain, magnetic field gradients are applied across the structure so that different places experience different magnetic fields, and therefore give signals with different frequencies and phases. So we can use the frequency and phase to determine which part of the signal is from which part of the brain. The unit measurement is a "voxel," analogous to a pixel in a 2-D image.

T1 (spin–lattice) weighted images depend on the relaxation of the longitudinal component of the net magnetization vector, that is the component aligned with the applied field. They are acquired by using short echo times (TE) and short repetition times (TR). In these images the cortex (gray matter) shows up as darker than white matter.

T2 (spin–spin) weighted images depend on the relaxation of the transverse component, that is the component perpendicular to the applied field. They are acquired using long echo times (TE) and long repetition times (TR). These images are useful for showing white matter lesions or cerebral edema.

T2 images are also used for diffusion weighted imaging (DWI), a technique for following fiber tracts that is described in Box 1.3.

fibers carry information between other areas, as well as to and from the lesioned area. This means that the behavioral impairment may also reflect the disruption to the activity of those distant areas. This is also true for the impairments that follow from surgical lobectomies or traumatic brain injury in which there is often shearing of the white-matter fibers.

There is a final problem that natural lesions do not obey the boundaries of the different cytoarchitectonic areas. It was Brodmann (1909) who first documented in detail the fact that the cortex is not uniform but is divided into different areas, each characterized by a different pattern of nerve cells. These can be visualized under a light microscope either by staining cortical sections for cell bodies (cytoarchitecture) or by staining them for the fibers within the cortex (myeloarchitecture). If the sections are inspected under the light microscope, different areas can be distinguished on the basis of the thickness of the cell layers, the density of the cells within them, and the types of cells that are present.

Figure 1.1 compares the cytoarchitecture of three neocortical areas in the brain of a macaque monkey, the primary visual cortex, primary motor cortex, and prefrontal association cortex. It will be seen that in primary sensory areas, layer IV is well developed. This is the inner granular layer, made up of small

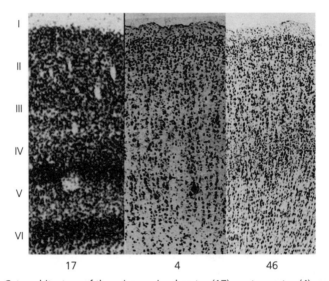

Fig. 1.1 Cytoarchitecture of the primary visual cortex (17), motor cortex (4), and prefrontal cortex (46). Numbers in Roman numerals denote the different cortical layers.

Adapted from Gerhardt von Bonin and Percival Bailey, The Neocortex of Macaca mulatta, Urbana: University of Illinois © 1947, University of Illinois.

granular or stellate cells, and it is to this layer that the sensory inputs are first relayed. The cortex is described as koniocortex after the Greek word "*konis*" meaning dust.

It can also be seen from Fig. 1.1 that the primary motor cortex lacks a layer IV, and is therefore said be agranular cortex. It is characterized by the presence of giant pyramidal cells, the Betz cells. These are particularly large because their axons reach to the spinal cord and there is a need for rapid transmission.

Association cortex is described as being "eulaminate" cortex, meaning that there is a relatively even development of all the layers. Whereas layer IV is missing in the motor and premotor cortex, the prefrontal cortex clearly differs in having a clear and continuous layer IV.

Brodmann (1909) allocated numbers to the different areas as distinguished on the basis of their cytoarchitecture. The original work was in German but it is available in an English translation (Garey, 2006). Some years later von Economo (1929) also studied the cytoarchitecture of the human brain, and he introduced a letter system to denote the different areas. One advantage is that letters can be combined to label intermediate areas. For example, in the inferior parietal lobe of the macaque monkey brain, area PFG is intermediate between area PG and area PF. It is now common to use numbers for some areas, for example, area 46 in the middle frontal gyrus, and letters for others, for example, TE for the inferior temporal cortex.

It is an advantage of such a labeling system that, in principle, equivalent areas can be identified across species. If the cytoarchitecture of a region in the human brain appears to be similar to that in a non-human brain, then the same label can be attached to suggest that they may be homologous. For example, Brodmann (1909) himself compared the human brain with that of an Old World monkey, the guenon, and he suggested that it was possible to identify many of the same areas in the two species. Later von Bonin and Bailey (1947) carried out a cytoarchitectonic analysis of the rhesus monkey, a species of macaque monkey. They adopted the lettering system of von Economo. More recently, Petrides and Pandya (2007) published their own map of the cytoarchitecture of the rhesus monkey brain, using numbers for some areas and letters for others. Figure 1.2 shows the complete map. It has become common in brain imaging studies to call the areas "Brodmann areas" (BA) irrespective of the system used.

In macaque monkeys, many of the boundaries between cytoarchitectonic areas occur in the depths of sulci or fissures. This means that it is possible to selectively remove particular areas. The surgery is performed with the use of an operating microscope so that one can distinguish the cortex from the underlying white matter and thus remove an area of cortex alone.

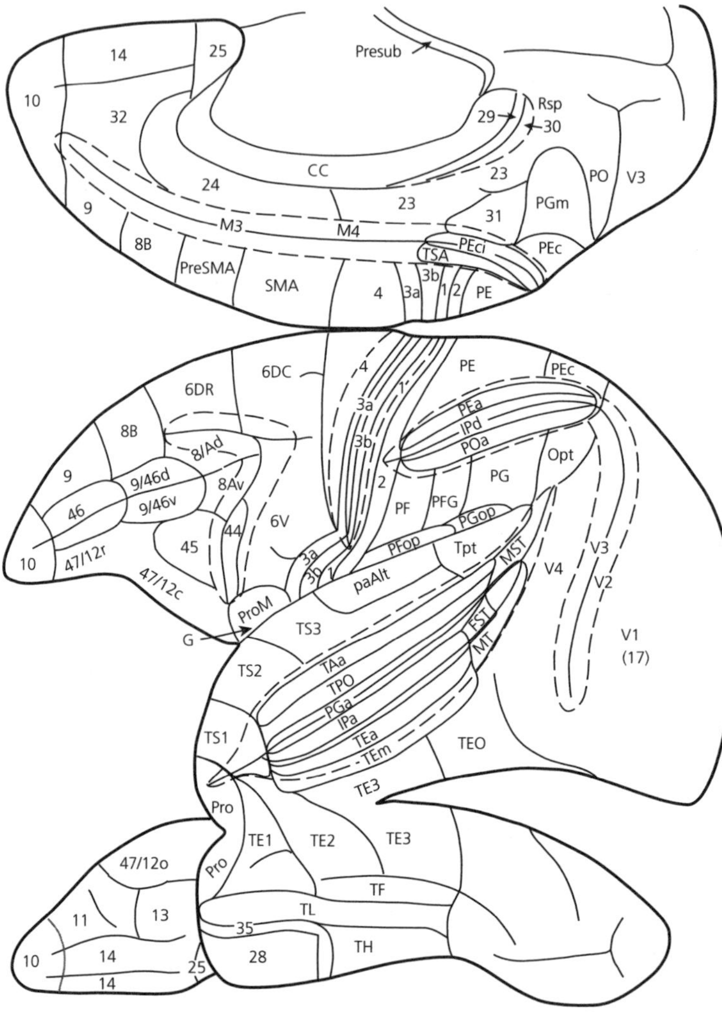

Fig. 1.2 Unfolded map of the neocortex in a macaque monkey.

Reproduced from Michael Petrides and Deepak N. Pandya, Efferent Association Pathways from the Rostral Prefrontal Cortex in the Macaque Monkey, Journal of Neuroscience, 27 (43), pp. 11573–11586; doi: 10.1523/JNEUROSCI.2419–07.2007 © 2007, The Society for Neuroscience.

Specific areas can also be experimentally lesioned using injections of selective neurotoxins such as ibotenic acid. These kill nerve cell bodies while leaving intact the myelinated nerve fibers that are passing through the tissue. The toxins do so by causing excitotoxic effects in which excessive stimulation of the cells leads to cell death. The fibers of passage are spared because there are no receptors on the fibers to take up the neurotoxin. Thus, in monkeys, though not in patients, it is possible to ensure that a lesion is discrete; that is to say, it is confined to the gray matter and to a particular area.

As in the case of studies with patients, the "double dissociation" is the gold standard for proving localization of function (Young et al., 2000). To give one example, monkeys can be tested on working memory tasks, and there are two ways of varying the difficulty of the task: one is to increase the delay between the presentation of the items and recall; and the other is to increase the number of items to be remembered at any one time. Monkeys with lesions in the inferotemporal cortex are impaired if the delay is increased but not if the number of items is increased; by contrast monkeys with lesions in the dorsal prefrontal cortex are impaired if the number of items is increased but not if the delay is increased (Petrides, 2000).

Chapter 4 will argue that the reason why it is possible to find dissociations of this sort is that the overall pattern of connections of each area is unique. It is an advantage of lesion studies in macaque monkeys that we have a very detailed map of these connections. Furthermore, lesions can be made that specifically target particular connections. For example, Browning and Gaffan (2008) cut a pathway in macaque monkeys that interconnects the anterior inferotemporal cortex with the ventral prefrontal cortex; the pathway is called the uncinate fascicle. It also exists in humans, but of course deliberate interventions of this sort are not permissible in the human brain, except in rare cases of surgery for intractable epilepsy. It is for this reason that our understanding of the human brain is still dependent in part on insights gained from studies of the brains of animals such as macaque monkeys.

However, though we cannot cut pathways in the human brain, the development of transcranial magnetic brain stimulation (TMS) has now given us a minimally invasive way of intervening deliberately with cortical activity, and thus for doing so in the human brain. For a detailed account of TMS we refer the reader to Wassermann et al. (2008). Box 1.2 provides a brief description of the method.

TMS and rTMS have proved of great value, and this will be documented in Chapter 7. However, there are two major limitations. One is that not all parts of the cortical surface are accessible by placing the coil over the skull. The other is that the strength of the pulses falls off with distance from the coil and this means they can fail to influence the cortex that is buried deep in sulci. For the same reason these techniques cannot be used for studying the functions of subcortical structures, such as the basal ganglia or amygdala. Given these limitations, these techniques cannot entirely replace studies of animals such as macaque monkeys.

Box 1.2 TMS and rTMS

A metal coil, shaped in a figure of eight or circle, is positioned over the scalp. The location is usually guided by a navigation device that allows the experimenter to view the position of the coil superimposed on the MRI scan of that subject.

The coil induces a brief magnetic pulse: this can be single, in pairs, or in a series of such pulses. The pulses influence the currents of the underlying cortical tissue. If a single pulse is applied (TMS), it can act to stimulate activity; for example, inducing the perception of a phosphene if applied over visual cortex or a muscle twitch if applied over motor cortex.

If a repetitive train of pulses (rTMS) is applied, it typically acts to disrupt the ongoing activity of the underlying cortex. The effects can be assessed in two ways.

First, if the train of pulses is applied *during* performance, it may cause an increase in reaction times. This is due to the short period of cortical disruption before normal activity is resumed.

Second, if the train of pulses is applied *before* performance, it may cause the subject to make errors. There are different techniques for achieving this. For example, one is to apply low-frequency rTMS pulses at 1 Hz for several minutes before testing, another to apply short bursts of rTMS pulses at the higher theta frequency. In either case there is a short time window of some minutes after the rTMS in which the activity of the cortex is abnormal (Di Lazzaro et al., 2008).

It is an advantage of applying rTMS before testing that the attention of the subject is not disrupted during performance by the noise, muscle, or skin sensations that occur during the operation of the coil or by muscle twitches caused by the stimulation if the coil is positioned near a muscle.

The wiring of the brain

Generalizations from the brains of other species depend on the assumption that the wiring of those brains is sufficiently similar to that of the human brain. For many years this assumption could not be tested, but the development of diffusion weighted imaging (DWI) has now made it possible to do so. We refer the reader to the book on diffusion imaging edited by Johansen-Berg and Behrens (2014) for details of the various methods. Box 1.3 gives a brief, though technical, account.

Box 1.3 Diffusion weighted imaging (DWI)

Water molecules in biological tissue are continually diffusing. The MRI signal can be sensitized to this movement.

As in standard MRI, the net magnetization of the spins of the hydrogen atoms aligns with the applied field. An oscillating radiofrequency pulse of the appropriate resonance frequency is then applied to rotate this alignment. In a diffusion imaging experiment, additional diffusion encoding gradients are added to vary the magnetic field along a particular direction in space, meaning that protons at different locations experience slightly different fields. Following a diffusion encoding gradient, a refocusing gradient is applied of the same magnitude but in the opposite direction. If a proton has moved between these two pulses, then it will not be completely refocused, resulting in a reduction in the signal due to the movement of the water.

Diffusion MRI provides measures of water diffusion along different directions in space. In tissue with a directionally oriented structure, such as a white-matter fiber bundle, water diffuses more easily along the axis of a fiber bundle than across it. This is due to the presence of physical barriers such as axon membranes and myelin sheaths, which hinder lateral diffusion across the axon.

Using diffusion MRI we can measure water diffusion along different directions in space and then fit a model to those measurements. For example, the diffusion tensor model allows us to estimate useful parameters describing diffusion at each point in space (a voxel) such as the magnitude of diffusion within the voxel and whether it is anisotropic. Anisotropy refers to the directional specificity of diffusion, in contrast to isotropy in which diffusion is identical in all directions.

In probabilistic tractography, the principal direction of the diffusion at each voxel is followed from one voxel to another, stepwise across the brain, so as to compute the most probable pathways from any given starting point (called the seed voxel).

There are many challenges for diffusion imaging, such as the fact that white-matter pathways can cut across each other; and sophisticated methods have been developed to deal with this issue (Wedeen et al., 2008). However, there are currently two overriding problems. These are that the axons cannot be visualized just as they leave the cortex in area A or as they penetrate the cortex in area B. Though improvements in spatial resolution make it possible to visualize fibers within the cortex (Song et al., 2014), they cannot yet be accurately distinguished at the gray/white-matter boundary. The danger is, therefore, that fibers of passage running under area A are mistaken for fibers that originate from, or terminate in, area A.

This problem can be avoided in experiments on animals by injecting tracers that are transported in vivo along the axons. Using this method, there are two ways of demonstrating that area A projects to area B. The first is to inject a tracer in area A: this is taken up by the cell bodies and is then transported in an anterograde direction to the terminals in area B. The second method is to inject a tracer in area B: this is taken up by the terminals in area B and is then transported in a retrograde direction to the cell bodies in area A. The location of the tracer can be identified in the histological material. The different tracers show up in different ways, for example, because they have a radioactive label, because they shine bright in fluorescent light, or because they promote reactions due to their property as an enzyme.

Unfortunately the same methods are not acceptable for studies of the human brain. It is true that a tracer is available that is visible to MRI because of its paramagnetic properties, so that the site to which the tracer is transported can be identified (Murayama et al., 2006). But it is not ethical to inject such a tracer into the brain of a human subject for research.

Nonetheless, the general accuracy of diffusion imaging can be checked by comparing the results with those obtained with tracers. Schmahmann et al. (2007) used a development of diffusion imaging to compare ten long association tracts in monkeys as visualized either by imaging or by the injection of radioactive tracers. These major tracts could be visualized with either method, and this acts as a preliminary validation for diffusion tractography.

Diffusion imaging can visualize tracts, but it is unlikely that it will ever reveal the detail available by using tracers. In one study alone, tracers were injected into 29 of the 91 cortical areas of the macaque monkey, and 1,615 connections between areas were described (Markov et al., 2011). Furthermore, in macaque monkeys tracers can be injected into specific layers so as to compare the internal connections of the different areas (Kritzer and Goldman-Rakic, 1995).

For the moment, therefore, we still need to depend on animal experiments for a very detailed knowledge of the wiring of the brain. This means that there is always the danger that there could be radical differences between the anatomy of the human brain compared with the brains of the chimpanzee or macaque monkey. Thus, we need to be clear what these might be.

It is unlikely that the basic unit of cortical computation, the cortical column (da Costa and Martin, 2010), has changed radically during the evolution of the human brain. Evolution is opportunistic, keeping what has worked well in the past.

Where we might expect differences is in the number of cortical areas and the way in which they are wired up. As brains get bigger there are pressures for regions to become subdivided so as to minimize the length of the wiring between cells with similar properties (Krubitzer and Huffman, 2000). Thus, there are many fewer cortical areas in a small monkey such as a marmoset than in a larger one such as a macaque (Kaas, 2007).

The same process has occurred in the evolution of the human brain. Take the parietal cortex as an example. The general organization of the human parietal cortex is as in the macaque brain, but there are more subareas (Caspers et al., 2006; Scheperjans et al., 2008). Furthermore, there has been some rearrangement of where particular functional areas are located. Rushworth et al. (2005) used diffusion imaging to chart the parts of the parietal cortex that are interconnected with the superior colliculus in the human brain. In macaque monkeys these are restricted to the inferior parietal cortex, including the ventral bank of the intraparietal sulcus. But in the human brain there are also collicular connections with the posterior part of the superior parietal cortex.

For these and other reasons, there are limits to the macaque monkey model (Passingham, 2009). Things would be improved if we had a detailed knowledge of the chimpanzee brain, but we do not since invasive procedures are not acceptable in the great apes, our closest ancestors. There is sometimes no alternative but to study the human brain itself, and its unique features: people are not simply big monkeys or even big chimpanzees.

There are many abilities of which only humans are capable, and that can therefore only be studied in people. Of these the most obvious is language. However, there are many other capacities that we believe to be unique to humans (Passingham, 2008). People can recall events or episodes from the past, re-experiencing them in the present, and they can imagine events far into the future (sometimes called mental time-travel). They can reflect on their own thoughts and on what others might be thinking or feeling (called a theory of mind). And they can control their own behavior so that it complies with the rules of their society, including legal or moral codes.

Functional brain imaging

The development of functional brain imaging has made it possible to study these abilities in the human brain. Since fMRI is non-invasive it has provided a vast impetus to research of this sort. At the time of writing there have been roughly 150,000 papers published using or referring to fMRI to study the brain.

Because the technique is non-invasive, it is now possible to carry out research on very large numbers of subjects. For example, the Human Connectome Project

(Van Essen et al., 2012) is collecting imaging data on 1,200 twins and their siblings, and the UK BioBank study is currently planning to include 100,000 subjects for MRI. A shared aim of these studies is to throw light on genetic factors that contribute to differences between individuals, in terms of brain structure and function.

The safety of the method also means that it is possible to study changes over time, as in child development. We do not know whether fMRI can cause subtle or long-term undesirable effects when the brain is very immature, but most centers now permit scanning of young children (Crone et al., 2009), while others may even scan *in utero*. This means that fMRI can be used to compare adolescents and adults (Cohen Kadosh et al., 2013) or even to study the transition of the same individuals through puberty (Klapwijk et al., 2013).

Similarly longitudinal studies can be carried out in old age. For example, Maguire et al. (2010) were able to study a patient as he developed semantic dementia. He was scanned three years running as his loss of knowledge set in. By the second year of study his semantic knowledge was partially preserved, but as well as decreases in activation, imaging could also detect increases elsewhere that were thought to reflect compensation.

The ability to repeat scans at different times also means that imaging can be used to study learning in the healthy brain and recovery after brain damage. For example, Floyer-Lea and Matthews (2004) used fMRI to compare the changes that occur when subjects learn a motor task in a single day with the changes that occur when the subjects are given daily practice over three weeks. Tomassini et al. (2012) have reviewed the use of fMRI to evaluate the potential of pharmacological interventions for promoting recovery in multiple sclerosis.

There is a final advantage of brain imaging. Whereas single-unit recordings are typically taken in animals in one or two selected brain regions, brain imaging can take measurements simultaneously over the whole brain. The brain is imaged while subjects perform tasks, and it is the whole brain, or more accurately the person, that carries out these tasks.

Given that one can visualize all the areas that are activated during a task, it is therefore possible to study the interactions between them. Chapter 6 will describe the concept of functional systems. These are made up of areas that are interconnected and that share similarities in their overall pattern of connections. This means that areas within such a system are more likely to interact with other areas in the same system than they are with areas in other functional systems.

If we are to understand how the brain works as a whole, we need to understand these interactions. It turns out that fMRI can detect slow fluctuations in the BOLD signal, either when the subject is resting or when the subject is performing a task (Raichle and Snyder, 2007). Functional systems can therefore be identified by the fact that areas within the system show positive covariance in their fluctuations; and different systems can be distinguished because areas in different systems fail to covary in this way (Dosenbach et al., 2007).

The same point is sometimes made by pointing out that the use of imaging can be extended beyond "brain mapping" or "functional specialization" to study distributed processing or "functional integration" (Friston, 2002). It is the single greatest advantage of imaging that it allows us to visualize the simultaneous workings of the integrated brain.

How to use brain imaging

It is the aim of this book to encourage those who carry out experiments with brain imaging to use it to explain mental phenomena, rather than simply to give functional labels to brain areas. Suppose that you are trying to understand the engine of a car. Of course, the first step must be to name the individual parts and find out what they do: the distributor distributes the fuel and the spark plugs ignite it. But the next step is to chart the layout of the system: the pistons are connected to the camshaft. And the final step is to work out the timing of events and how each part influences the other parts with which it is connected: the pistons work in a four-stroke cycle and the camshaft turns the alternator via the timing belt.

A car is a simple mechanical system, but the human brain is a vastly complex system. It has an estimated 10^{10} neurons, with some cells having over 25,000 synapses on them; and there are an uncounted number of interconnections between the different brain areas. It is also a biological system, one that was produced by evolution and that develops during life. Finally, it is a plastic system, one that adapts to life events via learning.

One way of trying to make progress is to study simpler systems, recording from "place cells" in the hippocampus of rodents (Burgess et al., 2005) or from the parietal cells of macaque monkeys while they make perceptual decisions about the direction of motion (Huk and Shadlen, 2005). However, recording is not enough. The empirical data need to be used to devise computational models of how navigation occurs (Penny et al., 2013) or decisions are made (Wong et al., 2007).

But if the aim of those studies is to help us to understand human brains, basic information is needed about the human brain itself. This book sets out how imaging can be used to provide that information. Diffusion imaging can be used to chart the connections, the layout of the system. PET and fMRI can be used to investigate the functions of the different areas and, in combination with

EEG and MEG, can be used to measure the interactions between them. Finally, TMS can be used to intervene so as to demonstrate causal influence within the system.

As in the case of the animal experiments, the empirical data need to be used to inform theoretical and computational models of how the system works. We need simulations both of how particular operations might be carried out and of how networks might work together, even if these simulations are greatly oversimplified. Imaging can then be used to see if it is possible to find activity that relates to particular terms in the model.

Summary

Imaging is just one of the methods of systems neuroscience. This chapter therefore places it firmly within anatomy and physiology. It emphasizes the importance of cytoarchitectonic differences as the basis for distinguishing between brain areas. It also says what can and cannot be achieved by studying macaque monkeys. A major limitation is that there are some abilities that are unique to humans.

The development of brain imaging has provided the means for studying these abilities. In this book the term "imaging" is used broadly to cover PET, MRI, fMRI, diffusion imaging, EEG, MEG, and even transcranial magnetic stimulation because MRI is used to navigate the coil. The methods of fMRI, PET, EEG, and MEG are alike in being whole brain methods, and this means that they can be used to visualize functional systems and the interactions between areas within those systems. To understand how the human brain supports complex cognition we need to know not only what transformations are performed by the individual areas, but also how the areas work together in systems. However, in order to make the problems tractable we need to produce computational models of how these systems work. Imaging can then be used to test the models and to measure their parameters.

Chapter 2

The signal

Abstract

Whatever brain imaging method is used, it is essential to understand the nature of the measurement that is taken. Positron emission tomography (PET) and functional magnetic resonance imaging (fMRI) record the activity of the brain indirectly. PET measures blood flow and fMRI measures the blood oxygenation level dependent signal (BOLD). The spatial and temporal resolution of these methods is therefore constrained by the fact that the signal is a vascular one. The spatial resolution is fully adequate for studying functional localization; but the temporal resolution is not adequate for studying the order of events in different brain areas. To do this it is necessary to use either electro-encephalography (EEG) or magneto-encephalography (MEG). However, though the temporal resolution of these methods is in milliseconds, the spatial resolution is of the order of a centimeter. Given the advantages and disadvantages of the different methods, it can help to combine fMRI with EEG or to carry out experiments in parallel using both fMRI and MEG.

Keywords

positron emission tomography, functional magnetic resonance imaging, the BOLD signal, spatial resolution, temporal resolution, electro-encephalography, magneto-encephalography, the inverse problem.

Introduction

The signal that is recorded by functional MRI (fMRI) is not a direct measure of cell activity. It measures the oxygenation of blood, not electricity. Although the electrical and metabolic activity of brain cells is closely related to the flow of blood and its oxygenation, it is important to understand the difference in order to design and interpret fMRI experiments. For example, the neurons themselves discharge with millisecond timing, whereas the fMRI signal unfolds nearby and over many seconds.

Brain cells are measured in microns, and so to record their individual firing it is necessary to insert microelectrodes. The procedure is painless because there are no pain fibers in the brain itself. Recordings are typically made in the brains of animals, in particular, rats and monkeys, but it is also possible to insert microelectrodes into the brain of human patients during surgery (Mukamel and Fried, 2012). Since the recordings can be made while the subjects are awake and performing tasks, it is feasible to relate the firing of individual cells to aspects of that task.

One way to do this is to characterize the tuning properties of each cell. A tuning curve plots the degree of activity that is evoked by different stimuli or that occurs during different cognitive states or movements. For example, cells in the motor cortex of macaque monkeys have directional tuning. None of the individual cells have tuning properties that specify the direction of movement with the precision of which the animal is capable. But if the tuning curves from all of the task-related neurons are combined, the population can specify each of these directions precisely (Georgopoulos et al., 1986).

Since it is the local population of cells that performs a particular operation, means are needed for identifying that operation at the population level. Brain imaging, whether by PET and fMRI or by EEG and MEG, offers the ability to do this non-invasively in the human brain. Each of these methods records in a different way, and thus they differ in the advantages that they offer.

Positron emission tomography (PET)

Both PET and fMRI are most commonly used to measure the perfusion of the brain. The principle on which they are based is that when neurons become active they need glucose and oxygen, and these are supplied by a local and short-term increase in the arterial blood supply. The local uptake was first firmly established by injecting deoxyglucose into the brains of rats, and showing that it was taken up in areas in which there was an increase in neuronal activity (Kennedy et al., 1974). Because, unlike glucose, deoxyglucose is not fully metabolized, it remains at the sites of uptake. The presence of the deoxyglucose can be detected in histological slices because a radioactive carbon label, ^{14}C, is attached.

Early human studies visualized the flow of blood by using radioactive ^{133}xenon as a label (Sveinsdottir et al., 1971). With an array of 32 detectors, two-dimensional pictures could be produced that used a color scale to show where there were increases in regional blood flow. PET came later with the development of new labels; tomography also made it possible to show the brain activity in three dimensions (Phelps et al., 1976).

PET can measure the uptake of deoxyglucose because this can be attached to a fluorine label (^{18}F) that emits positrons. The way in which these are detected is briefly described in Box 2.1. We refer the reader to the edited volume by Wahl and Beanlands (2008) for a more detailed account of PET and its applications.

The half-life of ^{18}F-fluorodeoxyglucose (^{18}F-FDG) is 110 minutes. This means that it is feasible to present tasks outside the scanner and then study the results afterwards in the scanner. This has its advantages. One is that the scanner environment is very restrictive and there are tasks that are not practical to present in the scanner. For example, the subjects may need to stand or make large movements with their head. One experiment investigated the vestibular system and so the subjects had to tilt their head (Becker-Bense et al., 2012). Labeled FDG was injected while the subjects did this outside the scanner, and the subjects were then scanned so that the uptake of FDG could be visualized.

The long half-life of ^{18}F-FDG also means that it is practical to scan animals. For example, the behavioral tasks or conditions can be presented before scanning but after the injection. The animals can then be scanned subsequently with PET while anesthetized. This technique has allowed comparisons to be made between scans taken from chimpanzees and scans taken from human subjects (Rilling, 2014).

Box 2.1 PET

A short-lived radiotracer isotope is incorporated into a biologically active molecule or water. One example is the incorporation of an ^{18}fluorine label into deoxyglucose so as to produce ^{18}F-fluorodeoxyglucose or ^{18}F-FDG. This is injected into the blood supply and circulates to the brain.

The tracer undergoes positron emission decay or positive beta decay. This decay can be detected because when a positron meets an electron, there is an annihilation reaction with the simultaneous emission of two photons at 180 degrees to each other.

A ring of detectors around the head measure this emission, by counting the number of times that photons arrive simultaneously at opposite positions in the array. The rate of these counts provides a measure of the concentration of the label at that location.

From the statistics of these coincidence events it is possible to reconstruct the accumulation of radioactivity at particular locations. This is an indirect measure of neuronal activity at those sites. If the PET image is co-registered with either a CT scan or an MRI scan, the locations can be identified accurately on the brain.

The long half-life is, however, a disadvantage for many psychological experiments. The reason is that it is often essential to present several tasks in a session, including experimental and control conditions; but the long-lasting label would give only one measure. However an isotope of oxygen, ^{15}O, has a half-life of roughly two minutes. By infusing $H_2^{15}O$, PET can be used to give a direct measure of regional cerebral blood flow (rCBF), and independent measurements can be made if they are taken some minutes apart. Even within the approved radiation exposure limits, it is practical to present up to twelve conditions in one session. A typical session might involve three runs of three different experimental conditions together with three runs of a control condition.

Whatever label is used, the PET method involves exposing the subjects to radiation. This is generally not acceptable if the subjects are women who might be pregnant or if they are children. The development of fMRI means that there is usually no need for PET for standard activation studies.

But this does not mean that there is now no use for PET. For example, it can be used to measure energy metabolism, as in the extraction of oxygen in hypoxia (Gaertner et al., 2012). And it can be used to study the role of specific receptors in health and disease. For example, ligands are available to study dopamine receptors in Parkinson's disease (Brooks and Pavese, 2011), as well as the 5-HT receptor in early schizophrenia (Hurlemann et al., 2008). PET continues to play an important role in studying the brain, alone and in combination with MRI (Siebner et al., 2014).

The BOLD contrast

It became possible to use MRI for functional brain imaging when it was shown that it was sensitive to the blood oxygenation level dependent (BOLD) signal (Ogawa et al., 1993). We refer readers to Huettel et al. (2009) for a detailed account. The nature of the BOLD signal is briefly explained in Box 2.2.

One cannot simply assume that the BOLD signal will give the same results as the PET measure of rCBF. The reason is that the transformation from rCBF to BOLD is non-linear (Mechelli et al., 2001). However, fMRI can also be used to measure local blood perfusion directly via the method of arterial spin labeling (ASL). One study compared perfusion, as measured by ASL, with the contrast agent gadolinium, timing its passage through brain areas (White et al., 2014). The two methods gave similar estimates. Another study compared blood flow as measured by ASL with measures of hemoglobin as assessed by near infra-red spectroscopy. As expected, flow as assessed by ASL related most closely to the total hemoglobin and oxyhemoglobin (Huppert et al., 2006).

Box 2.2 The BOLD signal

This signal relates to changes in the ratio of oxygenated to de-oxygenated blood. It resembles the oxygen extraction ratio that one can obtain with PET imaging, modified by local changes in blood flow and volume. The change in oxygenation ratio can be detected because de-oxyhemoglobin is paramagnetic. There is an increase in the MR signal with an increase in oxygenated blood and a decrease in the MR signal with an increase in deoxygenated blood.

The BOLD signal depends on $T2^*$ loss of magnetization. $T2^*$ is a time constant characterized by the combined effects of spin–spin interactions and field inhomogeneity. Because paramagnetic substances distort the surrounding magnetic field, the hydrogen protons experience different field strengths and thus there is a more rapid decay of the transverse magnetization $(T2^*)$.

If the BOLD signal is measured at the same time as near infra-red spectroscopy, it turns out that the signal is most closely related to the spectroscopic measure of de-oxyhemoglobin, as predicted on theoretical grounds (Huppert et al., 2006).

The standard sequence for acquiring the data is EPI (echo-planar imaging). Instead of measuring just one echo after each radiofrequency pulse, many echoes are measured. Typically, a slice of brain 2–5 millimeters thick can be imaged in 40–150 milliseconds, and therefore the whole brain in 1–3 seconds.

Whereas the PET signal is quantifiable in absolute units, since it is calibrated with a standard radioactive source, there is no such absolute unit with fMRI, and researchers rely on the detection of change in response to task events.

Although fMRI can be used to measure rCBF, there are disadvantages to ASL as a method. The signal to noise is less than BOLD–EPI based fMRI, so acquisition times are longer. Also, only part of the brain can be scanned at any one time and the image resolution is slightly worse. For these reasons most psychological studies measure the BOLD signal instead.

It is important to have some idea of the basic data that are gathered. The plots of the BOLD signal that come out of the analysis may appear smooth and clean. They are like the event-related potentials that emerge from electrophysiological experiments. But these plots result from averaging across many trials and across subjects.

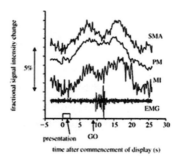

Fig. 2.1 BOLD signals for the motor cortex (MI), premotor cortex (PM), and supplementary motor area (SMA) on a go/no-go task.

Reproduced from Kaamil Ugurbil, Xiaoping Hu, Wei Chen, Xiao-Hong Zhu, Seong-Gi Kim and Apostolos Georgopoulos, Functional mapping in the human brain using high magnetic fields, Philosophical Transactions of the Royal Society B: Biological Sciences, 354, p. 1199, Figure 3 (c) 1999, The Royal Society.

Figure 2.1 shows the BOLD signal for a single subject and a single trial. The data were recorded in the motor cortex, premotor cortex, and supplementary motor area (SMA) (Ugurbil et al., 1999). The scans were performed with a magnetic strength of 4 Tesla. It is, of course, because the plots are noisy that the data are usually smoothed by averaging. However, the data are not only noisy but also highly variable from person to person and area to area (Handwerker et al., 2004).

The shape of the BOLD signal

Figure 2.2 illustrates the BOLD signal as recorded in visual cortex (Siero et al., 2014a).

The scans were performed with a magnetic field strength of 7 Tesla. The data are again for a single subject, but in this case the data are averaged across trials. Three curves are shown because the spatial resolution is such that the signal can be recorded from different depths within the cortex. Region 1 corresponds to layer 1, region 2 to the middle layers, and region 3 to the deep layers.

The fMRI signal can be visualized in one of several ways. One is to simply plot the "adjusted data," averaged over trials and corrected for motion artifacts or low-frequency drifts. Another is to show the "fitted" data, according to a model of the BOLD response. One can use a continuous set of impulse functions or one can use a set of Fourier basis functions, the advantage being that the shape of the BOLD response can be very flexible. However, the most common method is to fit a standard or canonical hemodynamic response function that is a close approximation to a "typical" time course, often with temporal and dispersion

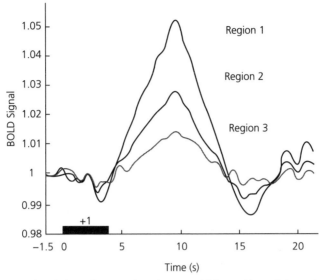

Fig. 2.2 BOLD signals from three sections (upper, middle, and lower) through the visual cortex. Black block = visual stimulation.

Reproduced from Jeroen C.W. Siero, Jeroen Hendrikse, Hans Hoogduin, Natalia Petridou, Peter Luijten, and Manus J. Donahue, Cortical depth dependence of the BOLD initial dip and poststimulus undershoot in human visual cortex at 7 Tesla, Magnetic Resonance in Medicine, Figure 4a, DOI: 10.1002/mrm.25349 Copyright © 2014 Wiley Periodicals, Inc.

derivatives that provide some variation in timing and shape. We refer the reader to Henson and Friston (2006) for a technical account of these methods.

The exact shape of the signal and the time for which it persists depend on several factors. The first is the method used to record it. If the measurements are taken from superficial gray matter, an initial negative dip is detectable at high field strengths (Fig. 2.2). The explanation of this dip is that there is an increase in oxygen consumption immediately after the event, and this precedes the increase in rCBF (Silva et al., 2000; Shen et al., 2008). The dip is either smaller or undetectable if measurements are taken at lower layers within the cortex (Fig. 2.2).

There is then a positive rise that typically reaches a peak 5 seconds after the stimulation. In Fig. 2.2 the presentation of a checker-board pattern is shown by a black block on the abscissa. The positive phase reflects the fact that after an event the local blood flow overcompensates for the increased demand for oxygen that arises from locally increased neural activity. This was first demonstrated using PET (Fox and Raichle, 1986). The positive phase persists for many seconds, but the exact time depends on whether the stimulation is phasic or continuous. In Fig. 2.2 the positive phase lasts for roughly 10 seconds.

The positive phase may then be followed by a brief undershoot. This can be seen most clearly in the plot for the superficial gray matter in Fig. 2.2. The undershoot is either smaller or not present at lower layers.

It is also possible to record a negative BOLD signal, which is a signal in which there is a prolonged negative rather than positive phase. There has been controversy over how a negative BOLD signal is generated and even whether it is of vascular origin. However, there is now an emerging consensus that the main contributor to negative BOLD is a decrease in cerebral blood flow and oxygen extraction ($CMRO^2$) (Huber et al., 2014).

The spatial resolution of the BOLD signal

In a typical fMRI experiment using a 3 Tesla scanner the activations, as measured by the positive BOLD signal, are represented in small tissue volumes measuring $3 \times 3 \times 3$ millimeters. As already mentioned, these volumes are referred to as voxels. This means that the spatial resolution is well within the limits of the volume of the different cytoarchitectonic areas. Thus, the standard spatial resolution is just what is required for asking questions about the functions of the different areas. It is true that within any voxels there are very many thousands of cells, but it is the population as a whole that performs the particular transformation.

No one pretends that recording at this level will enable us to work out how the individual cells in an area operate together so as to perform that transformation. To do this it is necessary to record from individual cells or groups of cells and to combine the results so as to calculate the population code. And it is perhaps for this reason that many of those who record from cells have too often shown a lack of interest in the results that can be obtained from brain imaging.

But in truth, single-unit physiologists sometimes also make statements about the *function* of the area in which they are recording. For example, the results of recording in prefrontal cortex have been said to support the view that the area is involved in working memory (Funahashi et al., 1989) or numerical coding (Nieder et al., 2002). Yet fMRI provides an equally powerful method for checking whether this is so.

If a finer spatial resolution is required, it can be achieved by using magnets of greater signal strength. Figure 2.2 illustrates the fact that it is possible to distinguish between the BOLD signals at three different depths through the cortex. Currently it is possible to achieve an fMRI voxel size of smaller than one millimeter by recording at 7 Tesla (Siero et al., 2014b), but this resolution is steadily falling with time. The thickness of the primary visual cortex averages 1.8 millimeters (Jiang et al., 2009), but most cortical areas are much thicker, with a mean of roughly 2.5 millimeters, and a range extending up to 4 millimeters (Fischl and Dale, 2000).

Thus, it is worth considering what questions can be answered as the spatial resolution improves. As already mentioned, it is already possible to distinguish the contribution to the BOLD signal at the sublayer level. Thus, Huber et al. (2014) have been able to show that for tasks in which there are positive activations, the BOLD response peaks at the cortical surface, but that for tasks in which there is a negative BOLD response the maximum response is in the deeper layers. And Shmuel et al. (2010) have been able to visualize the ocular dominance columns in the primary visual cortex.

However, the most exciting prospect concerns the functional organization within association areas. Functional patches have been demonstrated in the temporal and prefrontal association cortex. Wang et al. (1998) first recorded from cells in the inferotemporal cortex of macaque monkeys so as to find out what stimuli were optimal for driving the cells. They then presented stimuli with these features during optical imaging. The size of a functional patch was of the order of half a millimeter in diameter. In the prefrontal cortex of macaque monkeys, the full half hemispace is represented by a series of patches that are of roughly a third of a millimeter. Within these patches, pairs of cells can be found with tight correlations between their firing (Constantinidis et al., 2001). Thus, the best spatial resolution that can now be achieved at 7 Tesla is of the order of a functional patch.

So as to study functional organization in the human brain, Haxby et al. (2014) scanned with fMRI. They found that in the neocortex there are a large number of features that can be coded for in high dimensional representations, and that these representations repeat across cortical areas. This discovery depends on two techniques. The first is the introduction of a novel method for aligning the images of different subjects, based on function as well as anatomy. The second is the use of multivariate pattern analysis to discover what features are being coded for. These techniques will be explained in Chapters 3 and 6.

The temporal resolution of the BOLD signal

While the spatial resolution of the BOLD signal is more than adequate for functional studies, the temporal resolution is not. The reason is not related to the noise in the signal. It is possible to distinguish the time of the responses in two different conditions if the latencies differ by around 200 milliseconds (Friston et al., 1998). This can be done by measuring the difference in time at which the positive rise reaches half its maximum height.

The problem is that this method is only valid when comparing BOLD responses for two conditions *within* the same area. The reason is that there is a potential confound if the comparison is made *between* areas. This is that the size and shape of the responses can vary across areas (Handwerker et al., 2004) because of differences in the vascular bed. This has been shown in two ways. First, the ratio of blood flow to the metabolic rate of oxygen consumption $CMRO^2$ has been shown to differ between regions (Chiarelli et al., 2007). Second, the relation of the BOLD response to activity evoked by electrical stimulation is not the same in all the areas in which activations are found (Sloan et al., 2010).

Thus, if comparisons are to be made between the timing of activations in different areas, it is essential to control for possible differences in vasculature. Weilke et al. (2001) compared two conditions. In one the subjects made movements in response to an external cue and in this condition there was no statistical difference in latency between activation in the pre-supplementary motor area (Pre-SMA) and motor cortex. In the experimental condition the subjects initiated the movements on their own and in this condition the activation of the Pre-SMA occurred earlier than that of the motor cortex. This could not be due to differences in the vascular bed because that would have produced similar differences in the control condition.

The relation of the BOLD signal to cell activity

As explained in previous sections, the BOLD signal is an indirect measure of blood flow. Though it is clear that blood flow increases when neurons become active, it is less clear what aspect of that activity relates most closely to the BOLD signal. The way to find out is to measure the BOLD signal at the same time as recording from cells with microelectrodes. In an influential paper, Logothetis and Wandell (2004) reviewed what has been established both in their own and other laboratories. The results do not appear to differ greatly whether the animals are or are not anesthetized (Goense et al., 2008). The conclusions are summarized in Box 2.3.

Logothetis and Wandell (2004) have proposed that the BOLD signal reflects most closely changes in the local field potentials. These potentials reflect the summation of the dendritic synaptic activity of all the cells within the volume of tissue from which the recording is taken. To record these, the high frequencies are filtered out so as to remove the effects of action potentials. The remaining signal, the local field potential, can then be decomposed like the EEG into non-overlapping frequency bands. These are alpha (9–12 Hz), beta (13–30 Hz), and gamma (31–100 Hz). Magri et al. (2012) recorded BOLD and local field potentials simultaneously in anesthetized macaque monkeys,

Box 2.3 The BOLD signal and cell activity

In studies of the visual cortex of macaque monkeys, the BOLD signal appears to be related more closely to local field potentials than to the spiking activity of single cells (Goense et al., 2008). However, it is not the correlations that are critical. The key observation is that it is possible to record the BOLD signal in the absence of significant spiking activity, and also to record spiking activity without BOLD. This has been demonstrated in three ways.

First, it has been shown that in visual cortex there can be transient multi-unit activity that rapidly returns to baseline, whereas both the BOLD signal and local field potentials continue on (Goense et al., 2008).

Second, if a 5-HT1A agonist is injected into visual cortex, the multi-unit activity is greatly reduced, whereas there is no significant change in either the BOLD signal or the local field potentials (Rauch et al., 2008).

Third, if bicuculline is applied so as to increase the spiking output of the Purkinje cells in the cerebellum, there can be large increases in firing without any change in the rCBF (Thomsen et al., 2009).

Given these results, Logothetis (2008) has argued that the BOLD signal reflects most closely the fluctuations in the post-synaptic polarizations, which may or may not cause action potentials. It is likely that the signal is most sensitive to these fluctuations in cortical pyramidal cells. Local field potentials are less sensitive to depolarization in inter-neurons because these are variable in layout. The contribution of inter-neurons to the local field potentials can therefore be cancelled out.

and found that it was the gamma band that was most informative about the BOLD signal. However, the amplitude of the signal was also dependent on the relation between alpha and gamma power, and the latency on the relation between beta and gamma power.

Given that BOLD relates to the summed dendritic activity, it is therefore sensitive to modulatory effects on the post-synaptic cell. Direct evidence that the BOLD signal reflects modulatory effects comes from an experiment that used a perceptual manipulation called "generalized flash suppression." When moving dots appear abruptly around a visual target stimulus, they suppress the perception of that stimulus. The critical observation is that when cell activity was recorded in the visual cortex of a macaque monkey, there was no change in the spiking activity during suppression; yet there was an effect on the BOLD signal (Maier et al., 2008). This can be explained either by inhibitory synaptic inputs or by excitatory inputs that are below the threshold for driving cell activity.

The fact that the BOLD signal can reflect modulatory effects has proved useful for studies of the interactions between activations in different brain areas. In particular, top-down effects operate via feedback paths and there are suggestions that these paths have modulatory effects (Shipp, 2005). An example is the enhancement of activations in posterior areas as the result of goal-directed attention (Corbetta and Shulman, 2002). Chapter 6 considers these effects in more detail.

EEG and MEG

Whatever the relation between the BOLD signal and cell activity, it is necessarily indirect because it is vascular events that are measured. EEG and MEG record cellular events directly, and this means that they score in terms of temporal resolution. EEG records electrical activity by electrodes on the scalp or occasionally at the cortical surface; these are macro-electrodes, very much larger than those that are used for single cell recordings. MEG records the magnetic fields that are associated with this electrical activity. MEG uses superconducting quantum interference devices (SQUIDS) to detect the minute magnetic signals. We refer the reader to Sanei (2013) for a full account of how the recordings are made and analyzed.

The magnetic signals that are detected by MEG are generated perpendicular to the electrical signals. This means that MEG is particularly sensitive to signals from the pyramidal cells as they lie in sulci, even though the MEG signals rapidly decay with distance from the SQUID detectors. For this reason it can be helpful to carry out the same experiment with both MEG and EEG simultaneously so as to be most sensitive to cortical signals from one or other method.

Both methods can be said to measure brain "activity." However, the relationship of the signals to that activity is complex. It has been suggested that the EEG signal relates most closely to the extra-cellular activity caused by dendritic potentials and that the MEG signal to the intra-cellular activity caused by ionic currents (Buszaki, 2006). Claims of this sort can only be properly tested by measuring these signals at the same time as recording directly from the cells themselves.

Irrespective of the source of the signals, they have the advantage that they are recorded on a millisecond time base. This means that they can be used to record the order of events in the brain. One might think this implausible since the delays at the synapse are of the order of 2 milliseconds. However, any one area may take time to process the incoming information, perhaps involving the synchronizing of subpopulations of cells within the area. Furthermore, if communication between areas depends on the synchronization between the input and output cells, this too may take time.

In fact we have evidence for these delays. Hari et al. (2010) review studies that they have carried out using MEG in which they were able to follow the signals as they progressed across areas. In one study, for example, the subjects were presented with faces and required to copy the facial expression. The activity in the visual, temporal, parietal, and premotor cortex occurred at different times in succession: the delays between activation of successive areas varied from 20 to 90 milliseconds.

Oscillations

Whether recorded with EEG or MEG, the signals show periodic oscillations, and these can be separated into different frequency bands. By recording the EEG at the same time as multi-unit activity in animals, it has been shown that the relationship of the EEG to multi-unit activity is closest when there is an increase in the EEG power in the gamma band (Whittingstall and Logothetis, 2009). The variable amplitude of the gamma band has also been proposed to be the closest EEG correlate of the BOLD response (Scheeringa et al., 2011).

The relation between the power of the different spectral bands and cognitive operations has been studied by recording from an array of electrodes implanted intracranially in patients with epilepsy (Lachaux et al., 2012). These intracranial EEG recordings reveal high-frequency activity from 40 to 150 Hz. Different perceptual and cognitive operations are associated with different frequencies. For example, during reading there are differences in the mean frequencies for the visual, phonological, and semantic responses.

It is likely that the fluctuations in the gamma band serve an essential role in synchronizing activity within and between brain areas (Nikolic et al., 2013). It has been proposed that the effective communication between cells depends on coherence between their fluctuations in the gamma band (Fries, 2009). Maris et al. (2013) recorded local field potentials in macaque monkeys. The recordings were taken from pairs of sites *within* one area, the secondary visual area V4. The phase relation between different site pairs was influenced both by the presentation of visual stimuli and by the direction of attention. Roberts et al. (2013) recorded simultaneously in monkeys from sites in *different* but connected areas, the visual areas V1 and V2; and there was strong coherence between pairs when high-contrast gratings were presented.

It will be clear that, though it is possible to record slow fluctuations of the BOLD signal, a critical element of information processing is missed if all that is recorded is the amplitude of a signal and not its spectral components. For this reason, EEG and MEG are essential tools for studying the mechanisms via which the brain operates.

Combined use of fMRI and EEG or MEG

This does not mean that fMRI no longer has a place. This is because there is a fundamental problem in accurately localizing the source of the signals that are recorded by EEG and MEG. The localization requires a solution to the inverse problem of converting observed measurements into information about the brain itself. As explained in Box 2.4, the problem is that there is no single "correct" solution. We refer the reader to Henson et al. (2011) for a technical treatment of the issue.

The spatial resolution that can be achieved with EEG and MEG is of the order of a centimeter (Barkley, 2004). However, it remains to be established to what extent sources can be pinpointed from deep structures. Some success has been had in identifying the basal ganglia as a source (Attal et al., 2007), but it is as yet unclear what other deep signals can be resolved.

Box 2.4 The inverse problem

Inverse problems involve relating a set of observations to parameters of the system, whereas forward problems involve relating parameters of the system to observations.

The problem with localizing the brain sources that could account for any observations made with EEG or MEG is that there are many possible solutions. However, there are several ways of cutting down this number given prior knowledge about the brain. We mention several common solutions here.

The first is that the sources must lie in gray matter. Thus, if an MRI scan is taken for each subject, solutions are only acceptable if they suggest sources in gray matter (Dale and Sereno, 1993).

The second is that the orientation of the signals with respect to the cortical surface is known both for EEG and MEG. This orientation can be imposed on local patches of cortex.

The third is that, if the subjects are scanned with fMRI as well as with either EEG or MEG, the location of the signals in fMRI can be used to constrain the localization of the sources. This is not foolproof, however, since the MEG/EEG signals and BOLD–fMRI are sensitive to different neuronal populations and activity patterns.

Finally, one can impose regularization or smoothness on the solution, for example, by modeling that one area of the brain has properties that are similar to its close neighbors; this is a robust but inherently low-resolution solution. Alternatively, the model can assume that the activity is greater than in other regions, as in beamformer analyses.

Thus, an obvious strategy is to capitalize on the strengths of EEG and fMRI by carrying out the same experiment with both. It is now possible to record EEG in the fMRI scanner (Huster et al., 2012) and this has the advantage that one can be sure that the tasks are presented in the same way for the two modalities. It is true that one might worry that the EEG results could be distorted by the scanner environment, but a comparison of the EEG results obtained inside and outside the scanner suggests that the concern is needless (Bregadze and Lavric, 2006). It is also possible to carry out the same experiment using fMRI and MEG, though in this case the experiments must carried out successively (Dale et al., 2000). This provides the advantage of the good spatial resolution of fMRI and the good temporal resolution of MEG.

The imaging environment

In designing and analyzing imaging experiments, the user needs to take into account not only the nature of the signal, but also the conditions under which it is recorded. The various imaging techniques differ greatly in the experimental environment.

During PET, the head is held in the ring of detectors, but the body lies outside and relatively free movement of the arms is allowed. So, for example, subjects can be required to copy gestures or demonstrate the use of objects in mime (Rumiati et al., 2004). Furthermore, the subjects can be asked to speak, for example, reading words aloud (Price et al., 1994). This produces relatively little movement artifact in the emission signal.

By comparison, the MRI scanner is cramped, claustrophobic, and noisy. Furthermore, since the subject lies face-up in the scanner, the stimuli must be projected onto a small mirror. And the subject must lie still because movement in the scanner can produce artifactual signals, and this includes the movements involved in speaking.

These conditions put severe limits on the presentation of the task, the way in which the subjects treat it and the range of responses that they can make. These limits encourage the use of very simplified and artificial tasks. For example, in their normal environment people generate a wide variety of voluntary actions but this ability is often investigated in the scanner with simple button presses. It requires ingenuity to devise tasks that are rich and more typical of those encountered in everyday life. Fortunately virtual reality provides a way of introducing tasks that are more ecologically valid (Maguire, 2012).

The conditions are such that many subjects will be anxious, both about the noise and the need to stay still for up to an hour. These factors will produce variability in their attentional state and thus in the recorded images. It is for this reason that it is better to compare the images between two task conditions both of which engage attention rather than making comparisons with a resting baseline in which attention can wander.

It is a severe constraint that for most experiments it is necessary to avoid gross movement, which is why the responses are usually recorded via finger presses. So long as the arm does not move at the elbow, the subjects can press buttons without significant effect on the images. But this greatly limits the study of the motor repertoire. If the study requires gross movements, as in reaching and grasping, one may try to compensate for the distortions in the images using the recorded head movements as regressors in the analysis model (Barry et al., 2010), but even subtle movements can have systematic effects on the results and may bias group comparisons (Power et al., 2012).

It is less easy to record the movements of the jaw and mouth that are involved during speech so as to use them as regressors. For this reason, other techniques must be used if speech is to be permitted in the MRI scanner. One method is to detect trends in the data that might be accounted for by these movements and to remove them by a mathematical method (Gopinath et al., 2009).

Another is to use "sparse sampling." This depends on the fact that the peak of BOLD signal does not occur for five or more seconds after the movement, whereas the artifactual signal is restricted to the period during which the movement occurs. This means that if the scans only start some seconds after the word is spoken, the images will be free of motion artifact. In this way it has proved possible to study subjects who stutter (Watkins et al., 2008).

There is, however, currently no way of scanning with MRI in a free environment. This is what is offered by EEG, and this is why it is so useful in studies of children and even babies. For example, Marshall et al. (2013) were able to record cortical responses in babies of 14 months old while they made particular movements or observed others making the same movements.

Although the subjects are less free in MEG, they sit in a comfortable chair and look at a large screen in front on which the stimuli are presented. The arms are free rather than being constrained in a narrow tube. The conditions do not differ too radically from those of a psychologist's testing suite, except that the movements of the head are restricted.

This is only one of the reasons why the user should be encouraged to consider MEG. It is almost a direct measure of cortical activity, it records it in real time and it does so while the subject is relaxed and relatively unconstrained. It is true that the analysis of the signals has proved complex, but a variety of methods are now available, for example, in SPM, BrainVoyager, Freesurfer, and elsewhere. Packages such as these increasingly converge in integrating the solutions available for data analysis and source localization.

There is yet another reason for advocating the use of MEG. The history of functional brain imaging is that it started as a method for brain mapping, in other words as an anatomical technique. But the future lies in physiology. We need to know not only *where* particular operations are performed but also *how* the network operates so as to support human cognition (Bastos et al., 2012).

Summary

The spatial resolution of fMRI is adequate for answering many questions about the functions of particular cytoarchitectonic areas. Furthermore, at 7 Tesla the spatial resolution that can be achieved is now of the order of functional patches within areas, and this holds the promise of studying the functional organization of these areas. However, though it is possible to distinguish the time at which the BOLD signal rises in two different conditions within the same area, it is problematical to compare the times between different areas because of differences in the vascular bed.

EEG and MEG offer millisecond timing, but the problem of source localization remains troublesome, and the spatial resolution is thus limited. It is for this reason that laboratories increasingly combine fMRI with EEG or fMRI with MEG. EEG has the advantage of being relatively cheap and mobile. The cost of MEG and the complexity of analyzing the data have meant that MEG studies are not yet common in the literature. However, we see MEG as an increasingly important imaging technology, not least as the focus of brain imaging turns to physiology; that is to *how* the human brain supports complex cognition.

Chapter 3

Experimental methods

Abstract

Having recorded a signal, it is necessary to interpret its functional significance. The way in which this is done is to relate the signal to a psychological condition. As in other branches of science, an experimental condition is contrasted with a control condition. The interpretation is clearest when these differ in just one respect, though this can be difficult to achieve. Standard statistics are used to evaluate the significance of the difference. However, the analysis of imaging data can be onerous and many methods have been developed to avoid false-positive and false-negative results. These include robust correction for the number of statistical comparisons that are made, as the image is made up of thousands of voxels across many regions. Researchers also use targeted region-of-interest analysis; in this case the region must be specified beforehand. One must also study enough subjects: if small groups are used, the study may be underpowered.

Keywords

control conditions, subtraction technique, false positive, false negative, type I error, type II error, region of interest analysis, replication, number of subjects.

Introduction

The logic of imaging experiments is the same as the logic of scientific experiments in general. In physics or chemistry an experimental condition is compared with control conditions. Such comparisons between conditions can be made in biology, psychology, and medicine. For example, the bio chemist adds an enzyme and compares the product with the substrate without the enzyme. However, in the biological sciences comparisons can also be made between different groups of subjects. The doctor can compare the results for one group taking a drug and another group taking a placebo. In either case the result of the experiment is a *difference*.

The logic demands that, in order to interpret the effects of the drug, the experimental and control conditions should differ in just one respect; otherwise it will not be clear which is the critical factor. For example, there are two effects of giving a drug, one pharmacological and the other psychological; hence a placebo medication of identical appearance but without any pharmacological effects is needed to exclude psychological differences between conditions. It is the bane of psychology—and brain imaging—that, even if the stimuli are closely specified and the responses accurately measured, it is not possible to control completely the interpretation that the subjects place on the stimuli or the considerations that enter into their decisions. People have spontaneous thoughts and the experimenter has limited influence over these. The problem can be magnified when the subjects are lying in an enclosed scanner, perhaps anxious and disturbed by the repetitive noise.

A classic attempt in psychology to achieve the ideal experimental comparison between conditions involves the measurement of decision times. The original paper on this was by Donders in 1868, and because the paper is a classic it was republished in the 1960s (Donders, 1969). In one condition he measured simple reaction times (S): the subjects responded with the same finger whatever the stimulus. In the other condition he measured choice reaction times (C): the subjects responded with different fingers, depending on the identity of the stimulus. Since a finger is moved in both conditions, subtracting the simple reaction time from the choice reaction time (written as 'C – S') controls for the time to move a finger. The *difference* between C and S then provides an estimate of the time taken to make a decision.

The same logic applies in an imaging experiment. Take an experiment that was carried out by the authors (Rowe et al., 2005), in which the subjects were required to press one of four buttons on each trial. In the experimental condition, subjects chose which button to press; while in the control condition, they were required to press the button that was indicated to them. For convenience we will call the experimental condition the "internally generated" condition (I) and the control condition the "externally specified" condition (E). Both conditions involved finger movements, and thus in the comparison of I – E, the effect of moving fingers could be considered as having been subtracted out, leaving differences related to the choice of which finger to press. And the subtraction method appeared successful, since in the study by Rowe et al. there was no activation in motor cortex. But there was activation in the prefrontal cortex, and the assumption was that this reflected the choice associated with internal generation of action.

The problem of interpretation

As so often in science, the most obvious explanation is not the right one. The interpretation can be challenged because the two conditions differ in more than one respect. For example, in the internally generated condition (I), the subjects can prepare which finger to move during the inter-trial interval, even though they do not need to do so, and even though they do not know whether the next trial will be of the I or E type. In the externally specified condition (E), they cannot do this because they do not yet know which finger they will be required to move. So the prefrontal activation could reflect *preparation*, and other studies suggest that there is activation in the prefrontal cortex when subjects have been instructed to prepare the next finger movement (Rowe et al., 2002). It would be possible to control for preparation (P) by presenting the cues for the next trial earlier: the two conditions would then both include preparation, with the analysis comparing $[I + P] - [E + P]$.

Another respect in which the conditions differ concerns the relevance of the previous trial. In the externally specified condition, what happened on the previous trial is irrelevant to which button will be required on the next trial. In principle this is also true for the internally generated condition, but in practice subjects take into account what they did on recent trials when making choices about future responses (Zhang and Rowe, 2014). For example, they may think that they should vary their responses across trials in a particular way. In this case, the prefrontal activation could either reflect *memory* of previous trials or the use of previous trials as the *context* for generating the next movement.

To find out whether working memory is the critical factor, Taylor et al. (2008) compared a condition in which the subjects decided what to do (I) with a condition in which they were simply required to remember their last response (M). It turned out that there was activation for the comparison $[I + M] - [E + M]$, and this suggested that the prefrontal activation does not simply reflect working memory.

However, even if the activation in the prefrontal cortex does not reflect memory of previous responses, it could still be crucial that what the subjects do on trial n + 1 is influenced by what they did on trial n. To put it another way, the response on trial n + 1 is performed "in the context of" what was done on trial n.

To find out if this was the critical factor, Rowe et al. (2010) analyzed the data for the internal generation of movements in a sample of 57 subjects. Surprisingly, there was no prefrontal activation on the very first internally generated response trial. Yet, this was not for lack of statistical power because there *was* detectable prefrontal activation for a single trial in the middle of the series. So the prefrontal activation reflects the fact that subjects take previous trials into account when deciding on their next response: on the first trial there are no such previous trials to take into account.

Yet in a previous paper (Rowe et al., 2005) we had taken the prefrontal activation to reflect internal generation. This is a natural interpretation since the subjects were indeed instructed to generate actions at will. But it was the wrong interpretation.

The problem comes in part from labeling a task and then assuming that an activation fits that label. We called it "the internally generated task" (Rowe et al., 2005) and assumed that the activation reflected internal generation. The danger in labeling a task condition is that it may lead one (and other people) to ignore other explanations of the activations that occur when the task is performed.

This mistake is a general one, and even if the authors of a paper are careful to be precise and cautious in their specific interpretation, readers of the same paper may not be so careful. Funahashi et al. (1989) devised an oculomotor delayed response task for monkeys and called it a "working memory task." On each trial a spot of light was briefly presented followed by an unfilled delay and the monkeys were then required to indicate where the light had appeared by making a saccade to that location. When recordings were taken, roughly 50% of the task-related cells fired differentially, depending on the location, and continued to fire during the delay. For many years the conclusion drawn was that this area was involved in working memory. After all, the cells specified the location to be remembered and continued to do so during the delay.

However, there is another factor. The monkey's attention is drawn to the location of a light and, even when the light goes off, they could solve the task by simply continuing to attend to that location. Attention to the periphery is possible, even if fixation is maintained on a central point. A control is therefore needed in which the monkeys are required to attend to one location without their having to remember it.

This was achieved in a study by Lebedev et al. (2004). On each trial two cues were presented. The monkeys had to attend to one of them but to remember the other one. When that control was included, it turned out that 61% of the recorded cells coded for the attended location and only 16% for the remembered location.

This second example reinforces the point that problems of design are not unique to imaging. It emphasizes the need to conduct controlled experiments, and to challenge the simple or "obvious" explanation of a result; and this applies in brain imaging as in any other branch of science. The function of control conditions is to exclude explanations in which the experimenter is not interested. Thus, there should be as many control conditions as there are potential explanations. For brain imaging, it is often impractical to put all the control conditions into a single experiment and a series of connected studies may therefore be required.

Multiple factors and the interaction between factors

The problem of interpretation is complicated when there is no single critical factor but two or more factors that interact. For example, in an early PET study, Petersen et al. (1988) compared the activations for repeating (R) words with the activations for simply viewing (V) words. Thus, they performed the subtraction R − V. It was assumed that repeating words has no influence on the degree to which the words are processed. But this assumption may not be valid (Friston et al., 1996). In the passive condition, the subjects might view the words without concern for their meaning, whereas the requirement to repeat them might encourage further semantic processing.

The way to find out is to analyze not only the differences between conditions, but also how they may interact. In brain imaging, the most common method of analysis uses a general linear model (GLM), or the special case of a GLM known in other fields as an analysis of variance (ANOVA). In the simplest case it divides the variance into that part that is due to viewing (V) and repeating (R), together with that part that is due to an interaction between them (R × V). If repeating words recruits extra-semantic processing, the effect would show up as a significant effect of the interaction term.

As in psychology in general, analysis of variance provides a powerful means of evaluating the influence of the different factors in imaging experiments. Box 3.1 gives an example of a simple factorial design.

Analysis of variance can be used to find out how information is integrated in the brain. In the example given in Box 3.1, the integration is between kinematics (moving dots) and a particular configuration (of a person's limbs). A significant interaction term may reflect a specific conjunction of properties in a brain region, but it may also indicate synergism or antagonism between experimental factors.

In electrophysiology, analysis of variance can be used to look for cells that code for the integration between factors. For example, Wallis and Miller (2003) taught macaque monkeys a task in which the animals had to respond differentially to different cues and were rewarded with different amounts of juice. Whereas cells in the orbitofrontal cortex coded for the amount of reward, there were cells in the dorsal prefrontal cortex that integrated information about the appropriate response *and* the expected reward. The analysis of the cellular activity in the dorsal prefrontal cortex revealed a non-linear interaction between

Box 3.1 Factorial design

Factorial designs are a powerful and efficient way to examine the neural correlates of cognitive processes, especially where a task's processes may interact with the context in which it is performed. For example, Jastorff and Orban (2009) carried out an fMRI study to investigate the perception of biological motion. Point light displays were presented, and when these represented the movements of the limbs as people or animals walk, the displays were said to show "biological motion."

The design was a 2 × 2 factorial design. One factor was "Configuration." Either the shape of the displays accurately reflected the configuration of the limbs (Full) or it was distorted by scrambling the dots (Scrambling). The other factor was "Kinematics." Either the motion of the dots was an accurate display of walking (Biological) or the motion of the dots was up or down, thus not being an accurate display of walking (Translation). The design can therefore be set out as follows:

The statistical analysis looked for the main effect of configuration, the main effect of kinematics, and the interaction between these effects. This interaction is expressed as the difference between A and B versus the difference between C and D, or "[A – B] – [C – D]". A significant interaction in this study reflects what is special about biological motion rather than motion in general.

In the study there was a main effect of configuration in the occipito-temporal cortex, a main effect of kinematics in the MT/V5 complex, and an interaction in the fusiform gyrus. The interaction was in the area in which previous studies had reported activations when subjects view the human body. So the interaction was specific for the perception of a person walking.

responses and reward. This means that the degree of firing of the cells was greater than could be accounted for by the simple *addition* of the amplitude of the responses and reward alone. This is sometimes referred to as a "super-additive" interaction.

An analysis of variance, like linear regression and the Student's t-test, is a specific case of the general linear model. Linear regression relates the observed effect (dependent variable) to the task factor (independent variable) by estimating the regression parameter (β). The distribution of errors around the regression line is assumed to be Gaussian (also called "normal"). Multiple linear regression does the same thing for many independent variables at once. The different β weights provide an estimate of the degree to which each of the independent variables accounts for the variation in observations.

In the general linear models used for most brain imaging studies of the last 20 years, a set of measurements (the observed brain imaging data) is related to a "design matrix" that expresses the known experimental variables and the weighting parameters (β weights) of each of these variables (which are to be estimated). For a technical account of how the linear model is applied in the analysis of imaging data, we refer the reader to Poldrack et al. (2011). The present account is not meant to substitute for tutorial materials on how to set up the design matrix or calculate the parameter estimates, but to discuss the major principles in terms of their impact on experimental design and interpretation.

A variety of designs and methods of analysis are available to the user. Blocked designs present a series of the same trial types in blocks that last many seconds (typically 20–40 seconds), and the analysis then compares the averaged activations during the different blocks. Event-related designs present brief trials, usually in a random or semi-random order, and the analysis then collects together the data for each trial type separately, even if the responses to individual trials overlap in time, so as to compare the activations statistically using a model of the time course of activation (Mechelli et al., 2003). Many experiments combine blocks of one condition (an experimental context, such as attention or familiarity) with brief trial events that occur within that context. Parametric designs vary some factor systematically across a range of values, such as the number of items to be remembered, and then correlate this value with the degree of activation (Buchel et al., 1996). The decision as to which design to use will depend on the question asked and the demands for sensitivity (Amaro and Barker, 2006).

For block designs, event-related designs and mixed designs one can apply simple subtraction logic to the analysis, or more complex analysis of variance and general linear models. One can also combine tests, for example, using a test of one factor (e.g., the effect of movement versus rest) to define a set of brain areas as a "mask" within which one looks for the effect of another factor (e.g., the effect of having an illness affecting the motor system, such as a stroke or Parkinson's disease). Conjunction analyses test whether there are activations that are common to two or more task conditions (Friston et al., 2005).

The use of imaging for physiology

Each of these designs and analysis methods can be used to ask *where* there is activation during a particular task condition. The question is anatomical. But imaging is limited if it is restricted to "brain mapping." While it is important to establish localization of function, this should only be a preliminary to asking *how* the functions are performed.

So we strongly advocate that, wherever possible, imaging should use the same approach as electrophysiology. Consider the way in which the EEG is analyzed so as to detect event-related potentials (ERPs). As already mentioned, these are visualized by averaging across many trials. An essential step in doing this is to lock the record in time to particular events.

If the EEG record is time-locked to the presentation of a stimulus, it is possible to detect later fluctuations that relate to processing of that stimulus. These are referred to by polarity and order, the N100 or N1 (negative at 100 milliseconds), P200 or P2 (positive at 200 milliseconds) and so on (Fig. 3.1). Of particular interest, for example, is the mismatch negativity (MMN) that occurs at around 150 milliseconds after an unexpected event occurs in a series that is otherwise predictable. The MMN can be visualized by time-locking the record to the unexpected events.

The same technique of time-locking is used in single-unit physiology. For example, Weinrich et al. (1984) taught macaque monkeys to move a spot of

Fig. 3.1 Evoked potentials (ERPs) from the averaged EEG. N = negative, P = positive.

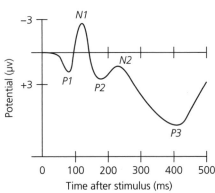

light to the left or right depending on the identity of the cue. A variable delay was interposed between presentation of the cue and the time at which the animals were allowed to respond. If the data were aligned to the presentation of the cue there was a brief phasic response, and if they were aligned to the response there was a similar phasic increase. However, the critical finding was that if the data were aligned to the presentation of the cue, there was continuous tonic or "set" activity during the delay period, in preparation for the response.

The method can as easily be applied to the BOLD fMRI time series. Toni et al. (1999) scanned subjects while they performed a visuomotor task in which there was a variable delay between the cue and response. Visual activations could be visualized by locking the record to the presentation of the cue and motor activations by locking the record to the time of the response. Figure 3.2 also shows that, as in the macaque monkey, in the premotor cortex there was an initial component that reflected the stimulus, a tonic component reflecting preparation of the response. and a final component at the time of the response.

Event-related methods can also be used to visualize areas in which there is a change in activation when an event is unexpected. Seymour et al. (2004)

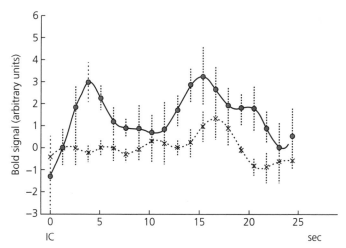

Fig. 3.2 BOLD signals in the dorsal premotor cortex (upper trace) and motor cortex (lower trace) for trials with a long delay. IC = instruction cue.

Reproduced from Ivan Toni, Nathaniel D. Schluter, Oliver Josephs, Karl Friston, and Richard E. Passingham, Signal-, Set- and Movement-related Activity in the Human Brain: An Event-related fMRI Study, Cerebral Cortex, 9 (1), pp. 35–49 doi:10.1093/cercor/9.1.35 © 2015, Oxford University Press.

compared the activations when a stimulus occurred that the subjects had not expected and when a stimulus failed to occur that the subjects had expected. There was a positive BOLD signal in the orbitofrontal and anterior cingulate cortex when the stimulus was unexpected and a negative BOLD signal when it was absent, though expected. These opposing effects are the same as predicted by single-unit studies in monkeys (Schultz and Dickinson, 2000).

Imaging offers other ways of studying physiology. By definition this involves changes over time, whether it be the beat of the heart or the rate of neuronal firing. In spite of its poor temporal resolution, the BOLD signal provides valuable information about time as well as amplitude.

For example, the duration of the BOLD signal is related to the length of time for which a stimulus is presented or a motor act is performed (Logothetis and Wandell, 2004). The duration can simply be measured using the points at which the amplitude is half its maximum. The full width half maximum (FWHM) is greater with the longer duration of stimulation presentation or motor response.

This relationship can be used to infer differences in the duration of cortical processing within a region. This was done in an imaging experiment by Richter et al. (2000) in which the subjects performed a mental rotation task. Pairs of complex objects were presented and the subject had to say whether if one was rotated it would match the other. The analysis looked for activations in which the width of the BOLD signal related to the time taken to make the judgment. There were activations in the parietal, premotor, and motor cortex for which this was true. Figure 3.3 plots the width of the BOLD signal in a single subject against the reaction times, and it is clear that the fit is very good.

There is, however, a limitation: for short trials, variations in the intensity of neuronal activity and variations in the duration of neuronal activity are almost indistinguishable from their resulting BOLD responses. The distinction can only be made if, as in the experiment by Richter et al, one has other evidence such as reaction times for differences in duration.

The amplitude of the BOLD signal serves as another important indicator of the underlying processing. This is best illustrated by considering the changes that occur during learning. If subjects are given a motor task to learn and they are trained by trial and error, there is strong activation at first in the dorsal prefrontal cortex (Fig. 3.4) (Floyer-Lea and Matthews, 2004). There could be many reasons: the task makes demands on attention, associative learning, and response preparation.

However, if the subjects are allowed to practice until the task becomes relatively automatic, these demands decrease. When the task is overlearned, the subjects no longer have to learn the associations and they no longer have to direct

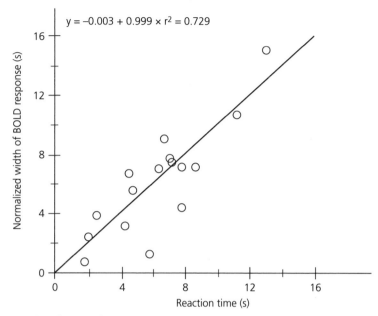

Fig. 3.3 Plot of width of the BOLD signal against the time taken to respond on a mental rotation task.

Reproduced from Wolfgang Richter, Peter M. Andersen, Apostolos P. Georgopoulos, and Seong-Gi Kim, Sequential activity in human motor areas during a delayed cued finger movement task studied by time-resolved fMRI, NeuroReport, 8 (5), pp. 1257–1261 © 1997, Wolters Kluwer Health, Inc.

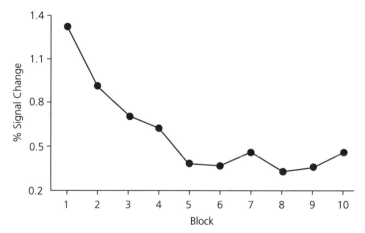

Fig. 3.4 Amplitude of the BOLD signal in the dorsal prefrontal cortex during learning of a motor sequence task.

Replotted from A. Floyer-Lea and P. M. Matthews, Changing Brain Networks for Visuomotor Control With Increased Movement Automaticity, Journal of Neurophysiology, 92 (40), pp. 2405–2412, Fig 3e, DOI: 10.1152/jn.01092.2003 © 2004, American Physiological Society.

their attention in advance to the response that they are going to make (Rowe et al., 2002). Figure 3.4 shows that, late in learning, the amplitude of the BOLD signal in the dorsal prefrontal cortex decreases until it is near the baseline level.

It will be clear that the BOLD signal can be used to study physiology, but there is a limitation in the examples presented so far. This can be illustrated by considering the study by Toni et al. (1999) on visuomotor learning. It is true that the analysis could visualize activations that related to the cue or response. But it could not distinguish whether cue A or B had been presented or whether the subjects had moved finger 1 or 2.

The problem is that in a single voxel there are very many thousands of cells. Although single-unit recording can find individual cells that code for cue A or B or for movement 1 or 2 (Asaad et al., 1998), the imaging methods described so far cannot draw similar distinctions. As a result they have not tackled the issue of neurophysiological coding.

The way in which fine-grained coding has begun to be investigated using fMRI is to analyze the pattern of activation *across* voxels, exploiting the uneven distribution of coding cells in neighboring voxels. This involves a "multivariate pattern analysis." The reader can find a detailed account of the method in Haynes and Rees (2006). Box 3.2 presents a simplified version.

Box 3.2 Multivariate analysis

This method was first applied to fMRI by Kamitani and Tong (2005) in an experiment on decoding the orientation of the lines that were presented to subjects in the scanner. The method analyzes the differences in the pattern of activation across a small group of voxels for the different stimuli, identifying a difference in the distributed signal even where no voxel individually differs significantly between conditions.

Figure 3.5 illustrates the method (adapted from Norman et al., 2006). This shows voxels in a one-dimensional array, whereas in the brain they are usually taken from a small three-dimensional volume of brain tissue or two-dimensional cortical sheet. Each column shows a trial, and the orientation of the bar for that trial is shown above the column. The degree of activation for each voxel is indicated by the shading.

The pattern of activation for the array of voxels will vary across trials, but it will be more similar for the same trial types (orientation in Fig. 3.5) than for different trial types. The aim of the analysis is to find a way of separating these patterns. The separation may best be achieved by a linear or non-linear function.

> ### Box 3.2 Multivariate analysis *(continued)*
>
> The classifier is trained on a series of trials (shown as run 1 and run 2) and then the accuracy of decoding is tested on a new series of trials (shown as test run 3).
>
> The analysis can be directed toward a pre-chosen area of voxels, for example, the visual cortex. Alternatively a "searchlight" technique can be used to interrogate where within the whole brain or cortex there are groups of voxels from which the information can be decoded significantly above chance.

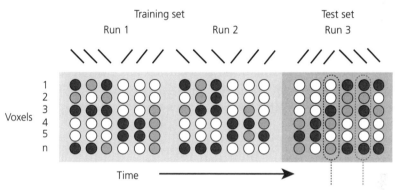

Fig. 3.5 Illustration of the use of multivariate pattern analysis. The voxels are shown as if in a column. The amplitude of the signal in each voxel is marked by the shading. The pattern across voxels is therefore shown in 2-D, whereas in the actual brain the pattern is read across voxels in 3-D. The orientations shown are given above the columns. The critical point is that, though there is variation from trial to trial with the same stimulus, the overall pattern for one orientation is different from the overall pattern for the other orientation.

Adapted from Trends in Cognitive Sciences, 10 (9), Kenneth A. Norman, Sean M. Polyn, Greg J. Detre, James V. Haxby, Beyond mind-reading: multi-voxel pattern analysis of fMRI data, pp. 424–30, Copyright (2006), with permission from Elsevier.

In the experiment by Kamitani and Tong (2005), mentioned in Box 3.2, different orientations were presented across trials. This meant that the pattern of activation could be related to the stimuli that were presented. The classifier could be trained to separate the populations because it was known what stimulus was shown on any particular trial.

However, multivariate analysis has also been used to decode cognitive states such as memories (Chadwick et al., 2010) and intentions (Haynes et al., 2007). Here there are no external stimuli and thus the classifier can only be trained if there is feedback at the end of the trial as to what the subject was remembering or intending.

Given sufficient sensitivity, it is also possible to decode from single voxels. Jerde et al. (2008) scanned at the ultra-high magnetic strength of 7 Tesla. They presented mazes and required the subjects to attend to one of four different orientations on each trial. Tuning curves were plotted for each voxel, and 51% of the voxels in the superior parietal cortex had a tuning curve with a peak for one of the orientations (Fig. 3.6). These curves are similar to those found for single cells in parietal cortex in macaque monkeys performing the same task (Crowe et al., 2004).

Voxels tuned to a particular orientation tended to occur in clusters. There was an average of 22 voxels for each cluster and a separation of 9.4 millimeters between clusters with the same tuning.

Whether a multivariate analysis or single voxel analysis is used to decode, there is nothing magical in the procedure. There is no difference in principle between using experimental conditions to predict activations in the brain (encoding) and using activations in the brain to predict the experimental conditions (decoding).

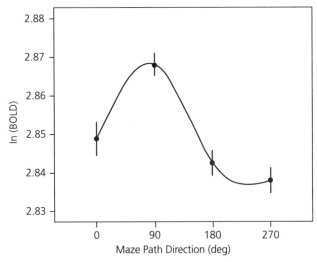

Fig. 3.6 Tuning curve for a voxel in parietal cortex, plotting the amplitude of the BOLD signal against the orientation of the maze exit.

Reproduced from Experimental Brain Research, 187 (4), pp. 551–561, Ultra-high field parallel imaging of the superior parietal lobule during mental maze solving, Trenton A. Jerde, Scott M. Lewis, Ute Goerke, Pavlos Gourtzelidis, Charidimos Tzagarakis, Joshua Lynch, Steen Moeller, Pierre-François Van de Moortele, Gregor Adriany, Jeran Trangle, Kâmil Uğurbil, Apostolos P. Georgopoulos © 2008 Springer International Publishing AG. With kind permission from Springer Science and Business Media.

There are currently still important unanswered questions about the mechanisms underlying the accuracy of decoding by multivariate pattern analysis methods, and their limits (Haxby et al., 2014). In an attempt to clarify the mechanisms, Shmuel et al. (2010) scanned the visual cortex at 7 Tesla. At a fine scale they could discriminate the ocular dominance columns, but at a coarse scale of several millimeters, the multivariate analysis was also able to discriminate the eye to which the stimulus was being presented. The power to do this was contributed both by gray matter and by the distribution of the blood vessels. The combination of neuronal and vascular information suggests that the spatial scale at which coding occurs neuronally need not be the same as the scale at which decoding is most sensitive using fMRI.

Detecting small signals

If fMRI is to be used for physiology, the methods need to be as sensitive as possible because the signals can be small, of the order of as little as 1% change. So it is critical that the signal-to-noise ratio is good. This ratio can be improved by scanning at higher magnetic field strengths (Zwanenburg et al., 2010) or by using specialized coils (Carmichael et al., 2006). This increases the chance that small effects can be detected.

The problem is that, however optimal the methods, fMRI is less sensitive to individual neuronal responses than is single-unit recording, and so there is a danger that an effect that is real is missed. This is referred to as a "false negative" or "type II error." This error can matter. Take the experiment already mentioned by Floyer-Lea and Matthews (2004). They studied motor sequence learning and the activation in the prefrontal cortex fell near to baseline when the motor sequence task had become automatic (Fig. 3.4). Given the variance around each value (not shown in Fig. 3.4) there was no significant activation in the dorsal prefrontal cortex by the end of the session. One might think that this meant that the prefrontal cortex is no longer involved when the task is overlearned.

But we know from work on macaque monkeys that this is not so. Rainer and Miller (2000) trained monkeys on a task that required them to recognize objects. An object was presented, followed by a delay before the animal made its response. If the objects were new, there was sustained activity during this period, and we know that this reflects, in part, preparation for the response (Rainer et al., 1999). However, if the animals had been overtrained so that the objects were familiar, the delay activity was minimal, though it could still be detected just before the response. It is quite possible that after overtraining, similar activity was present in the imaging study, but that lack of sensitivity meant that it was not detected.

It will be clear that if imaging is to be used for physiological studies, we cannot neglect small signals. In the early days of imaging, the balance was different because the concern was with functional anatomy. Short studies with few subjects (say 12 or fewer, each scanned for several minutes) can be quite adequate to detect large effects (Friston, 2012), and imaging has had great success in mapping out the different functional areas in this way. But in neurophysiology, small effects can be of as much interest as large effects. And the same is true in brain imaging.

The danger of false signals

There is, of course, a danger in relying on small effects, and this is that they may be due to chance variation. This is referred to as a "false positive" or a "type I error." Any experiment, whether in physiology, psychology, or social science, has to be alert to errors of this sort. The problem is that if in the analysis many comparisons are made, some of them may turn out as statistically significant when actually these are false positives.

The issue is particularly acute in imaging experiments. The reason is that the statistics are usually performed on many thousands of voxels. The problem is slightly reduced because each voxel is not independent of its neighbors, since the data are usually smoothed by the properties of the BOLD signal and often smoothed further by the experimenter—by averaging over a set of neighboring voxels. Nonetheless, a correction for the number of comparisons is still required.

The danger of relying on uncorrected statistics was famously illustrated by Bennett et al. (2009). They scanned a dead salmon on a test involving the perception of social situations, and when uncorrected values were used, the whole brain analysis produced "activations." The point of the experiment was, of course, precisely to show that the danger of depending on uncorrected values is that they can mislead you because of false positives. In the case of a dead salmon, there is no argument.

Given that a correction is needed, there is a choice. The Bonferoni correction is strict and protects against false positives, but it fails to take into account the spatial correlation between voxels (Bennett et al., 2009). An alternative is to place limits on the false discovery rate (FDR) to ensure that, for example, only 5% of the significant results represent false positives (Benjamini and Hochberg, 1995). However, in fMRI the use of FDR is appropriate if applied to a statistical analysis of clusters of activation, but not if applied to voxel-based statistics (Chumbley et al., 2010).

One way of controlling for false-positive rates is to appeal to random field theory (Kiebel et al., 1999). In this application images are treated as continuous processes and activations are regarded as topological features like peaks. A statistical parametric map is then a collection of statistics reflecting the activation at any point in the brain. By using a suitable statistics' value as a threshold, it is then possible to accurately control the false-positive rate for activated voxels, and the clusters that these significant activations form.

Region of interest analysis

Though correcting for multiple comparisons should protect against false positives, it can lead to false negatives. One way of increasing sensitivity is to make use of prior knowledge. The experimenter may have a prior expectation concerning the area in which activation is likely to occur. In this situation a region of interest can be defined for this area. This can be done by specifying a geometric volume centered on this area or by defining an anatomical mask. Both methods serve to decrease the number of statistical comparisons made, because there are fewer voxels to test.

It is an attractive idea to draw an anatomical mask, but in practice it can be problematical. The reason is if macroscopic landmarks like sulci are used to draw the mask, they may not match the borders between cytoarchitectonic areas. If larger masks are used, such as the superior parietal cortex (Scheperjans et al., 2008) or the inferior parietal cortex (Caspers et al., 2006), they will include many different cytoarchitectonic areas, and so the hypothesis underlying the masked region risks becoming so general as hardly to be an hypothesis at all.

For this reason it can be better to define a small region by choosing a coordinate that lies clearly within a particular cytoarchitectonic area. The region of interest can then be defined by a small circle round this coordinate. The coordinate itself can be derived in one of several ways. A peak can be used from a previous study in which similar, even if not identical, conditions were included. Or the experimenter can run a pilot study and use the peak to center the region of interest in a subsequent and independent study. Or the experimenter can define a region on the basis of one contrast and then run an analysis for that region using an independent ("orthogonal") contrast.

But, however the anatomical region of interest is chosen, it must be defined *before* the experiment and not after the results are obtained. The reason is that the justification for the procedure is that there is a *prior* expectation. You must metaphorically put the defined region of interest, for example, its coordinates, in a brown envelope before the experiment. It is too easy to define regions of interest post hoc, when they should be a priori, and we confess to a concern about how many researchers and laboratories take a biased approach in their use of regions of interest.

One misuse of region of interest analysis has been much discussed. This concerns what has been called "double dipping" (Kriegeskorte et al., 2009). This refers to the practice of carrying out two statistical tests on the same voxel. Box 3.3 explains the issue.

If properly conducted, a region of interest analysis has the advantage of sensitivity because there are fewer corrections for multiple comparisons. The results are also easier to interpret because prior knowledge or theory is used to constrain the inferences. Such an analysis is entirely appropriate where the interest is indeed limited to a specific question. For example, Weber et al. (2009) were interested in the visual analysis of a natural category (mammals). The question was whether the degree of similarity in the neural activation for two exemplars was related to the degree of similarity as judged by the subjects

---

Box 3.3 Double dipping

The term refers to the practice of carrying out an analysis of activations (usually for the whole brain), and then picking a significant area of activation from that analysis so as to carry out a second non-independent statistical test in it. An example would be to look for activation related to angry faces (versus rest) in an area that has been identified from the contrast of all-faces versus rest, where the angry faces are included in the same group of all-faces.

Another example would be to correlate the activation at a voxel with a measure of performance when performance was used to identify the voxel. The reason is that if the initial whole brain analysis has already shown that there is a correlation at a voxel, it is extremely biased ("cheating") to pick that voxel and then carry out a second similar test to show the strength of that correlation.

More formally, use of the same data for both selection and selective analysis will give invalid statistical inference if the analysis statistics are not independent of the selection criteria. Double dipping is occasionally deliberate ("voxel shopping"), but it is easy to commit unintentionally if one has not considered the potential relationship between tests used for defining a region of interest and the second test of interest (Kriegeskorte et al., 2009).

There is no such problem if the region of interest is defined before the analysis. The reason is that it is independent of the data being analyzed (Poldrack and Mumford, 2009). It is also valid to use a contrast from within a given dataset to define a region of interest, provided that the two stages of analysis are independent. This is often done if the experimental design is fully factorial.

on psychophysical tests. To answer the question, the authors first looked for activations for intact versus scrambled pictures; this contrast is independent of any analysis of similarity. There was activation for the contrast in six regions. The second stage of the analysis therefore compared the degree of neural similarity in just these regions with the degree of similarity as reported by the subjects.

As imaging advances, so the research questions will indeed become more sophisticated and more specific. The identification of the relevant areas is a stepping-stone to asking the more important question as to how they function. But tasks are performed by the brain (and body) as a whole, and thus a whole brain analysis can also be appropriate. This is particularly the case where the question concerns the interactions among all the areas that are involved. There is also an advantage of a whole brain analysis that is easily overlooked: there may be activations in areas that had been not expected, and these may merit following up. It can be such unexpected findings that lead to new avenues of research.

Number of subjects

Apart from region of interest analysis there is another way of increasing sensitivity, and this is to acquire more data. For questions that rest on understanding differences between individuals, or that ask what is typical of a population of subjects, increasing the number of subjects increases sensitivity more rapidly than lengthening the time for which each subject is scanned. Ideally, a power analysis should be carried out to tell the experimenter how many subjects are needed, given the effect size and variability. This could use existing knowledge of similar tasks and make explicit assumptions so as to guide software like "Powermap" (Joyce and Hayasaka, 2012) or the power calculation model developed by Mumford and Nichols (2008). However, the problem is that the experimenter does not usually have all the information that is needed to carry out an analysis of this sort.

With unlimited funds or an unrestricted pool of subjects, one might argue that one should scan as many subjects as possible. But funds are not unlimited. Unfortunately this has led to a very high number of inherently underpowered studies that have not been able to deliver the insights that one would demand for the combined effort and cost. This is a problem that is not restricted to brain imaging, but also applies to other areas of neuroscience (Button et al., 2013).

So as to investigate how many subjects may be required, Murphy and Garavan (2004) scanned 58 subjects. The task was a go/no-go task in which the activation for no-go trials was compared with the activation for go trials. The data were analyzed at different significance levels from $p < 0.01$ to $p < 0.000001$ (uncorrected) and for different numbers of subjects (from 4 to 58). The most important finding was that, compared with the results for the full sample, the data for groups of 20 subjects produced many false negatives.

Button et al. (2013) analyzed the results of 461 individual imaging studies in 41 separate meta-analyses, so that the reliability of the results could be assessed. The median statistical power of the studies was just 8% (i.e., an expected false-negative rate of 92%). This leads to the "winner's curse" in which published studies that find evidence for an effect provide a greatly inflated estimate of the size of that effect. Similarly, there is a considerable reduction in the positive predictive value of a result from an underpowered study, which is the probability that it reflects the true effect.

It is particularly important to recruit large samples where the effects are small and variable, such as the influence of genetic variations on physiology and cognition. For example, Munafo et al. (2003) calculated that in studies of individual differences, as many as 1,500 subjects will often be necessary to produce reliable results. That is one reason why the Human Connectome Project aims to recruit as many as 1,200 twins and their siblings (Van Essen et al., 2012), and another consortium is collecting resting state data for 1,414 subjects from 35 different imaging centers (Biswal et al., 2010). This is a leap forward from the typical 12–20 subjects used in the last two decades of fMRI, but clearly increases cost and calls for coordination across studies of large numbers of individuals (Shafto et al., 2014).

Replication

Recruiting large samples can protect against both false negatives and false positives. But there is another way of checking whether a positive result is unreliable, and this is to try to replicate it. It is essential for scientists to check their own results, if only to prevent themselves from wasting the next five years up a blind alley. It is particularly unfortunate that journals treat a failure to replicate as of less interest than positive results, while inflated effects or biased results of an initial publication become seen as a gold standard by virtue of precedence.

No-one disputes that in imaging it is easy to find replicable results where the effect sizes are very large. Take, as an example, the activations that can be recorded when subjects are tested on the n-back task. On an n-3 task, a series of items is given and the subject is required to say whether the present item is the same as the one presented three items previously. The task is complex. The subject has to constantly update the last few items in the series, avoid responding when the item was 2 as opposed to 3 back, and so on. Several hundred fMRI studies of this task have been published, with children and adults in health and disease. The results indicate large effects that are very robust across groups and over time: even with 25 subjects, the results are replicable when the same subjects are retested 15 days later (Plichta et al., 2012).

But many of the effects that are reported in the imaging literature are small, and there has been insufficient emphasis on the need for replication. The issue is not one that is peculiar to imaging. Consider the search for genes or groups of genes that predispose to psychiatric illnesses. Ten years ago, Munafo and Flint (2004) revealed that less than a third of genetic associations that have been reported were replicable. Large-scale studies using ultra-high-resolution imaging and whole-genome sequencing are beginning to expose hundreds of genetic modifiers of neurological and psychiatric illnesses. These are expressed across the brain and in terms of connectivity, as well as structure or activity. Rigorous approaches to "imaging genomics" will be required to ensure the reliability of these discoveries (Medland et al., 2014).

There are also areas of psychology in which there is an urgent need for replication. In social psychology "priming" has been used to set up dispositions in subjects of which they are not aware. For example, there have been many studies that have claimed that if subjects are presented with sentences containing words such as "clever" or "old," this influences their future behavior, even though they are not aware of the influence (Bargh, 2006). In response, Kahneman wrote an open letter to researchers on social priming stressing the need to replicate such studies. As a result, in 2012 the journal *Perspectives on Psychological Science* (American Psychological Association) devoted an issue to the problem of replication in psychology.

Imaging has to face up to the same issue, but it can do so. As mentioned in Chapter 1, at the time of writing there have been roughly 150,000 studies using fMRI to study the brain. It is of great concern that within this literature there are not many studies that simply tried to replicate a finding. It is an inadequate excuse to cite the expense of doing so, especially in view of the excess of underpowered studies.

Imaging results have high impact, and therein lies a danger. There is pressure to publish in the best journals. This can lead to a failure to check the reliability of one's own study before submitting it for publication. Journal editors may also devalue results that are either negative or "mere" replications. These effects are not trivial, as can be seen from the study by Boekel et al. (2015). They attempted to replicate 17 effects from five influential studies that reported correlations between regional gray or white matter and cognition. To do this they both replicated the studies and reanalyzed the data using Bayesian statistics to evaluate the evidence in favor of the null hypothesis. In only 1 of 17 cases was there evidence of replication.

The publication pressure also affects the way in which studies are written up. Tressoldi et al. (2013) have analyzed the way in which statistical results are presented in the fields of neuropsychology, psychology, and medicine when they are published in high-impact journals. These included *Nature* and *Science*. The review showed that the presentation of the statistical results tended to be less satisfactory than in specialist journals with lower impact. Remarkably, articles in high-impact journals were less likely to include information on confidence intervals, effect sizes, and prospective power. There were even many articles that presented histograms without error bars.

The result is that others can be misled because they are unable properly to evaluate the strength of the claims. There is a simple solution: it is in the hands of each scientist to try to replicate, to use unbiased methods, to plan properly powered studies, and to present the information necessary for others to evaluate the evidence.

Summary

The experimental approach used in imaging is no different from that used in other branches of science. It is that of the controlled experiment. However, there are several issues that are particularly difficult to deal with in functional brain imaging. One is that it is hard to achieve the ideal in which experimental conditions differ in just one respect. Another is that fMRI is relatively insensitive as a method, so it is easy to miss small signals. This is particularly true when a statistical correction is applied for a whole brain analysis. A region of interest analysis can be used to overcome this problem, but only if the region to be analyzed has been defined before the experiment and independently. A final problem is that many studies are currently underpowered because the number of subjects is too small. While this may be adequate for detecting large effects, it can obscure small effects, even though these can be more interesting and more important for understanding the physiology of the brain.

Chapter 4

Anatomy

Abstract

Once the statistical analysis has been performed, the location of the activations has to be established. The importance of this step lies in the fact that the location provides a link to the anatomical connections, since it is these that constrain the functions of the area. Each cortical area has a unique overall pattern of extrinsic connections, and it is this connectional fingerprint that provides the anatomical basis for functional localization. Thus, it is critical that an activation is assigned to the correct area, and that the localization is not described in terms of a general region, if within that region there are subareas with different connections. One can account for the function in terms of the anatomical connections. The identification of the correct cytoarchitectonic area usually depends on the warping of the image so that it fits a standardized template and the use of a probabilistic atlas to identify the most likely area for the activation.

Keywords

anatomical fingerprint, cytoarchitectonic maps, diffusion weighted imaging, comparative anatomy, Talairach coordinates, MNI template, normalization of the image, automatic labeling, JuBrain probability atlas.

Introduction

The usual result of an fMRI experiment is a set of activations at particular locations in the brain. It is obvious to anyone who uses the technique that it is essential to ensure that the activations are statistically significant (see Chapters 2 and 3). If they are not, the paper should be rejected. What may be less obvious is that the same is true if they are not allocated to the correct anatomical location.

This judgment may appear to be harsh, but consider what you would say if you were reviewing a paper by a neurophysiologist. The author says that the cell recordings were from the premotor cortex, but it is clear to you from the brain sections shown in the paper that the cells were in fact in the motor cortex. You would not accept the paper or its conclusions about the premotor cortex.

In other words, location is critical. There are two reasons. The anatomical connections of the premotor cortex are not the same as those of the motor cortex; for example, there are projections from the prefrontal cortex to the premotor cortex but not to the motor cortex (Lu et al., 1994). The functional properties of the cells also differ; most of the cells in the premotor cortex code for the spatial goal of the action, whereas cells in the motor cortex are more likely to code for the kinematics of the movement (Shen and Alexander, 1997).

The differences in cytoarchitecture between the motor and premotor cortex reflect differences in their connections. There are giant pyramidal cells, called "Betz" cells, in the motor cortex but not in the premotor cortex. As mentioned in Chapter 1, these Betz cells send their axons down the spinal cord and the ones on the medial surface are particularly large because they reach the motor neurons for the legs. Unfortunately, during cell recordings it is not possible to visualize these cells and thus delineate the border between the premotor cortex and motor cortex. Nor is there a sulcal landmark to mark the transition. However, the border can be plotted in the histological material because the cells can be viewed down a microscope (di Pellegrino and Wise, 1991). This means that after the study, the neurophysiologist can show you which electrode tracts were confined to the premotor cortex and which strayed into the motor cortex.

It is unfortunate that those using brain imaging cannot be as certain of the cytoarchitectural area in which they find an activation, since they do not have the histological material to examine. Instead they are dependent on published cytoarchitectonic maps. As a consequence the allocation of the activation to the correct area is only as good as the methods that are used to create such maps and to warp a subject's brain image to the same anatomical space as the cytoarchitectonic map.

Over the years the methods for creating and aligning cytoarchitectonic maps have both improved. In an early study of the theory of mind, the frontal activation was said to lie in medial prefrontal area 8 (Fletcher et al., 1995). The only method for allocation that was available at that time was reference to sections in the atlas by Talairach and Tournoux (1988), which represented an approximation of Brodmann's areas drawn onto a single adult brain. With subsequent better methods for allocation, it is clear that the activation actually lies in the anterior cingulate cortex (Amodio and Frith, 2006).

Unfortunately the mistake mattered. Area 8 is involved in the direction of eye movements and covert attention (Corbetta et al., 1998), whereas the anterior cingulate cortex is involved in monitoring and self-reflection (Passingham et al., 2010). Area 8 is connected with the superior colliculus (Fries, 1984) and brainstem oculomotor nuclei (Segraves, 1992), whereas the anterior cingulate cortex is connected with the retrosplenial cortex and the hippocampal system (Kobayashi and Amaral, 2003). So any account of how theory of mind was achieved would be misconceived if the activation was taken to lie in area 8.

The point of allocating activations correctly is that it allows them to be interpreted in terms of what is known of the brain. There is no point in simply citing BA (Brodmann area) numbers by rote without reference to the functional anatomical significance of each area. The term "blobs" is sometimes used to describe the islands of activations that lie above a threshold for statistical significance, and this encourages the treatment of the images as if they were just pictures with the activations treated as indicator variables. If this is done, the exercise can become an expensive kind of phrenology, with the blobs seen as a set of disconnected bumps, rather than elements of an integrated network.

The problem with the phrenologist's bumps on the skull was that they bore no relation to the brain itself (Young, 1990). Fortunately, the activations do relate to changes in the brain and they carry important information. If the cytoarchitectonic labels are applied correctly, they are informative both of the likely connections of the area and of the functional properties of neurons in that region. It is these that both allow the area to do what it does, and help the researcher to understand its functions.

Cytoarchitecture as a link to connections

The reason why the cytoarchitectonic label provides a link to the anatomical connections is that each area has a unique pattern of extrinsic connections. This is evident from the map of cortical connections produced by Young (1993) for the macaque monkey. The point was emphasized by Passingham et al. (2002) who compared the different subareas of the prefrontal cortex.

To do this they plotted the connections of each area, using information collected in a database of connections in the macaque monkey brain (www.cocomac.org). The development of this database is described by Stephan (2013). In the study by Passingham et al. the connections were shown in the form of a radial plot, and the specific pattern of connections for each area created what the authors called a "connectional fingerprint." The analogy was with the "receptor fingerprints" illustrated by Zilles and Palomero-Gallagher (2001). In a radial plot of the receptor fingerprint of an area, the different receptors are presented round the circumference with their density shown on the radius. The connectional fingerprint of an area shows the different regions with which it is connected round the circumference, with the strength of each connection shown on the radius (Fig. 4.1).

Blumenfeld et al. (2014) have since written software that allows the user to plot the connections of any cortical area, using the Cocomac database as the source of the information. In their paper they illustrate, for example, the connections of the dorsal prefrontal (areas 46 and 9/46) and ventral prefrontal (areas 47 and 45B) cortex. The graphs clearly show that these areas differ markedly in the overall pattern of their connections.

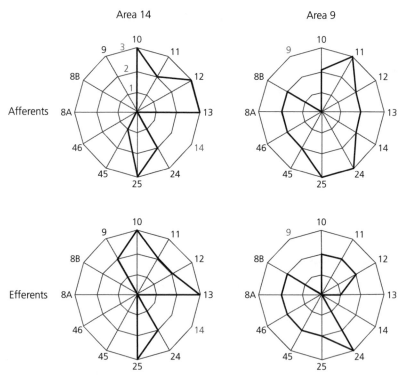

Fig. 4.1 Connectional fingerprints for prefrontal areas 9 and 14 based on data from macaque monkeys. The afferents (top figures) or efferents (lower figure) are shown round the circumference, and the strength of the connections is shown along the radius.

Reprinted by permission from Macmillan Publishers Ltd: Nature Reviews Neuroscience, 3(8), Richard E. Passingham, Klaas E. Stephan and Rolf Kotter, The anatomical basis of functional localization in the cortex, pp. 606–16, doi:10.1038/nrn893 © 2002, Macmillan Publishers Ltd.

Multidimensional scaling can be used to demonstrate that the overall pattern of connections of each area is unique (Passingham et al., 2002). If two areas have the same pattern of connections, they should appear in the identical position in the plot in two-dimensional space. In fact all the areas for which this test was run turned out to be distinctive (Fig. 4.2).

All these results suggest that the functions of each area are determined—or at least constrained—by the pattern of extrinsic connections. Each area can be seen as transforming a set of inputs into a set of outputs. The inputs determine the information received and the outputs determine the sphere of influence of that area. This is not to deny that there are also differences between areas in their internal wiring (Kritzer and Goldman-Rakic, 1995), and these too must have an influence on an area's function. But the extrinsic connections have a major influence over what the area can do because they limit the information on which it can operate.

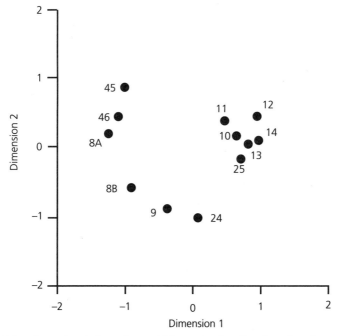

Fig. 4.2 Two-dimensional plot, using multidimensional scaling, based on the connectional fingerprints of the different prefrontal areas in the macaque monkey brain. The numbers refer to the Brodmann areas.

Reprinted by permission from Macmillan Publishers Ltd: Nature Reviews Neuroscience, 3(8), Richard E. Passingham, Klaas E. Stephan and Rolf Kotter, The anatomical basis of functional localization in the cortex, pp. 606–16, doi:10.1038/nrn893 © 2002, Macmillan Publishers Ltd.

The fact that each area has a different pattern of connections can also be used to plot the borders between different areas. This was first demonstrated using diffusion imaging for the border between the pre-supplementary motor area (Pre-SMA) and supplementary motor area (SMA) on the medial frontal surface of the human brain (Johansen-Berg et al., 2004). Since then the technique has been used to distinguish other areas, such as the dorsal and ventral premotor cortex (Tomassini et al., 2007), and Broca's areas 44 and 45 (Klein et al., 2007). The borders as delineated on the basis of connections can be compared with the borders as delineated on the basis of cytoarchitecture. This has been done for Broca's areas 44 and 45, and there is a good match (Klein et al., 2007).

The pattern of connections as visualized by diffusion imaging can also be plotted in the form of a connectional fingerprint. For example, Fig. 4.3 shows the fingerprints for the dorsal and ventral premotor cortex (Tomassini et al., 2007). It will be seen that the fingerprints for the dorsal and ventral premotor cortex are quite distinct.

Given that diffusion imaging can be used to plot connectional fingerprints for the human and macaque monkey brain, it is also possible to test whether there are areas in the two species that share the same connections. Croxson et al.

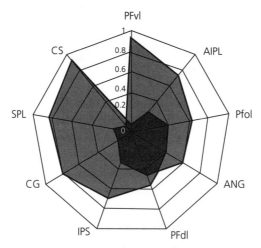

Fig. 4.3 Connectional fingerprints for the dorsal and ventral premotor cortex, based on data from diffusion weighted imaging. The letters refer to the areas.

Reproduced from Valentina Tomassini, Saad Jbabdi, Johannes C. Klein, Timothy E. J. Behrens, Carlo Pozzilli, Paul M. Matthews, Matthew F. S. Rushworth, and Heidi Johansen-Berg, Diffusion-Weighted Imaging Tractography-Based Parcellation of the Human Lateral Premotor Cortex Identifies Dorsal and Ventral Subregions with Anatomical and Functional Specializations, Journal of Neuroscience, 27 (38), pp. 10259–10269; doi: 10.1523/JNEUROSCI.2144–07.2007 © 2007, The Society for Neuroscience.

(2005) produced masks for different prefrontal areas in the macaque monkey and human brain. These were based on the pattern of sulci, but the areas so delimited roughly correspond to the major cytoarchitectural divisions. Croxson et al. seeded voxels in the white matter of the parietal and temporal cortex in human and macaque monkey brains, and they found that the connections with the prefrontal cortex were remarkably similar in the two species. Furthermore, in general the results for macaque monkeys fitted with what we know from the use of tracers.

There is another way of plotting connections. This is to make use of the principle that, if two areas are strongly connected, the BOLD signals in the two areas tend to covary when the subject is at rest, even if the areas are far apart. The covariance of spatially distinct areas is known as functional connectivity, and there is a close relationship between anatomical and functional connectivity (Bullmore and Sporns, 2009).

The principle of joint anatomical and functional connectivity lies at the heart of "connectomics" research (Behrens and Sporns, 2012), and is supported by theoretical analyses of complex systems such as the brain (Sporns et al., 2000), as well as empirical validation in human and animal models. For example, in a study on macaque monkeys, the pattern of functional covariance as shown by DWI was compared with the connections as documented by the injection of tracers (Vincent et al., 2007). It has also been shown that a lesion to the anatomical connections between two regions alters their functional connectivity (O'Reilly et al., 2013). In general, high covariance is a reasonable marker that two areas are connected, although only a few indirect connections between two areas may be sufficient to support functional connectivity.

Studying the pattern of covariance therefore provides a means for comparing the connections in the human and macaque monkey brain. It also indicates whether there are areas in the human brain for which there is no equivalent in the macaque brain. If areas in the two species have the same overall pattern of connections, the assumption is that they are homologous areas. If, on the other hand, areas are found in the human brain that covary in a way not found in the macaque monkey brain, the assumption is that they are new to the human brain. Rushworth and colleagues have used this method to compare the areas of the dorsal (Sallet et al., 2013) and ventral prefrontal cortex (Neubert et al., 2014) in the human and macaque monkey brain. There appears to be an area in the ventral frontal pole that is new to the human brain. Using the same method, Mars et al. (2013) have also shown that there is an area at the temporo-parietal junction that appears to be new to the human brain. However, these claims will be strengthened by replication in other species, and the identification of the evolutionary step between macaques and humans at which the new function appeared.

The link between connections and function

So far we have suggested that the operation that is performed by an area is dependent on the pattern of extrinsic connections. If this is true, it should be possible to show that areas that differ in their function also differ in their connections. This can be investigated in relation to the fusiform face area (FFA) and the parahippocampal place area (PPA).

The FFA is an area in the ventral temporal lobe that is activated when faces are shown, whereas the PPA lies more medially and is activated when scenes are shown. Saygin et al. (2011) used diffusion imaging to plot the pattern of connections for each voxel in the FFA in a series of individual subjects. They then tested whether the same connections were a reliable predictor of activation in the FFA in a new series of individual subjects. The procedure was successful for 22 of the 23 new subjects.

There were also connections that were poor predictors of activation in the FFA. Connections with the PPA were negatively related to activation of the FFA. Though the FFA and PPA both receive visual inputs from the pre-occipital cortex (Yeterian and Pandya, 2010), the FFA does so via the lateral occipital complex (LOC) and the PPA from the transverse occipital sulcus, an area that is also activated when scenes are presented. If rTMS is applied to the lateral occipital complex, it impairs the categorization of objects; whereas if it is applied to the transverse occipital sulcus, it impairs the categorization of scenes (Dilks et al., 2013). Thus the FFA and PPA appear to derive distinct visual inputs.

It is, of course, obvious that the functions of a visual area are determined in part by the nature of its sensory inputs. But the principle that function is related to connections can be shown to hold for higher regions. For example, Beckmann et al. (2009) used diffusion imaging to distinguish nine subareas within the human cingulate cortex on the basis of their overall pattern of anatomical connections. Beckmann et al. then reviewed 171 functional studies. There was a good fit between the areas that were selectively activated in particular task conditions and the subareas as established by tractography.

It will now be clear why it is essential that imaging studies correctly identify the areas that are activated. The cytoarchitectonic subdivisions relate to connectional subdivisions. Thus, any attempt to say *how* an area performs a particular operation must specify how the connections of the area allow it to do so.

The point can be illustrated by returning to an example discussed earlier in the chapter. We mentioned that if subjects are presented with tasks that test for theory of mind, the activation is in the anterior cingulate cortex (Amodio and Frith, 2006). This is significant because there are projections from the upper bank of the superior temporal sulcus (STS) to the anterior cingulate cortex

(Saleem et al., 2008), and there is activity in the STS when monkeys (Jellema and Perrett, 2003) or human subjects (Grezes et al., 2001) watch people moving. So the anterior cingulate cortex has inputs that could carry information about the movements of others.

This has proved to be an important clue. Sallet et al. (2011) have measured the resting state covariance between the superior temporal sulcus and the anterior cingulate cortex in macaque monkeys. It turns out that the larger the social group in which the animals are kept, the greater the covariance between the STS and the anterior cingulate cortex. The most likely explanation is that this is because of the need to make use of signs to predict what others will do (Rushworth et al., 2013). So the human ability to make judgments about the mental states of others is probably derived from a mechanism for using external signs to predict behavior. It is consistent with this hypothesis that monkeys with lesions in the anterior cingulate cortex no longer respond to the social signals of other monkeys (Rudebeck et al., 2006).

Talairach atlas

This example shows why accurate localization is essential. The crucial insight would be missed if the activation was wrongly allocated to prefrontal area 8. As already mentioned, this mistake was originally made because of the use of the atlas by Talairach and Tournoux (1988). Talairach was a neurosurgeon and for illustrative purposes he put labels for the Brodmann areas on the brain sections. But because Talairach simply drew the areas on by eye using Brodmann's two-dimensional diagram (1909), it is not acceptable to assign a peak to a cytoarchitectonic area using this atlas. Since the labels are a fiction, there is no advantage to automating the error, despite the availability of software to do so, such as the "Talairach daemon" (Lancaster et al., 1997).

The Talairach coordinate system and standardized anatomical space

It is essential to distinguish between the specific Talairach template or space and the generalized Talairach coordinate system. The Talairach template refers to the brain sections in the Talairach atlas (Talairach and Tournoux, 1988) as drawn on the single subject, a 60-year-old woman. The sagittal and coronal sections are simply reconstructed from the horizontal sections.

The generalized Talairach coordinate system refers to the system that was devised by Talairach et al. (1967) to identify any location in the brain by means of three coordinates; it is illustrated in Fig. 4.4. This system dominates the

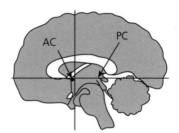

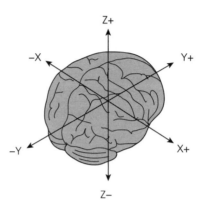

Fig. 4.4 Talairach coordinates. AC = anterior commissure, PC = posterior commissure. The AC–PC line is the line through these coordinates. The VCA line is the line drawn vertically through the anterior commissure.

Upper: © Mark Cohen, 2000.
Lower: © Chris Rorden, 2002.

communication of the sites of brain activations from fMRI, and the start or end sites for tractography. In this system, the AC–PC line is defined as the line through the anterior and posterior commissure and the VCA line is defined as the line drawn vertically through the anterior commissure at 90 degrees. The natural symmetry of the brain provides the third axis so "x," "y," and "z" coordinates can be defined with respect to these lines.

Any location or activation peak can now be specified in the volume. The x value gives the laterality either side of the midline, with a negative value indicating the left hemisphere and a positive value the right. The y value gives the anterior to posterior extent, with a negative value indicating posterior to the VCA line and a positive value anterior to this line. The z value gives the height, with a negative value indicating below the AC–PC plane and a positive value above this plane.

It is now standard to report activations using the Talairach coordinate system but to use a series of brains, rather than a single brain, as a template or reference space. Most studies of the last 20 years refer to a template produced at the Montreal Neurological Institute (MNI), based on the average of 152 brains. The average ensured that the template is representative—or at least representative of the population of healthy young adults from which the 152 were drawn. When studying other groups, such as children or older adults, or comparing patients to controls, an unbiased template may be needed that is more appropriate for the study population and this can be created specifically. However, even study-specific templates use a Talairach system of coordinates and are warped to a close approximation of a common reference such as the MNI template, so as to aid the reporting of locations and comparisons across studies.

Localization and visualization

There is now a vast and rapidly evolving array of resources for localizing activations. The Neuroimaging Informatics Tools and Resources Clearinghouse (www.nitrc.org) currently provides an effective means to find, compare, and access neuroimaging software, including those that we discuss in more detail here and alternatives. Common analysis tools for fMRI and DWI, such as SPM, FSL, AFNI, BrainVoyager, Caret, and FreeSurfer, come with their own visualization options and these are increasingly able to interlink through common data formats for brain imaging. Other more specialist packages, like the Brain Connectivity Toolbox (www.brain-connectivity-toolbox.net), bring together a sophisticated set of tools to analyze and to present graphically or numerically the nature of brain activity and connectivity.

For new users, however, a simple package such as MRIcro or MicroGL (www.MRIcro.com/) is easy to learn to use, and allows the user to enter a set of coordinates and see where this lies in anatomical brain space, using, for example, the MNI template. The averaged image of the MNI template appears blurred, because of variability between the brains that are included in the average, but new "averaging" tools (e.g., Diffomorphic Anatomical Registration Through Exponentiated Lie Algebra, DARTEL; Ashburner, 2007) improve on this and can themselves be represented back in MNI space. Alternatively, one can see where the peak lies on a single "representative" brain, with the caveat that this brain differs in some details of its gyral and deep anatomy.

If brains are normalized to the MNI template, it is tempting to resort to a program to find out the most likely location for your activations in the brain. Two tools are the Automated Anatomical Labelling atlas (www.cyceron.fr/web/aal_anatomical_automatic_labelling.html), which labels 5 subcortical structures and 40 cortical areas (Tzourio-Mazoyer et al., 2002), and the Harvard–Oxford atlas (www.cma.mgh.harvard.edu/fsl_atlas.html), which labels 21 subcortical structures and 48 cortical areas.

However, the usefulness of these programs is currently limited. Whilst they have a useful role in standardization of regions of interest, they fail to provide sufficient anatomical detail of the neocortex. They use general terms such as the anterior cingulate gyrus and do not provide divisions within this so as to distinguish, for example, whether the area lies on the dorsal convexity, in the cingulate sulcus, or under the genu of the corpus callosum.

There are published brain atlases to aid the user to make further distinctions. The book by Duvernoy (1991) gives labeled sections for forebrain structures and the book by Naidich et al. (2009) does so for the brain stem and cerebellum. But, exact MNI coordinates are not shown because the sections are real and from individual brains. It is possible to look up a coordinate in MNI space in the atlas by Mai et al. (2011) for the cortex and the atlases by Schmahmann et al. (1999) and Diedrichsen et al. (2009) for the cerebellum. However, one must understand the processing steps each atlas author has taken to bring anatomical information into the standard space represented by the MNI template.

None of these atlases provide cytoarchitectonic labels. Fortunately, many of the cytoarchitectonic areas can now be located using the JuBrain Cytoarchitectonic Atlas (http://www.fz-juelich.de/inm/inm-1/EN/Forschung/JuBrain/_node.html). This is readily available as a toolbox in both SPM (Eickhoff et al., 2005) and FSL, but could be used with any major imaging software. The borders between the different cytoarchitectonic areas have been specified by using an automated procedure that measures the density of the gray matter across the different layers (Schleicher et al., 1999). The JuBrain atlas has used this technique on ten or more brains that were scanned whole before being cut into many thousands of slices for cytoarchitectonic analysis (Amunts et al., 2007). This means that the atlas can give the probability that a particular coordinate in MNI space lies within a particular cytarchitectonic area.

The usefulness of the JuBrain atlas depends on the accuracy of the algorithms that are used to fit the brains in any particular study to the standard space. Klein et al. (2009) compared 14 different methods for this registration, and these differed greatly in the degree to which they brought identical structures into line. The best methods, however, proved impressively accurate. It is true that, even after registration, there is more variability in the boundaries of higher order association areas than primary sensory and motor areas (Fischl et al., 2008). But, there is hope that with further refinement in these methods, atlases such as JuBrain will allow the allocation of areas identified by functional or structural imaging to cytoarchitectonic areas with confidence.

Given that each area has a different pattern of connections, an alternative method is to use the patterns of connectivity to distinguish between areas, using, for example, resting state covariance from fMRI or anatomical connections from DWI. Already two maps have been published for the whole brain (Blumensath et al., 2012; Craddock et al., 2012). But it is not necessary to depend only on atlases. Instead, each experimenter can take the areas that are identified in their own study and plot the likely connections using the resting state covariance or DWI data. There is hope that one day this might become common practice, with publishing tools and open databases to communicate this information.

Common problems in localization

Given the limitations of current automated programs, the experimenter needs to know enough neuroanatomy to form their own judgment as to the most likely allocation, and to be aware of the uncertainty over the identification of activations in highly variable regions. It is easy to make mistakes when doing this, and we present some common problems and challenges here.

The first mistake is that the activations should not just be localized on the basis of a lateral projection of a surface-rendered image of the brain, although this has become one of the commonest ways to publish results. The problem is twofold. A lateral view is a two-dimensional representation of a convexity. It is easy to think that activations lie on the surface, when in fact they lie in the underlying sulci and "shine through" so as to appear as if they are on the surface. For example, a peak may appear to lie on the inferior parietal surface, when in fact it lies in the depths of the intraparietal sulcus. This particular error has been repeated again and again in the literature. It can be avoided by looking at the peak on coronal sections. Another method is to study the peak on an "inflated" brain in which the sulcal tissue is shown on the surface of an expanded cortex. This inflation is standard in Caret or FreeSurfer. However, it can take time to become familiar with these representations, since they preserve the topology but not geometry of the natural brain space.

The second mistake is to check the coordinates on a single plane; for example, the horizontal plane. Some structures are easily detected in the horizontal plane but many others are not. Different structures show up best in different planes. For example, peaks in the superior temporal sulcus are best localized in a parasaggital section, whereas peaks in the amygdala are best localized on a coronal section. It is for this reason that the common practice of simply presenting the activations on a series of horizontal (axial) sections can be very unhelpful. The point of presenting figures is to allow the readers to form their own judgments; but they are unable to do so if the data are presented in a form that is uninterpretable. Electronic publishing and data tools are increasingly able to support the dissemination of three-dimensional images to solve this problem.

The third mistake is to rely on overarching terms such as "basal ganglia," "cerebellum," or "insula." These structures contain subareas with quite distinct connections and so different functions, and if these are ignored the wrong conclusions will be drawn from a study. In the following sections, we discuss some of the regions that are especially vulnerable to conclusions that are based on general descriptions.

Basal ganglia and cerebellum

The basal ganglia consist of input nuclei (the striatum), output nuclei (the globus pallidus and substantia nigra, pars reticulata), and nuclei with modulatory influences (the subthalamic nucleus). Furthermore, several different cortico-subcortical loops run through the striatum (caudate nucleus and putamen) and pallidum (Alexander et al., 1991). These originate in different cortical areas, and in the case of the frontal areas, there are reciprocal projections back to the same areas via the thalamus. The different loops have also been identified in the human brain by using resting state fMRI (Choi et al., 2012) or DWI.

This is not to say that the loops are totally independent: we know that neighboring cortical areas project to overlapping regions in the striatum (Averbeck et al., 2014). Nonetheless, the different cortico-striato-thalamo-cortical loops are involved in radically different functions. So it really matters whether a striatal activation lies in an area that connects with the motor cortex, the frontal eye field, or the orbitofrontal cortex. Their connectivity and pharmacology are radically different.

Just as different loops run through the basal ganglia, so different cortical areas project to the cerebellum via the pons, and in the case of the frontal areas there are reciprocal projections back to the same areas via the thalamus (Middleton and Strick, 2001). The cerebellar regions that are connected with the prefrontal cortex are especially well developed in the human brain (Balsters et al., 2010). So again it will matter whether the activation lies in an area that connects with motor cortex or, for example, the prefrontal cortex.

Insula

The insula forms the tissue at the bottom of the Sylvian fissure where it flattens out. It is this area that is characterized by autonomic inputs (Mesulam and Mufson, 1985). The insula is quite distinct from the adjoining frontal or parietal operculum. The opercular areas lie on the lateral bank of the sulcus, and there is an opercular part for each of the frontal and parietal areas on the lateral convexity (von Economo, 1929). Yet the term "insula" is often wrongly used when the activation lies in an opercular area. We cite two examples, but similar errors have been made by many groups. One study looked for the area of overlap in lesions that cause an impairment in the coordination of speech, and reported that it lay in the insula (Dronkers, 1996); yet it is likely that the true location was the premotor or motor sector of the frontal operculum. Other studies have reported activations related to inhibiting responses as lying in the insula (Kelly et al., 2004); yet it is likely that they lie in the opercular part of the caudal ventral prefrontal cortex (Monchi et al., 2001).

Angular gyrus

The angular gyrus is a complex region at the border between the temporal and parietal cortex. It includes the posterior part of the superior temporal sulcus, area Tpt, which may play a role in language (Galaburda et al., 1978), another area that appears to be involved in attention (Bzdok et al., 2013), and an area that is activated when subjects make judgments about the mental states of others (Mars et al., 2013). It is possible that a single region has three such very different functions, but given the functional and anatomical complexity of this area, it is more likely that three regions with three different functions lie in close proximity. Therefore, it may be true, but it is unhelpful, to report simply that an activation lies in the angular gyrus.

Anterior cingulate cortex

Activations have been reported so commonly in the anterior cingulate cortex that the term ACC is often used. But again this is a large and complex area. The convexity cortex includes three distinct cytoarchitectonic areas, 24, 32, and 25, and there is a clear functional distinction between activations in dorsal cingulate and ventral cingulate areas (Koski and Paus, 2000). On the basis of the pattern of connections alone there appear to be six separate areas within the anterior cingulate cortex (Beckmann et al., 2009). Some activations that have been attributed in the literature to the cortex on the convexity are actually in the cingulate motor areas, which lie in the sulcus (Rushworth et al., 2007).

Dorsolateral prefrontal cortex

The situation is arguably worse with the dorsolateral prefrontal cortex, often called the DLPFC. In macaque monkeys the term "dorsolateral prefrontal" was first used for the whole of the lateral prefrontal convexity (Pribram et al., 1952). It was then used for the tissue in the principal sulcus plus the superior prefrontal convexity (Mishkin, 1964). Sometimes it is taken to include the tissue in the upper limb of the arcuate sulcus in monkeys (Goldman and Rosvold, 1970) and sometimes not. In the imaging literature, the term DLPFC has been used in just as inconsistent a fashion, with wide variation in the anterior border with the pole and the posterior border with the frontal eye fields. It is sometimes used to include the inferior frontal sulcus and superior frontal gyrus, in addition to the middle frontal gyrus. Terms such as the dorsolateral prefrontal cortex should be defined precisely or not used at all. On the basis of the pattern of connections, there appear to be at least seven separate areas on the dorsolateral surface (Sallet et al., 2013), and this suggests physiological and functional differences within the area.

The overall lesson is that the point of allocating activations to specific areas is that it provides a link to the anatomical connections and the constraints on function. There is no advantage in allocating to very general areas if there are subareas with different connections. Anatomy matters.

Summary

Just as one must get the statistics right, so it is just as critical to get the anatomy right. The brain is not an amorphous lump. The different brain areas have different patterns of connections. Since it is these connections that determine in part what the area does, we cannot understand how the brain does what it does unless we locate the activations correctly. Atlases can help with this if used critically and with precision. It is the locations that provide the key to the connections and so enable the understanding of brain function.

Chapter 5

Functional specialization

Abstract

A critical step in finding out how the human brain supports cognition is to identify the operations that are performed by the individual parts. In the case of the cortex the parts are the different cytoarchitectonic areas. Just as connectional fingerprints can be established for each area, so their functions can be discerned by functional fingerprints. These show the degree to which an area is engaged across a wide range of cognitive tasks. The aim of comparing these plots for different areas is to work out the transformation that the different areas perform, from input to output. Given the complexity of the brain it can help to produce computational models of how it works and to relate the operations that are carried out by different areas to different components or parameters of the model.

Keywords

functional fingerprints, parameter estimates, reverse inference, operations, transformation, multivariate analysis, computational models.

Introduction

In the last chapter we argued that the functional specialization of an area depends on its anatomy, in terms of its precise location and connectional fingerprint. This chapter considers how to characterize that specialization. In doing so it introduces the notion of a "functional fingerprint."

This term is used by analogy with a connectional fingerprint (Passingham et al., 2002) and receptor fingerprint (Zilles and Palomero-Gallagher, 2001). In the same way it is illustrated by a radial plot: the difference is that here the functional data are shown round the perimeter and the strength of the functional relation is plotted on the radius. The functional data could come from imaging studies

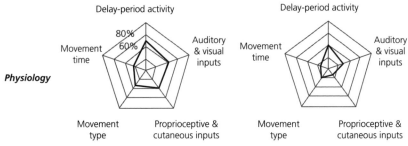

Fig. 5.1 Physiological fingerprints for the supplementary motor area (left) and ventral premotor cortex (right) based on single unit data. The types of activity are shown round the perimeter and the extent of the firing on the radius.

Reprinted by permission from Macmillan Publishers Ltd: Nature Reviews Neuroscience, 3 (8), Richard E. Passingham, Klaas E. Stephan and Rolf Kotter, The anatomical basis of functional localization in the cortex, pp. 606–16, doi:10.1038/nrn893 © 2002, Macmillan Publishers Ltd.

or from lesion studies, but we illustrate the principle using electrophysiological data. This serves as a reminder of the need for brain imaging to inform us about physiology.

Figure 5.1 provides an example of a functional fingerprint for the supplementary motor area (SMA) and the ventral premotor cortex (PMv). Five functional criteria are shown round the perimeter and the degree to which the cells are active in relation to each is shown on the radius (Passingham et al., 2002).

The advantage of plots of this sort is that they provide a ready summary of the available data, and can therefore give clues as to the fundamental operation that is performed by each area. The way in which they can do this is illustrated in Fig. 5.2, which shows data for the SMA and PMv for just two tasks: a visually guided motor task and a memory guided motor task. A scale of 1–7 is used. On this scale, 1 means that the cells are exclusively active on the visually guided task; and 2 and 3 that they are more active on this task. Correspondingly, 5 and 6 mean that the cells are more active on the memory guided task; and 7 that the cells are exclusively active on this task (Mushiake et al., 1991).

The histograms in the lower part of Fig. 5.2 show that there is a strong tendency for cells in PMv to fire during the visually guided task and for the cells in the SMA to fire during the memory guided task. The same distinction is clearly made in the radial plots above in Fig. 5.2 (Passingham and Wise, 2012). Functional fingerprints are, therefore, a way of visualizing the functional differences between areas.

We suggest that plotting these is the first of three stages in the interpretation of function. As a worked example, consider the ventral premotor cortex and the anterior inferior parietal (AIP) area with which it is interconnected (Borra

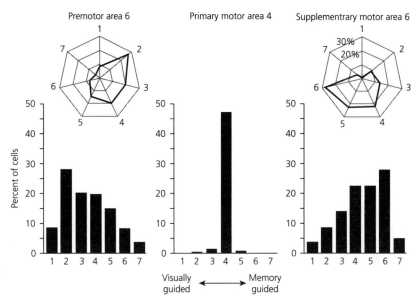

Fig. 5.2 Physiological fingerprints for the ventral premotor cortex (left), motor cortex (center) and supplementary motor area (right). For the histograms below: 1, 2, and 3 mean exclusively firing, mainly firing, or tending to fire on a visually cued task; 6, 7, and 8 mean tending to fire, mainly firing, or exclusively firing on the memory guided task; and 4 means firing equally on the two tasks. The radial plots are shown above.

Reproduced from H. Mushiake, M. Inase, and J. Tanji, Neuronal activity in the primate premotor, supplementary, and precentral motor cortex during visually guided and internally determined sequential movements, Journal of Neurophysiology, 66 (3), pp. 705–718 © 1991, American Physiological Society.

et al., 2008). There are more visual cells in AIP than in PMv, but more motor and visuomotor cells in PMv than AIP (Raos et al., 2006). This suggests that parietal AIP is fundamentally a sensory area with both visual and tactile inputs (Grefkes et al., 2002); whereas premotor PMv is fundamentally a motor area, with outputs to the primary motor cortex (Muakkassa and Strick, 1979) and the spinal cord (He et al., 1993). Though there are cells that fire during movement in AIP (Raos et al., 2006), these could derive their firing either from back projections from PMv or from proprioceptive input from the periphery.

The second stage is to specify the *operation* that is performed by an area. Thus, the key to PMv is the visuomotor cells. These fire not only when a piece of food is shown, but also when the animal prepares to grasp it. They are involved in the transformation from an object as seen to an object as grasped and so felt.

The final stage is to say *how* this transformation is performed. This involves detailed electrophysiology and anatomy. But, for a system with networks of interacting nerve cells, it also involves computational modeling. Although reaching appears to be a relatively simple task, the specification of how it is performed requires expertise in engineering as well as electrophysiology (Shadmehr and Wise, 2005).

Imaging functional specialization

The same three stages apply to studies that use brain imaging. It is an advantage of brain imaging that there have by now been very many thousands of studies and the results of many of these can be gathered into a database. Examples are the Open fMRI project (http://openfmri.org) and the BrainMap database (http://brainmap.org). So it is increasingly possible to plot functional fingerprints for different areas. Figure 5.3 shows fingerprints for the dorsal anterior cingulate cortex and the rostral agranular insula (Sporns, 2014). Subregions of these two areas are strongly interconnected (Vogt and Pandya, 1987).

As expected, the functional fingerprints of the two areas are similar but not identical. The differences relate to their different inputs and outputs. For example, there are stronger somatic activations in the insula and stronger executive activations in the anterior cingulate cortex. The dysgranular insula has strong somatic inputs, whereas the anterior cingulate cortex does not (Saleem

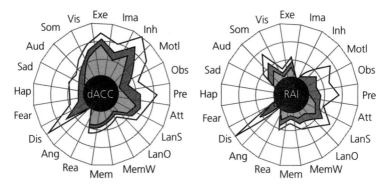

Fig. 5.3 Functional fingerprints for the dorsal anterior cingulate cortex (dACC, left) and rostral agranular insula (RAI, right) based on imaging data. Different aspects of the data are shown round the circumference such as "Mem" = memory and "Exe" = executive.

Reprinted by permission from Macmillan Publishers Ltd: Nature Neuroscience, 17 (5), Olaf Sporns, Contributions and challenges for network models in cognitive neuroscience, pp. 652–660 doi:10.1038/nn.3690 © 2014, Macmillan Publishers Ltd.

et al., 2008); and there are outputs to motor cortex from the caudal cingulate motor area but not from the insula (Dum and Strick, 2005).

The data for Fig. 5.3 were taken from the BrainMap database, but there are three problems. One is that, as mentioned in the previous chapter, the areas are poorly specified anatomically. Another problem is that the database draws on data from many different laboratories that vary greatly in methods and quality. But the most critical problem is that, though BrainMap provides functional labels for a series of coordinates throughout the brain (Lancaster et al., 2012), the functional task labels are relatively crude. For example, "Mem" refers to memory and "Att" to attention. These are labels for broad classes of tasks rather than specific operations, even though the source data may have derived from a precisely controlled experiment that was designed to identify specific processes.

For these reasons it can be better to be selective, analyzing the results of studies that fit stringent criteria. For example, Duncan and Owen (2000) carried out a meta-analysis by picking five studies that had specifically manipulated the cognitive demands of a task. The aim was to choose studies that manipulated the task demands by varying one parameter. For example, one study manipulated perceptual difficulty, another memory load, and yet another the degree to which the task had been learned.

There was activation in the dorsal prefrontal cortex in all cases. This suggests that the dorsal prefrontal cortex is involved when tasks are attentionally demanding, even though the different tasks make different demands. This led Duncan (2010) to characterize the dorsal prefrontal cortex as being part of a "multiple-demand system." The next chapter will describe this system in detail.

Two lessons emerge from the study by Duncan and Owen (2000). One is that it can be dangerous to try to interpret the function of an area by relying on one task alone. Many previous studies had reported activation in the dorsal prefrontal cortex when subjects performed working memory tasks, and this had led the authors to conclude that the key to the area is working memory. Yet there is activation within the dorsal prefrontal cortex when subjects are given difficult perceptual discriminations with no working memory load (Crittenden and Duncan, 2014).

There is another lesson to be drawn. A meta-analysis of the sort carried out by Duncan and Owen can protect against an error that it is easy to make. This is to suppose that, because other studies report activation of the dorsal prefrontal cortex during working memory tasks, the activation in the current study reflects working memory. The problem is that this conclusion involves what has been called a "reverse inference" (D'Esposito et al., 1998). In a seminal paper, Poldrack (2006) set out the logic of such an inference. It is briefly explained in simple terms in Box 5.1.

Box 5.1 Reverse inference

The logic of a reverse inference is as follows:

1. Area A is activated in the present study.

2. In other studies area A was activated during the process or condition X.

3. Therefore in the present study it is activated because of X.

   This inference may or may not be valid.

   If A is also activated during processes Y and Z, or if it is not known whether A is activated during Y and Z, the inference is not valid.

   If A is *only* activated during X, it is valid.

Note the implicit reliance on evidence that A is not activated in Y or Z, despite the fact that classical statistics are not able to prove such a null hypothesis. Bayesian methods can be used to estimate the confidence one has that A is not activated in Y or Z but unfortunately these are rarely used.

Meta-analyses across multiple studies of multiple tasks X, Y, and Z provide a pragmatic tool for understanding the functions of an area, from a range of tasks that have, and have not, been associated with activation of area A. But, though meta-analyses include a range of studies, they are still unable to prove the null hypothesis. Reverse inference may be useful to raise a hypothesis about the functions of area A, but too often it is used on its own to draw conclusions about the reason for activation of an area during an experiment.

The paper by Poldrack gives a general probabilistic formulation, based on conditional probabilities.

The dangers of reverse inference should warn against cherry picking results from the literature. The best way of trying to protect against such an inference is to assess the function of an area across as wide a set of conditions as possible. Preferably, comparison should also be made with the activations in other areas across the same conditions.

This was done, for example, by Hope et al. (2014) in a study of word repetition. The stimuli were either auditory or visual. There were four types of auditory stimulus: spoken words (Word), pseudowords (Pseu), the sounds made by objects or animals (Sou), and humming (Hum). There were also four types of visual stimulus: visually presented words (Word), visually presented pseudowords (Pseu), pictures of objects and animals (Pic), and colored patterns (Col).

Finally, there were four tasks. In two the subjects repeated the sounds they heard or the names of the visual stimuli. In two the subjects pressed the key when the stimulus was the same as the one that had occurred one-back. For simplicity we present the result for only two of these tasks, repeating sounds (auditory speaking) and visual one-back.

The results were visualized by plotting the parameter estimates. As mentioned in Chapter 3, these are the β weights, where β is the slope in a regression model of the BOLD response. They provide an estimate of the degree to which each condition causes the observed activations, analogous to the 1–7-point scale used for electrophysiological fingerprint plots in Fig. 5.1.

Figure 5.4a plots the profile of the parameter estimates for Broca's area. The activations were greater when the subjects heard sounds, whether they had semantic content (Word, Sou) or not (Pseu, Hum). There was also significant activation in the visual one-back conditions. The reason is that the task involves working

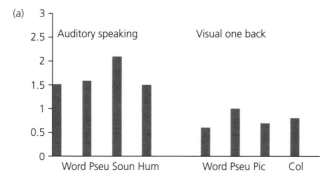

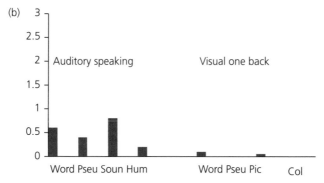

Fig. 5.4 Parameter estimates for (a) Broca's area (coordinate –36 12 6) and (b) the inferior prefrontal cortex (coordinate –36 30–12). The tasks are given above, and the conditions below. For conditions see text. For error bars see Hope et al. (2014).

Replotted using data from Hope TM, Prejawa S, Parker J, Oberhuber M, Seghier ML, Green DW, Price CJ, Dissecting the functional anatomy of auditory word repetition, Frontiers in Human Neuroscience 8 (246), doi: 10.3389/fnhum.2014.00246, 2014.

memory, and we know that an articulatory code is used even when the stimuli are visual (Conrad, 1972). Thus, the profile for Broca's area reflects phonological processing.

Figure 5.4b plots the profile for the inferior prefrontal cortex, area 12/47. Here the activations were significantly greater when the subjects heard meaningful (Word, Sou) rather than non-meaningful words (Pseu, Hum). There was no significant activation in the visual one-back condition. Thus, the profile reflects semantic rather than phonological processing.

Operations

The next stage is to specify the operations that are performed. Once again it is helpful to make use of the very detailed knowledge that we have of the properties of cells in macaque monkeys when approaching the brain imaging data. Box 5.2 provides some examples of these cells. The list is not exhaustive (Passingham and Wise, 2012).

Box 5.2 Coding by single cells

Specific stimuli

Specific responses

Polymodal coding

Quantity, time, distance

Temporal order

Categories of stimulus

Abstract value

Associations between stimuli

Conjunctions between stimuli, responses, and value

Sequences of responses

Rapid cumulative increase before response selection

Retrospective coding of prior stimulus

Prospective coding of future response

Match or non-match

Abstract conditional rule

Prediction error for reward

Prediction error for sensory consequences

Of course, the functions of an area are not performed by single cells but by subpopulations of many cells. Plots of the changes that occur over time suggest that different subpopulations are active at different times (Takeda and Funahashi, 2004). Imaging provides a summary measure at the population level and this can be useful in indicating the operation that is performed. To illustrate this, we will take the ventral visual system as an example, following the transformations that occur from initial input to later processing.

Conjunction in hierarchical coding in the ventral stream

In the visual system, as in all sensory systems, a set of subordinate cells feed information onto superordinate cells (Cadieu et al., 2007). Here the critical operation is one of conjunction. Cells in visual area V4 have larger receptive fields than those in areas V2 or V1 (Desimone et al., 1985). This can be explained if we suppose that a set of cells with small receptive fields, each for a different part of one visual field, are fed onto higher order cells, which are then able to fire irrespective of the exact position of the stimulus within that field. There is anatomical evidence that such a conjunction is possible: there is a noticeable increase in the number of spines on the layer three pyramidal cells as one progresses from V1 through V2 to V4 and inferotemporal cortex (Elston, 2007).

Cells in V4 (Desimone et al., 1985) and the inferotemporal cortex (Tanaka, 1997) also respond to more complex stimuli than cells in V2 or V1. The implication is that a set of cells that respond to elements are fed onto higher order cells, which can thus combine these elements. So Grill-Spector et al. (1998) presented images in which the number of elements varied from 1 to 1,024. Using fMRI they then showed that, whereas V1 responds well to the images that are scrambled into very many elements, areas V4 and inferotemporal cortex respond best to images that are complete.

Multivariate pattern analysis (see Chapter 3) can also be used to study coding of such conjunctions. For example, Carlin et al. (2011, 2012) used multivariate imaging in combination with models of information processing to study the way in which facial and eye cues are interpreted. They identified a hierarchy of visual areas in which anterior regions in the temporal lobe encode the conjunction of head and eye positions that reveals the direction of gaze, whereas posterior regions encode the orientation of the head irrespective of gaze or more basic physical features of the visual image.

The next stage in sensory processing is to form conjunctions between cells in the different sensory streams. We know, for example, that there are polymodal cells in the upper bank of the superior temporal sulcus in macaque monkeys

(Bruce et al., 1981) as well as in the ventral intraparietal (VIP) area (Avillac et al., 2005). The conjunction of vision, touch, and hearing in VIP can be demonstrated by presenting stimuli in each modality. So Bremmer et al. (2001) scanned with fMRI and found activation in VIP in human subjects, irrespective of whether visual, tactile, or auditory stimuli were presented.

Matching and associations

Sensory information, whether unimodal or polymodal, needs to be compared with information that is held in memory. Recognition requires the operations of matching and non-matching of stimuli. These operations can be studied by presenting exemplars and then presenting for recognition either the same pictures or pictures that are dissimilar. In an imaging study, Ishai and Yago (2006) presented faces that the subjects had either seen or not seen before. The activation in the fusiform gyrus was greater when the subjects recognized the faces (match) than when they did not (non-match). There are also cells in the inferotemporal cortex of macaque monkeys that respond differently to familiar and novel visual stimuli (Baylis and Rolls, 1987).

There is a difference between simply recognizing stimuli and identifying them. Identifying requires the operation of associating the stimulus with an identifier. The stimulus is "an X" or "a Y."

The ability to identify can be studied in human subjects by asking them to name the stimulus. Hocking et al. (2009) scanned subjects while they named objects, and found activation in the perirhinal cortex when the stimuli were all of one category and visually confusable. And it has been shown that the progressive loss of tissue in this area in fronto-temporal dementia produces an impairment in just the same stimulus conditions (Kivisaari et al., 2012).

The association between names and their referents is arbitrary, and it has therefore to be learned. The process can be studied by teaching subjects the names of novel faces. Tsukiara et al. (2002) found activation in the ventral prefrontal cortex during new learning. However, when the subjects were asked for the names of faces they had already learned, activation was observed in the temporal lobe. Chapter 7 considers the significance of this effect.

The learning and retrieval of such arbitrary associates has also been studied in macaque monkeys. Miyashita and colleagues have done this by teaching that fractal A goes with fractal B (Miyashita, 1990). After learning, there are cells in the perirhinal cortex that fire both on presentation of A and on presentation of B, even though there is no visual similarity between A and B (Sakai and Miyashita, 1991). Thus, the operation that is performed by the perirhinal cortex is that of conjunction (Bussey et al., 2005).

Retrospective and prospective coding

Once the stimuli have been recognized and identified, the next step is to decide on the appropriate response. However, there are situations in which it is not possible to respond at once, and in those cases it is necessary to bridge the delay. This can be done either by continuing to code for the stimulus or by continuing to code for the response. Both involve sustained or set activity.

One way of finding out whether the delay-period activation represents the stimulus presented is to use a multivariate pattern analysis. This was done by Sreenivasan et al. (2014) in an experiment in which the subjects were presented either with faces or with scenes. After a delay of 9 seconds, a probe stimulus was presented and the subjects had to say whether it did or did not match the sample. This design means that during the delay the subjects could not know what response would be appropriate, since they could not predict what probe would be shown.

The multivariate analysis showed that during the delay it was possible to decode the type of stimulus from activations in the extrastriate cortex, including the lateral occipital complex (LOC). The delay-related activations in visual areas must therefore reflect retrospective coding of the stimulus that had been presented. Area LOC includes the posterior inferotemporal cortex and, in macaque monkeys, there are cells there that continue to fire during an unfilled memory delay (Miller et al., 1991).

Delay-period activation can also be found in the prefrontal cortex (Lewis-Peacock and Postle, 2008). So as to distinguish retrospective and prospective coding, Lewis-Peacock and Postle taught subjects associations between pictures of people, objects, and scenes. So, for example, the picture of person A might be associated after a delay with object B. A multivariate analysis was used to decode whether the delay-period activation reflected memory of the first member of the association (retrospective coding) or expectation of the second memory of the association (prospective coding).

The technique was essentially the same as that used by Rainer et al. (1999) in an experiment with macaque monkeys. They taught the monkeys that picture A was associated, after a delay, with picture B, even though these were not visually similar. In the experiment with human subjects, as in that with monkeys, both types of coding could be found. However, prospective coding was stronger than retrospective coding toward the end of the delay.

Conjunction of response and value

After presentation of a stimulus, a response is required whether or not a delay is interposed. In experiments on monkeys the response that is rewarded is the one that the experimenter has allocated as "correct." The monkey has, therefore, to evaluate the different potential responses in the light of its past experience of reward. Chapter 3 has already mentioned that there are cells in the dorsal prefrontal cortex that fire when the monkey prepares to make a saccade in a particular direction for a specific number of drops of juice (Wallis and Miller, 2003). And there are cells in the orbital frontal cortex that code for the abstract value of the reward (Padoa-Schioppa and Assad, 2006).

Human subjects can also be taught to make choices on the basis of reward. Boorman et al. (2011) presented subjects with three pictures on each trial. Under each picture there was a display of the number of points that could be gained if that picture turned out to be the correct one. The subjects tried a picture, and were then informed whether it was correct. If it was, a red bar lengthened so as to represent the amount of reward gained. The other two pictures were then presented and the subject was given the opportunity to choose between them. For purposes of exposition, we call these two pictures the "alternatives," since neither had initially been chosen on that trial.

So the set-up was such that, in making their decisions, the subjects could take into account not only the number of points available on the present trial, but also the likely value of a choice based on the past history of rewards. There were voxels in the lateral polar prefrontal cortex in which the activation reflected the value of the better of the two alternatives. Thus, human subjects can keep track of the values of potential alternatives. The fundamental operation is that of forming a conjunction between the representation of a particular choice and its value.

Computational models

The previous section presented examples of the way in which imaging can be used to specify the operations that an area performs. However, the description of the operations has been in terms such as "sensory coding," "prospective coding," or "conjunction of response and value." These are the terms of ordinary language.

If we are to understand the operations in more detail, we need terms that are more precise and that precision is offered by mathematics. The final stage in the analysis is, therefore, to account for the operations that an area performs in terms of computational models of the operations underlying the functions of an area. We provide three examples of the way in which activations can be related to parameters in formal computational models.

Accumulation-to-threshold models

The first example concerns decision-making or the selection of responses. Gold and Shadlen (2007) presented an account of how decisions, such as perceptual decisions, can be made in the form of an accumulation-to-threshold mechanism. There are two basic forms of accumulation-to-threshold model. In the first, separate cell populations are each coupled to a different response, and separately accumulate evidence in favor of their output as increases in their activity. When the activation of one of the accumulators (representing the accumulated evidence) has reached a critical threshold, the subject is committed to that output. This type of decision is analogous to a horserace, each accumulator trying to be "first past the post." A second mechanism applies to two-alternate forced choice decisions, in which a single accumulator changes its activity according to the evidence in favor of either one percept/response (to a positive threshold) or the other (to a negative threshold). These simple models are able to capture a wide set of behavioral and psychophysical phenomena, and have direct neurophysiological support (Ratcliff et al., 2003; Churchland et al., 2008). They can also, therefore, be used to inform experiments that use brain imaging.

We illustrate this application with reference to the supplementary motor area (SMA). When monkeys spontaneously reach for a target in the absence of an instruction cue, a significant minority of the cells in the SMA start firing early before movement (Romo and Schultz, 1987). In this study, the mean time for 43 of the 266 cells recorded was 1,430 milliseconds before movement. The activity of these cells increased until it reached a peak 370 milliseconds before movement. When humans were asked to choose which hand with which to make a response, many SMA units progressively increased their firing rates over approximately a second prior to the response. Many were selective for one or other response, and the neurophysiological activity could accurately predict which response was to be made (Fried et al., 2011).

Imaging data capture this effect and show its extent throughout the motor system, using computational models of the decision process. For example, Rowe and colleagues (Rowe et al., 2010; Zhang et al., 2012) adapted the horserace model to account for a decision between multiple alternative responses, even when the neural generators of adjacent finger presses cannot be distinguished by fMRI. In the critical condition, there were no external stimuli to specify which action to take and the subject decided from trial to trial which finger to move. A ballistic accumulation-to-threshold model was developed for how this might be implemented neurally, providing an estimate on each trial of the total accumulated activity for the "winning response" that was executed and the "losing responses" that were never made.

The analysis of the fMRI data then looked for BOLD activations that related to this model prediction as opposed to other potential differences between trials. There was a maximal activation in the SMA. Furthermore, the analysis was able to capture the tendency of subjects to choose not to repeat previous responses (Zhang et al., 2012). This was modeled by the selective inhibition of the accumulators, and here the activation was in the ventral prefrontal cortex. This is consistent with the findings of a study that applied TMS to this region so as to study the mechanism via which responses are inhibited (Neubert et al., 2010).

Monitoring volatility in an uncertain world

When subjects make decisions, they take into account the success or otherwise of decisions made in the past. Behrens et al. (2007) have given a Bayesian account of optimal decision-making when the past history is characterized by changes in the likely consequences of particular decisions. The frequency with which these changes have happened in the past is referred to as the "volatility" of the environment. This can be illustrated by considering a simple reversal task. Choosing response 1 is rewarded on successive occasions, but there is then a switch such that choosing response 2 is now rewarded. The volatility relates to the frequency with which reversals occur, rather than the probability of reward per se.

Behrens et al. presented a Bayesian formulation of sequential decisions that included updated estimates of the reward probability (r), the volatility (v), and changes in the volatility (k). They looked for activations that related both to monitoring of the outcomes and estimates of the volatility (v). There was a single activation that met these criteria, and this was in the anterior cingulate cortex.

Behrens et al. then carried out an analysis on the rate of learning. A subject who places more weight on the recent outcomes when the volatility is high should learn more quickly than a subject who does not. Conversely, continuing to place weight on earlier response outcomes will help to learn in an unpredictable but non-volatile environment. So Behrens et al. applied a delta learning rule to separate phases of the experiment with high and low volatility, and estimated the subjects' learning rate in each phase. They found that the learning rates were higher in phases with higher volatility. The corresponding fMRI results indicated that the activation in the anterior cingulate cortex increased with volatility when the subjects monitored the outcomes of their decisions.

It is, therefore, significant that in macaque monkeys there are cells in the anterior cingulate cortex that fire when the response is rewarded or when reward fails to occur (Procyk et al., 2000). This firing decreases if the task becomes routine (Procyk et al., 2000). However, the cells continue to fire in a changing environment, when the associations between response and reward are less reliable (Amiez et al., 2006).

So the combination of imaging with a formal model of optimized behavioral decisions was able to identify a highly specific process. And the results are consistent with what we know from single-unit recording in monkeys.

Prediction error

It is well established in the field of psychology that learning occurs when the consequences are not as expected (Rescorla, 1976). When an unexpected reward occurs, or an expected reward fails to occur, there is a prediction error. The physiological correlates of these error signals have been identified in monkeys. For example, if a stimulus is presented that predicts an unexpected reward, then dopamine cells in the substantia nigra fire when the reward is received. However, if the trials are repeated, then as learning occurs the cells fire earlier within the trial after the predictive stimulus; and they eventually stop firing in response to the actual reward (Schultz, 1998).

Schultz et al. (1997) presented a temporal difference model to account for this effect. The account is mathematical. It states that at the beginning of learning the expected reward at time t [V(t)] is zero, and that this is true for all times within the trial until after the reward or UCS (unconditioned stimulus) has been presented. On the next trial a positive prediction error is generated when $V(t_{ucs})$ is compared with $V(t_{ucs} - 1)$. Learning occurs as a result of this prediction error, and as it progresses, so V(t) is updated for each time going back to t_{cs}, that is to the time of the CS (conditioned stimulus).

O'Doherty et al. (2003) tested this model in humans, using whole brain imaging. They presented their subjects with one of three fractals on each trial, and there were three possible outcomes: a rewarding glucose taste, a neutral taste, or no taste. The measure of learning of the association between fractal and taste was the degree of anticipatory pupillary dilation. The fMRI analysis looked for activations that related to the prediction error that was generated by the temporal difference model.

Activations were found that related to this error signal as estimated from the model. These were in the ventral striatum, which receives dopamine inputs from the substantia nigra, and in the orbitofrontal cortex, which is connected with the ventral striatum. This accords with evidence from macaque monkeys in which there are cells in both areas that fire after the predictive stimulus, during the delay in expectation of the reward, or after presentation of the reward itself (Schultz et al., 2000).

However, there are differences between the areas in the proportions of cells of the different types, reflecting the distinct functional fingerprints of the two areas. For example, there are more cells in the orbitofrontal cortex that fire after a visual predictive stimulus, consistent with the strong connections of this area with the inferotemporal cortex that conveys processed visual information (Saleem et al., 2008).

Human cognition

In previous sections we have often referred to data from macaque monkeys when trying to explain how a particular operation occurs. But there is an obvious objection. This is that, as mentioned in Chapter 1, the special advantage of imaging is exactly that it can be used to study abilities of which macaque monkeys are *not* capable. Of these the most obvious are language and complex social interactions that rely on a theory of mind.

Though Broca's area is not unique to humans (Petrides et al., 2005), the ability to read is. And, as already mentioned, in the human brain Broca's area is involved in the transformation from visual text to articulation (Hope et al., 2014). It might appear that there is no way of studying the cellular mechanism other than by direct recording from cells during surgery on patients (Engel et al., 2005). However, this is too pessimistic. We suggest that problems of this sort are tractable if approached in several steps.

To illustrate this approach, we consider "mentalizing" (Frith and Frith, 2006); this is the ability of people to reflect on the thoughts of others. As already mentioned in Chapter 3, humans are not unique in being able to read social signs. Monkeys can use these to predict the behavior of others, and their ability to do so depends on the anterior cingulate cortex (Rudebeck et al., 2006) as it does for humans (Amodio and Frith, 2006). What is different about people is that they are capable of metacognition: they can think about their own thoughts, and this means that they can use social signs to interpret what others are thinking.

The first step is to identify any common ground across species. For example, there are basic tasks that both monkeys and human subjects can perform; so one can scan monkeys and human subjects so as to find the areas that are activated in common in people and monkeys. The next step is to study the connections of these areas (see Chapter 4) and characterize the patterns of cell activity in macaque monkeys. From this one can specify an hypothesis of a possible mechanism that could operate both in monkeys and people. The final step is to see whether the human ability can be accounted for by the development of these more basic operations. For clarity we number the steps in the following paragraphs.

1. The first step involves scanning human subjects and macaque monkeys while they watch videos of actions. When macaque monkeys (Nelissen et al.,

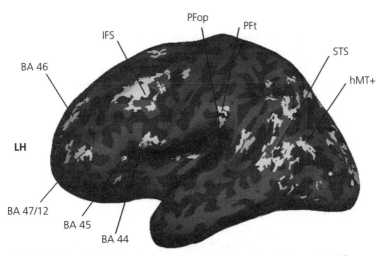

Fig. 5.5 Activation in the left anterior inferior parietal cortex (PFop and PFt) for observing actions.

Reprinted from Brain Research, 1582, R.E. Passingham, A. Chung, B. Goparaju, A. Cowey, and L.M. Vaina, Using action understanding to understand the left inferior parietal cortex in the human brain, pp. 64–76. doi: 10.1016/j.brainres.2014.07.035, Copyright (2014), with permission from Elsevier

2011) or human subjects (Passingham et al., 2014) do so, there are activations in the motion area MST and the upper bank of the superior temporal sulcus (STS). Figure 5.5 shows the data for human subjects.

Both MST and the upper bank of the STS send projections in the macaque monkey brain to the inferior parietal area PFG (Rozzi et al., 2006) and there are cells in PFG that respond to biological motion (Rozzi et al., 2008). As a result, there are also activations in the parietal area PFG of monkeys (Nelissen et al., 2011) and parietal areas PFt and PFop of human subjects (Fig. 5.5) (Passingham et al., 2014) when they watch videos of actions. It has been suggested that areas PFt and PFop in the human brain are homologous with the area PFG in the macaque monkey brain (Passingham et al., 2014).

2. The next step is to study the neuronal mechanisms. In macaque monkeys there are cells in area PFG that have mirror properties, firing both when a monkey acts and when it observes a similar action (Bonini et al., 2010). And many cells show similar properties in the ventral premotor cortex (Bonini et al., 2010). The repetition suppression technique has been used to show that there may be similar cells in the anterior inferior parietal cortex in the human brain. There

is less activation in the region when subjects observe an action if they have recently executed that same action (Chong et al., 2008). This suggests that the same cell populations are involved in observation and execution.

However, the inferior parietal cortex is not the only area that receives an input concerning biological motion. There are also projections to the anterior cingulate cortex from the upper bank of the superior temporal sulcus (Saleem et al., 2008). When human observers watch videos and make judgments about the beliefs (Grezes et al., 2004b) or intentions (Grezes et al., 2004a) of others, there are activations in the superior temporal sulcus and anterior cingulate cortex. And this is also true when subjects view videos of themselves as actors (Grezes et al., 2004a).

Thus a possible mechanism involves the operation of mirror neurons. These have been reported in the anterior cingulate cortex both in macaque monkeys (de Araujo et al., 2012) and in patients during surgery (Mukamel et al., 2010). The activity in the anterior cingulate cortex during viewing can be accounted for by the input from the upper bank of the superior temporal cortex. The activity there during action can be accounted for by the connections of the cingulate convexity with the cingulate motor areas in the cingulate sulcus (Morecraft et al., 2012).

3. The studies mentioned so far are limited in that they simply involve the observation of actions. So, further steps are needed to account for the role of the anterior cingulate cortex in judging the intentions of others. We suggest that a clue as to how this might be done is provided by Fig. 5.6, which shows a series of activation peaks from human imaging, shown on a midsagittal view of the anterior cingulate cortex (Passingham and Wise, 2012). The references for the different peaks are given in the text there.

Peak (1) marks an activation observed when subjects are required to attend to their actual movement (1), whereas peak (2) marks an activation when they are required to attend to their *intended* movement (2). These peaks are in adjacent regions. The intermediate peaks (3), (4), and (5) mark activations when subjects are required to attend to their own internal states. These relate not to intentions but to bodily states.

The remaining peaks lie more anteriorly. These relate to situations in which the subjects are required to think about themselves or others. Number (6) marks activations when subjects are required to use trait words to describe either themselves or others. Peak (7) refers to activations when subjects monitor and reflect on their own performance and peak (8) to activations when subjects remember episodes in their own life. Peak (9) marks the average coordinate for tasks in which the subjects are required to reflect on the mental states of others.

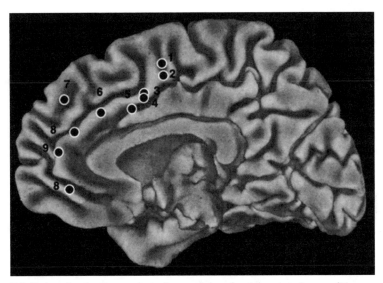

Fig. 5.6 Series of activation peaks in the medial prefrontal cortex. For conditions see text.

4. A trend is apparent here. The posterior and intermediate peaks (1–5) relate to the self, the bodily self, its actions and intentions. The more anterior peaks (6–8) relate to the ability to reflect on the self. This involves metacognition (Lau and Rosenthal, 2011).

In moving from monkeys to humans, the advance to metacognition could be achieved by differentiating out a new anterior band of cortex, and indeed there is no equivalent in the macaque monkey brain of the human paracingulate area 32 (Passingham, 2008). But the comparative studies and neural mechanisms in paragraphs 1–3 provide a clear framework with which to test hypotheses about the human mechanisms for mentalizing.

We do not pretend that in this worked example we have achieved a full understanding of the theory of mind. Our aim is rather to suggest how a problem of this complexity can be tackled despite limitations in the animal models that would otherwise be amenable to direct neurophysiological investigation. The approach involves treating imaging as a branch of neuroscience, not photography, and relating the results of brain imaging to the evidence from cells and their connections.

Summary

The aim of imaging neuroscience is to understand how the human brain works. This involves specifying the functions that are performed by the different areas. We suggest three key stages. The first is to characterize the difference between areas, and here it is helpful to plot functional fingerprints. The second stage is to specify the operations or transformations that each area performs. The final stage is to account for these operations in terms of a computational model, looking for activations that relate to parameters in the model. This approach supports even challenging areas of investigation into functions that are special features of human cognition.

Chapter 6

Functional systems

Abstract

The different areas of the brain do not work in isolation. Instead they operate as integrated systems. These systems can be identified because areas within the same system have a similar, though not identical, pattern of connections. Because the areas are also interconnected, the activations of areas within a system tend to covary over time, whether the subject is at rest or engaged in a task. Thus the different systems can be identified on the basis of the degree to which they covary or are activated independently. There are two aims in studying functional systems. One is to identify the nature of information that flows from one area to another. The other is to characterize the causal structure of the system. Several methods are available to do this, and these have been particularly useful for studying top-down effects, as in the voluntary control of attention.

Keywords

functional systems, resting-state covariance, graph theory, psychophysiological interactions, structural equation modeling, dynamic causal modeling, top-down effects, flow of information.

Introduction

While specialized areas perform specific operations, they do not act in isolation. They form part of functional systems with interacting components that are interdependent. However, the term "systems" is often misused, simply being applied to the pattern of activations found in an experimental condition. A group of activations does not constitute a "system" unless it can be shown that the areas that are activated are closely connected, and that one part of the system can influence another part.

It is important to distinguish two ways in which systems of the brain can be visualized. The first is via the use of tracers or diffusion imaging, so as to demonstrate "anatomical" or structural connectivity. Two or more areas can be regarded as being part of a system if they have similarities in their connections. For example, tracer studies have shown the cortex in the intraparietal sulcus and the cortex in the dorsal prefrontal area 46 have many cortical and subcortical outputs in common (Selemon and Goldman-Rakic, 1988). The anatomical connections between regions impose constraints on the flow of communication, and are thus important determinants of the functional properties and efficiency of the brain (Deco et al., 2011). As mentioned in Chapter 4, a comprehensive description of the structural networks of the brain, encompassing their elements and connections, is known as the "connectome" (Sporns et al., 2005),

The second way in which systems can be visualized is by studying the statistical dependencies between activations in different areas, so as to demonstrate "functional connectivity." For fMRI, these statistical relationships are readily assessed by measuring the covariance between the time series of activations in different areas while subjects perform tasks or by measuring the coupling between the intrinsic activations that can be observed at rest. If there is high covariance between the activation of two areas, it is also likely that they are connected by one or by only a few synapses (Johnston et al., 2008). Other methods to examine the statistical dependencies can be used such as the rates of change of activity in relation to activity elsewhere (dynamic causal modeling, DCM), lagged autoregressive models, or Granger causality modeling. DCM is described later in this chapter and Granger causality in the next.

The fact that there is a covariance between activations in areas A and B says nothing about whether A is driving B or B is driving A. Indeed neither might be true since the data could be explained if both are influenced by C. The directional influence within a system is referred to by the term "effective" connectivity, and is an important aspect of causality in brain systems. Demonstrating effective connectivity with fMRI data, as for direct neurophysiological data, requires a model or set of models for the causal interactions between A, B, and C. If one does not have a priori evidence for a particular model on the basis of the connections, then differences in how well the models explain the observations can be used to support inferences about the most likely organization of the functional system. The different models imply different hypotheses about the functional system, and it helps to be explicit about these hypotheses.

In this section we illustrate how the workings of a system can be studied in terms of its anatomical, functional, and effective connectivity. We suggest that it is most useful to adopt four stages in the analysis of a system. The first is to identify the system on the basis of its anatomical and functional connectivity.

The second is to characterize the function of the system as a whole. The third stage is to study the directional flow of information within the system, by which one element influences another.

However, there is a final stage. Just as the aim of functional localization is to identify the transformation that is performed by each area, so the aim when studying a system must be to identify what information is being transmitted between areas. Here multivariate methods offer promise. Imaging is no longer simply a matter of measuring activations: it concerns the flow of information (Kriegeskorte et al., 2006).

The core system

The system we have chosen to illustrate has been referred to as the "core system" (Markov et al., 2013). This identification has been made on the basis of the anatomical wiring of the macaque monkey brain. The diagram is detailed and so new methods are needed to describe the internal structure and to understand the principles that shape its organization. One way of doing this is to use graph theory, building on the pairwise relations between parts of the network so as to assess the topological relationships among them. An advantage of graph theory is that it can be applied to any complex and dynamic system; there are robust organizational principles that apply across species from the nematode worm to humans. It can also be applied across widely different spatial and temporal scales and across different types of data, such as fiber tracings, diffusion weighted imaging, fMRI, and MEG (Bullmore and Sporns, 2009).

As mentioned in Chapter 1, Markov et al. (2014) have gathered extensive data in a single study of the macaque monkey brain. They injected 29 different areas with tracers, so as to reveal their inputs. The methods used were particularly sensitive and connections were counted even if they were minor. As a result, the average number of steps required to connect one region to any other in the resulting map is much shorter than in other maps (Markov et al., 2013). Here path length is defined in topological terms, referring to the number of connections and not to geometric distances. The model of the cortex that emerges is of a set of highly connected "hubs" forming a central core with a periphery of less connected nodes. The central core consisted of 13 hubs and the periphery of 17 nodes.

Figure 6.1 shows a simplified version of the core system. Posterior areas include the polysensory area in the upper bank of the superior temporal sulcus, the inferior parietal area 7a extending into the intraparietal sulcus, and the medial parietal area 7m. Prefrontal areas include the caudal prefrontal areas 8m, 8l, and 8B, the more anterior prefrontal areas 9/46 and 46, and the frontal

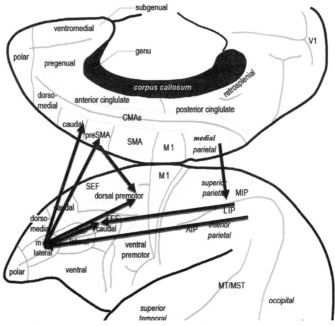

Fig. 6.1 Simplified diagram of the connections of the core system in a macaque monkey brain. For references see text.

polar area 10. The output areas are the dorsal and ventral premotor cortex and the rostral cingulate motor area.

In the macaque monkey many of these areas have also been described as forming part of a "rich club" of highly connected hub regions that are disproportionately connected to each other (Harriger et al., 2012). Van den Heuvel and Sporns (2011) used diffusion weighted imaging to chart connections in the human brain and found a similar rich club of interconnected regions. This included the medial parietal cortex, the superior parietal cortex, and the dorsal prefrontal cortex. Rich clubs and hub regions provide high computational efficiency in a complex system, optimizing metabolic efficiency while conferring remarkable robustness to non-selective lesions.

As already mentioned, even simple nervous systems, such as that in the nematode worm, adhere to many of the same topological principles as the human brain (Towlson et al., 2013), but the scale and complexity in primate brains permit unique functional properties. It is of note that many of the core areas identified by Markov et al (2013) are unique to the brains of primates (Passingham and Wise, 2012). This is true, for example, of areas AIP and LIP in the intraparietal sulcus, of the ventral premotor cortex (PMv), and of the granular prefrontal cortex including areas 8, 9/46, and 46. The core system, as identified in the brain of the macaque monkey, is thus fundamentally a primate system. It is this system that has been elaborated in the human brain for more complex cognitive and executive functions. Genovesio et al. (2014) have made tentative suggestions as to how this elaboration could have occurred.

The functions of the core system

The term "core" system is used here to refer to the anatomical system as identified by Markov et al. (2013). Within this system there are functional hubs. For example, we know that it includes subsystems that play a role in attention or task control (Vincent et al., 2008), and that there are functional subdivisions even within the dorsal prefrontal cortex (Cieslik et al., 2013).

The subsystems can be identified by measuring covariance during task performance. Dosenbach et al. (2007) used graph theory to characterize different clusters. They found one that included areas that were activated both when new tasks were initiated and when the outcomes were monitored. This cluster comprised the cortex in the intraparietal sulcus and the medial parietal cortex, the dorsal prefrontal cortex, and the dorsal and ventral premotor cortex. Another cluster of areas was also activated during the maintenance of task set (the implicit or explicit task "rules"). This comprised the polar prefrontal cortex and the cortex in the anterior cingulate sulcus.

The areas identified in this study are activated across a wide variety of tasks (Dosenbach et al., 2006). However, it is one thing to show that the same areas are activated irrespective of task and another to show that this is true for the same voxels within each region. Fedorenko et al. (2013) gave seven tasks, chosen on two criteria. One was that the tasks should be diverse and the other that the difficulty of the tasks could be varied. There was activation in the core frontoparietal system on all tasks. Even when the analysis was performed for single subjects, it could be shown that the same voxels were activated across tasks.

As mentioned in the previous chapter, Duncan (2010) has suggested that the core system be described as a "multiple-demand" system. Homologous core systems are identifiable by fMRI in both humans and macaque monkeys (Stoewer et al., 2010). However, as already mentioned, there is no suggestion that the different components of the system contribute in the same way. So as to compare the information coded by different areas, Woolgar et al. (2011) therefore performed a multivariate analysis of the data from an fMRI study. By comparing the results it is possible to make suggestions as to the information that is transmitted between areas.

Woolgar et al. taught subjects tasks in which there were four stimulus locations and four response locations. The subjects learned which response location was appropriate given each of the stimulus locations, and the color of the background specified which of two stimulus/response mapping rules applied. This is a visual conditional motor task. Tasks of this sort are commonly used in human and animal studies of cognition, and have the advantage that they involve simple transformations from a stimulus to a correct output. They also involve flexible responding, with one response being appropriate at one time and another response at another, depending on the context. These features of the task enable one to decode the neural representations of stimulus codes and response codes, and the rules that associate them, whether the neural activity is recorded cell by cell or by fMRI.

Woolgar et al. found patterns of activation in the intraparietal sulcus and inferior frontal sulcus that reflected the stimulus locations and the mapping rule. There was an activation in the anterior cingulate sulcus that reflected the stimulus locations, mapping rule, and response, though the statistics for this did not quite reach significance. Finally, there was an activation in the motor cortex that reflected the response. These results suggest that the different areas carry out particular transformations and that their outputs then influence later areas. The flow through the system can be thought of as one in which information is transferred.

The same tasks can be given to macaque monkeys. In an experiment by Yamagata et al. (2012), a color cue was presented followed, after a delay, by two targets, located either on the left or the right of the screen. One color specified touching the left of the two targets and the other touching the right of the two targets, irrespective of the location of the two targets on the screen. Yamagata et al. recorded in three areas: the dorsal prefrontal cortex, ventral prefrontal cortex, and dorsal premotor cortex. The dorsal prefrontal cortex included areas 46d and 46v, both of which are part of the core system as defined by Markov et al. (2013). Roughly 8% of the cells in the ventral prefrontal cortex coded for the color of the instruction cue. Roughly 14% of the cells in the dorsal prefrontal cortex coded for the behavioral goal; these were found mainly in 46v as it borders on the inferior prefrontal convexity. The goal reflects the mapping rule rather than the response location. Finally, there were cells in the dorsal premotor cortex that coded for the behavioral goals and also cells that coded for the response. These results bear a striking resemblance to those of the imaging study by Woolgar et al. (2011).

The results of both studies indicate that the core system as a whole codes for the input/output rules that govern behavior. However, the different components differ in the strength of their association with different aspects of rule coding.

The current context is coded most clearly by the ventral prefrontal cortex, the current rule for mapping stimulus to goal is coded most clearly by the ventral part of the dorsal prefrontal cortex, and the motor response is coded most clearly in the motor cortex itself. So the results speak to the transfer of information between areas.

The reason why the core system can act as a multiple-demand system is that it can learn to generate any correct output (an action or goal) from any input (the cue), depending on the current situation (the context) (Passingham and Wise, 2012). This is true whether the goals are for the hand (Yamagata et al., 2012) or the eyes (Asaad et al., 1998). In the case of human subjects, the goals can involve words (Frith et al., 1991) or the choice of the item that completes the series on a test of reasoning (Bunge et al., 2005).

A system that can learn to generate any output for any input is necessarily one that is flexible. Different goals are appropriate depending on the context, and the context changes frequently between trials. That this is a critical factor is confirmed by experiments in which human subjects are given the opportunity to generate the goals at will. The activation in dorsal prefrontal area 46 is greater the number of switches, and this is true whether the subjects have to choose between finger movements (Rowe et al., 2010), numbers (Jahanshahi et al., 2000), or rules (Zhang et al., 2013).

Interactions within a system

The flow of information within a system depends on interactions between areas. But since the system is flexible, these interactions depend on the current task. To put it more generally, they are context dependent. There are several ways of investigating such interactions. We describe three of these, and illustrate them by showing how they can be used to understand the core system.

The two main hubs in the core system are the cortex in the intraparietal cortex and the dorsal prefrontal areas 9/46 and 46 (Selemon and Goldman-Rakic, 1988). Both the cortex in the intraparietal sulcus (Johnson et al., 1993) and the dorsal prefrontal cortex (Wang et al., 2002) send projections to the premotor areas.

Psychophysiological interactions

One way of investigating interactions in this system is to look for what have been called "psychophysiological interactions" (PPIs) (Friston et al., 1997). The method is described in Box 6.1.

We illustrate the use of this method in a study that compared the influence of the parietal and dorsal prefrontal cortex on the Pre-SMA and cingulate motor

Box 6.1 Psychophysiological interactions (PPI)

If the physiological interaction between two areas varies as a function of the psychological context, there is said to be a psychophysiological interaction. PPIs can be used to test hypotheses about effective connectivity, although they can also serve as descriptive markers of functional connectivity.

The commonest method to identify a PPI measures the relation between the activations in two areas over time. It uses a regression model to test whether the relation between the activations differs as a function of task condition or context. The model accommodates the gradual transition in fMRI signals between task conditions arising from the hemodynamic response. The PPI can be visualized by plotting the range of activations in area A against the range of activations in area B, and doing so separately for two tasks or conditions.

If the slopes are the same for the two conditions but the intercepts differ, this indicates a main effect of task/condition on activity. If the slopes differ between the two conditions, this will be expressed in the interaction term, hence the title "psychophysiological interaction." PPIs, therefore, provide a method for looking for context-dependent differences in the interactions between two areas. Higher order interactions may also occur, if, for example, the PPI is present in one group more than another, or on a drug more than placebo.

It is important to realize that the activations in areas A and B could be greater in task/condition 2 than in task/condition 1 without there being a change in the regression slope for the activations of area A against area B. In other words, PPIs are not simply an artifact of increased activation.

areas. Lau et al. (2004) used the task devised by Libet et al. (1983a) to study when subjects first become aware of their intention to move. In one condition, the subjects were required to report when they were first aware of actually moving their finger, and in the other condition, to report when they were first aware of "the urge to move."

When the two conditions were compared, there was activation in the Pre-SMA when the subjects attended to their intention as opposed to the movement itself. For the same comparison there was also activation in the dorsal prefrontal cortex and the cortex in the intraparietal sulcus. So Lau et al. plotted the activations in these two areas against the activation in the Pre-SMA. There was a significant PPI for the dorsal prefrontal cortex against the Pre-SMA, but not for the cortex in the intraparietal sulcus against the Pre-SMA.

It is important to recognize two limitations of what can be inferred from these results. First, as plotted, the PPI suggests that it is the prefrontal cortex that influences the Pre-SMA. But the data could also be plotted the other way round: in other words, the activations for the Pre-SMA could be plotted against the activations for the dorsal prefrontal cortex. A significant PPI could, there-fore, also suggest that it is the Pre-SMA that influences the prefrontal cortex. Other information would be needed to justify assertions about the direction of influence.

The second limitation is that the lack of a significant PPI for the parietal cor-tex does not mean that the parietal cortex plays no part in the awareness of intention. In fact, when tested on a similar Libet paradigm, patients with par-ietal strokes fail to report awareness of their intention before the time of the movement itself (Sirigu et al., 2004). In other words, even if the enhancement in the Pre-SMA is not driven by the parietal cortex, the perception of that enhance-ment involves the parietal cortex.

Structural equation modeling

There is another way of studying psychophysiological interactions. This is to use structural equation modeling (SEM). The method is briefly described in Box 6.2. For more details we refer the reader to Horwitz et al. (1999).

Rowe et al. (2002) used SEM to compare the influence of the cortex in the intraparietal sulcus and the dorsal prefrontal cortex on the premotor cortex. There were three critical conditions. In one the subjects performed a simple automatic sequence of finger movements. In another they were specifically instructed to attend to each move by thinking about it in advance, and in a third condition their attention were distracted because they were required to search for visual targets at the same time as performing the sequence.

In the anatomical model, the parietal cortex and prefrontal cortex both pro-jected to the premotor cortex, and in turn the premotor cortex projected to the motor cortex. When the subjects were required to attend to their actions, there was a significant increase in the path coefficient for the link between the pre-frontal cortex and premotor cortex. But when the subjects were distracted, there was a significant decrease in the coefficient. There was no significant change for either condition for the path between the parietal cortex to the pre-motor cortex.

This experiment considers the output pathways. However, there are also top-down projections from both the prefrontal cortex and parietal cortex. The cau-dal prefrontal cortex projects to the inferotemporal cortex (Webster et al., 1994), area V4 (Ungerleider et al., 2008), and the MT/V5 complex (Stanton et al., 1988). The cortex in the intraparietal sulcus projects to the same areas: the

Box 6.2 Structural equation modeling (SEM)

SEM interprets the relations between observed variables in terms of causal influences among them, including latent or hidden variables that mediate the influence between them. SEM was first used in other disciplines; for example, in psychology where motivation is a latent variable or in economics where consumer confidence is a latent variable.

SEM was first applied to imaging data by McIntosh and Gonzalez-Lima (1994). The analysis is based on the covariance matrix between the observed variables, estimating the path coefficients, and hidden variables that best explain the observed data. Although time series from brain regions can be the variables, the method is stationary and does not consider the dynamic properties of the brain or temporal lags.

The analysis looks for the solution that minimizes the differences between the observed covariance and that implied by a model. It is usually used to identify the change in the path coefficients from one experimental condition to another, and is therefore conceptually similar to a PPI, but it differs in that it uses a model that specifies directional influences.

The covariance matrix can also be interpreted in terms of an anatomical model, which constrains the possible routes of influence. The anatomical model is based on what is known of the connections within the system. However, to avoid an unidentified model, it needs to be relatively simple, without too many connections or reciprocal connections. Otherwise there are more parameters to estimate (path coefficients) than there are data points (inter-regional covariances). The anatomical model is agnostic as to whether the connections are mono-synaptic or poly-synaptic.

It is important to note that changes in connectivity between two regions cannot simply be inferred from the changes in their activity from one condition to another. For example, in the experiment by Rowe et al. (2002) described below, when the subjects attended to action, there was no change in the path coefficient between the parietal and premotor cortex, even though there was an enhancement of the activation in both areas.

inferotemporal cortex (Webster et al., 1994), V4 (Ungerleider et al., 2008), and the MT/V5 complex (Ungerleider and Desimone, 1986).

Imaging has been used to compare these paths. Buchel and Friston (1997) carried out a study on attention to motion. In one condition the subjects simply watched moving dots and in another they performed a task, detecting when there was a change in the display. Structural equation modeling was used to analyze the data. It indicated that the top-down projection from the prefrontal cortex influenced the path coefficient for the connection between the parietal cortex and the MT/V5 complex.

Rowe et al. (2005) carried out a study on attention to color. They compared conditions in which either a single color was presented or an array of colors from which the subjects had to choose. In this more demanding condition there was an increase in the path coefficient for the pathway from the prefrontal cortex to a visual area processing color. This lay on the borders between the caudal temporal lobe and V4.

It is clear that SEM has advantages over PPIs, by linking the analysis to explicit models of brain networks and being able to compare models. However, there are limitations. Although it fits a model that embodies directed connections, it cannot easily compare models that are not a subset of each other. Furthermore, it is restricted to models of very limited complexity. This is because the data to which the model is fitted (empirical covariance matrix) contain relatively few data points, so limiting the number of free parameters (connections) in the model. In addition, models with reciprocal connections may have unstable solutions. The other fundamental limitation of SEM is that it fails to take into account the dynamics of the system.

Dynamic causal modeling

These are some of the reasons why an alternative method, dynamic causal modeling, was devised to analyze imaging data (Friston et al., 2003). Box 6.3 gives a brief account. We refer the reader to Penny et al. (2004) for a fuller discussion of the advantages, and to Stephan et al. (2010) for a tutorial guide.

As with structural equation modeling, DCM can be used to study top-down influences. Vossel et al. (2012) carried out an experiment on attention to the left or right visual field. The Posner paradigm (Posner et al., 1984) was used in which a central cue tells the subject whether the target is likely to appear in the left or right visual field. This cues the direction of covert attention.

The basic anatomical model consisted of the frontal eye field, the cortex in the intraparietal sulcus, and the prestriate cortex, with the connections between them being shown in both directions. Twenty models were then compared, which differed in the patterns in which they showed the direction of influence. For example, some of the models tested suggested that it was from the frontal eye field to the parietal cortex or prestriate cortex, and others that the influence was in the reverse direction.

The model favored by Bayesian selection gave the direction of influence as being from the frontal eye fields to the parietal cortex and from the parietal cortex to the prestriate cortex. Furthermore, when attention was paid to one

Box 6.3 Dynamic causal modeling (DCM)

DCM was developed by Friston et al. (2003) as a method for interpreting imaging data in terms of effective connectivity. DCM has a number of distinct features.

- First, it describes the dynamic response of a brain area: in others words how it changes over time, rather than stationary relationships with events in other brain regions and the external world.

- Second, it distinguishes the neuronal level of interactions from the measured signal. For example, for blood-oxygen level dependent fMRI it contains a "forward model" of neurovascular coupling at each region. By optimizing the parameters of this model or "model inversion," one can infer interactions at the level of neuronal activity from the measured signal.

- Third, instead of traditional measures of goodness of fit, it compares different models based on a criterion from Bayesian statistics; this is called the "model evidence." This trades the accuracy or fit of a model against its complexity and thus prevents "overfitting." Based on the model evidence, one can determine the most convincing model from any set of alternative models, including models in which A influences B versus models in which B influences A, and even compare models which are not nested in each other. This is referred to as Bayesian model selection.

An anatomical model is constructed as in SEM, although with fewer constraints. In particular, DCM does not have the same restrictions as SEM on the number of connections, and it can accommodate forward and reverse connections between nodes. Many possible directions of influence can be elaborated in a series of models of effective connectivity, each with different responses to changing task or sensory conditions. These can be thought of as different system architectures, and can be evaluated using Bayesian model selection.

The sense in which DCMs are "causal" is that they quantify how hidden states influence each other and so cause the observed data. However, the results obtain only for the range of models tested, and DCM is generally applied to hypothesis testing rather than network discovery. Nonetheless, by imposing constraints on the models, it is possible to recover the networks from a very large set of possible models.

There is empirical support for the DCM approach from other methods. For example, the physiological connectivity parameters in DCM correlate

> **Box 6.3 Dynamic causal modeling (DCM)** *(continued)*
>
> with direct measures of cortico-cortical coupling, as suggested by TMS (Boudrias et al., 2012), or diffusion weighted imaging of anatomical tracts' connectivity (Rae et al., 2015). The model of neurovascular coupling has also been validated by recording neuronal activity at the same time as fMRI. David et al. (2008) recorded the EEG intracranially in rats at the same time as recording BOLD responses, and they were able to show that the influence of one area on another could be correctly inferred from the fMRI data, once the model of neurovascular coupling was taken into account.

side, there was an increase in the influence from the parietal cortex to prestriate cortex on that side, but a decrease from the parietal cortex to prestriate cortex on the opposing side.

The results of the imaging studies reviewed above suggests that, irrespective of whether attention is paid to motion (Buchel and Friston, 1997), color (Rowe et al., 2005), or location (Vossel et al., 2012), the attentional enhancement in visual areas is driven by the prefrontal cortex. The reason is that, as already mentioned, it is this area that receives information about the instruction cue or context (Yamagata et al., 2012).

Context-dependent interactions

In experiments on macaque monkeys, the instruction cue is typically visual, but in experiments with human subjects, it is usually verbal. In an experiment by Sakai and Passingham (2006), the subjects were presented at the beginning of each trial with words telling them which of two tasks they had to perform. When later presented with a word, the subjects were either to judge the number of syllables in the word (phonological task) or the meaning of the word (semantic task).

There was activation in the ventral prefrontal cortex that reflected the task that the subjects were going to perform. If the task was to judge the number of syllables, this prefrontal activation correlated with later activation in an area involved in phonological processing. If the task was to judge the meaning of a word, it correlated with later activation in an area involved in semantic processing.

This is an example of context-specific connectivity (Friston et al., 1997; McIntosh, 2000; Stephan and Friston, 2010). In context 1 area A interacts with area B; but in context 2 area A interacts with area C (Passingham et al., 2012). This principle holds both for the influence of context on responses and for the

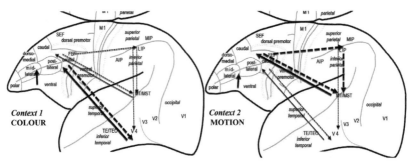

Fig. 6.2 Simplified diagram to show how the core system might operate when the tasks are either to attend to color (left) or to attend to motion (right).

influence of context on attention to the task relevant cues. As Duncan (2013) has stressed, the core system allows both for flexibility in responding and for flexibility in switching attention from one moment to another.

Figure 6.2 provides a simplified diagram of how these attentional effects might work. It does so for a task that has been given to macaque monkeys (Lauwereyns et al., 2001). The stimuli were colored moving dots and there were two types of trial: color trials and motion trials. On color trials, the rule was that the subject should make response 1 if the dots were red and response 2 if they were blue. On motion trials, the rule was that the subject should make response 1 if the dots were moving to the left and response 2 if the dots were moving to the right.

In the study by Lauwereyns et al. (2001), there were cells in the prefrontal cortex that were sensitive to the dimension that was relevant for that trial. This is consistent with the hypothesis that the caudal prefrontal cortex sends a top-down signal to the caudal inferotemporal cortex and V4 on color trials and to the MT/V5 complex on motion trials. Where attention is to spatial location, as on motion trials, there is also a top-down effect from the prefrontal cortex to the parietal cortex and thence to the MT/V5 complex. The effect of these signals is to enhance the relevant stream and so select which pathway is available for forward processing.

In Fig. 6.2 the feedback paths are marked with dotted lines. The output pathways are not shown, but Shipp (2005) has pointed out that there is a similarity between the feedback paths and the output paths through the premotor and motor areas. This is that the feedback paths avoid the granular layer IV, terminating in the supragranular and infragranular layers (Markov and Kennedy, 2013) and the output paths also terminate in these layers because there is no granular layer IV. Both pathways are selective: the feedback paths select between sensory streams, whereas the output paths select between responses.

There are two reasons why the same system is involved in both response selection and attentional selection. One is that covert spatial attention is bound up with overt attention via eye movements (Astafiev et al., 2003). The other is that at any one time a multitude of stimuli are available, but the ones that are the target of attention are determined by the task in hand. Attentional selection is for action (Allport, 1986).

Figure 6.2 shows the connections as established for the macaque monkey brain. However, it also shows the directionality of the top-down effects as established by imaging studies. These are the studies by Rowe et al. (2005) for color, by Buchel and Friston (1997) for motion, and by Vossel et al. (2012) for location. Imaging could show these effects because of two advantages. The first has been mentioned in Chapter 1, and this is that, in contrast to monkey neurophysiology, it is a whole brain method, and so it is possible to visualize changes in prefrontal, parietal, and temporal cortex at the same time. The second has been mentioned in Chapter 2, and this is that imaging is sensitive to modulatory changes (Logothetis, 2008), and this means that it can measure attentional enhancement, which we know to be the result of top-down influences (Gee et al., 2008).

The medial system

The previous section has used the core system to illustrate how imaging can be used to find out how a system is structured and how it operates. This involves investigating both how areas within a system interact and also what information is transmitted. The same approach can be used when studying other brain systems. We consider two such systems. We outline the connections of each system as established through anatomical and functional connectivity. We then describe ways in which the flow of information can be studied.

Figure 6.3 shows a simplified version of the anatomical connections of the medial system as demonstrated by anatomical experiments on macaque monkeys.

One clue to the functions of the medial system is that it is more strongly interconnected with the parietal and dorsal prefrontal cortex than with the temporal lobe (Barbas, 2000; Kobayashi and Amaral, 2003). Whereas it can derive proprioceptive and somatic input from the parietal cortex, it receives little visual input from the ventral visual stream passing through the inferotemporal cortex. These findings are consistent with the claim in the previous chapter that the medial system is involved in representing the individual and the individual's actions rather than in representing the state of things in the outside world (see Fig. 5.6).

It also helps to explain the fact that areas on the medial surface are more active when subjects are at rest than when they have to react to external stimuli

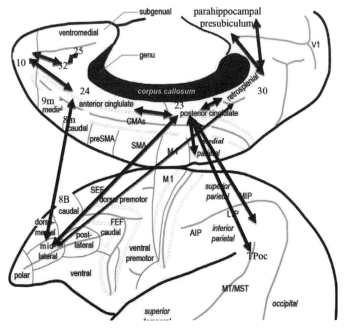

Fig. 6.3 Simplified diagram of the connections of the medial system in a macaque brain. For references see text.

so as to perform a task (Raichle and Snyder, 2007). In experiments on human subjects there is a relation between the number of spontaneous thoughts that the subjects report and activation in these areas during rest (Mason et al., 2007). These thoughts can relate to personal experiences in the past or thoughts about the future (Mason et al., 2007).

The regions that are deactivated during task performance have been described both for macaque monkeys and for human subjects (Mantini and Vanduffel, 2013). They include the medial prefrontal cortex, the anterior cingulate cortex in front of, and below, the genu of the corpus callosum, and the posterior cingulate cortex. These areas can be shown to form a network on the basis of intrinsic coupling in their temporal covariance (Buckner et al., 2008). The term "default network" was initially proposed, the idea being that the "default mode" is the state when the subjects are at rest rather than being engaged in an experimental task (Raichle et al., 2001).

However, characterizing this system on the basis of deactivations alone may be misleading. The reason is that, if the system is defined in this way, it includes neither the retrosplenial cortex nor the hippocampus (Mantini and Vanduffel, 2013). These areas are not deactivated when subjects move from rest to task performance. Yet we know that when subjects are required to remember episodes in their past life, there is conspicuous activation in the retrosplenial cortex and hippocampus, as well as other areas in the medial system (Summerfield et al., 2009).

The apparent discrepancy can be explained in two ways. The first is to suppose that the retrosplenial cortex and hippocampal system are active when subjects are at rest, but that they *remain* active when subjects are given tasks to perform. This is plausible since the core system is involved in task control and it is strongly interconnected with the medial system. There are direct projections, for example, from the dorsal cortex and medial prefrontal cortex to the retrosplenial cortex (Kobayashi and Amaral, 2003) and presubiculum (Goldman-Rakic et al., 1984, Morris et al., 1999).

The second way of explaining the apparent discrepancy is to appreciate that there is an alternative way to characterize the medial system. This is to define it by analyzing the resting covariance between areas on the medial surface. The system, as so defined, includes the retrosplenial cortex and hippocampus within the anatomical subclusters (Andrews-Hanna et al., 2010).

Functional imaging can also be used to investigate how the areas within the medial system interact with each other and with the core system when subjects perform tasks. Maguire et al. (2000b) studied interactions within the system when subjects remembered episodes in their own life, rather than events that did not involve themselves. The retrieval of personal events was specifically associated with an increase in the effective connectivity between the parahippocampal cortex and the hippocampus.

To compare these areas with the rest of the medial system, Bonnici et al. (2012) used multivariate analysis to distinguish between recent and less recent memories. They found that both recent and remote memories are represented in the hippocampus and ventromedial frontal cortex, but that there is a stronger representation of remote memories in the ventromedial frontal cortex.

Methods such as DCM could now be used to analyze the interactions between these areas during the encoding of new autobiographical memories and the retrieval of either recent or remote memories.

The same medial areas that are involved in retrieving memories of personal events are also involved in imagining future events (Addis et al., 2007; Hassabis et al., 2007). One reason could be that when subjects imagine future events they may construct them from elements that they hold in memory. Zeidman et al. (2014) specifically instructed subjects to construct scenes in their imagination, and there were activations throughout the system that is activated during remembering scenes. The authors then used a method for calculating a global PPI (McLaren et al., 2012) to investigate what areas covaried more strongly with the hippocampus during constructing scenes than perceiving scenes.

Of note was that these areas included the superior and middle frontal gyrus. This is significant because imagining involves the spontaneous generation of goal items, and, as already mentioned, there is activation in the middle frontal gyrus when subjects generate responses, whether they be finger responses (Rowe et al., 2005) or random numbers (Jahanshahi et al., 2000). Furthermore, there is activation in the prefrontal cortex when subjects are instructed to imagine finger movements (Gerardin et al., 2000). Again DCM could be used to compare models that differ in the influence from different areas and the direction of information flow.

As already mentioned, feedforward and feedback paths run to different laminae. The aim must, therefore, be to understand the transfer of information in terms of the influence exerted by the different layers. As an example of what has already been achieved, Maass et al. (2014) compared the projections from the superficial layers of the entorhinal cortex to the dentate gyrus with those from CA1 and the subiculum to the deep layers of the entorhinal cortex. To resolve the layers the authors used fMRI at 7T.

They then used multivariate pattern analysis to decode the information in the system. The subjects viewed scenes that were either novel or familiar. When they viewed novel scenes, decoding was best from the activations in the superficial entorhinal cortex, dentate gyrus, and CA2/CA3. When they viewed familiar scenes, decoding was best from the activations in CA1 and the deep layers of the entorhinal cortex. This suggests that input pathways are involved in encoding novel scenes and that output pathways are involved in the recognition of familiar scenes.

The ventral system

The previous section described activations when contrasting the recall of personal events with the recall of objects (Hassabis et al., 2007). When the reverse comparison is run, there are activations in the inferotemporal cortex and the ventral prefrontal cortex. These form part of the ventral system.

This system is illustrated in Fig. 6.4. Though for simplicity this is shown for vision alone, it also includes the auditory and tactile streams. As already described in the previous chapter, inferotemporal cortex receives inputs from the primary and secondary visual areas (Desimone and Ungerleider, 1989). However, as shown in the figure, there is also a top-down projection from the ventral prefrontal cortex (Borra et al., 2011).

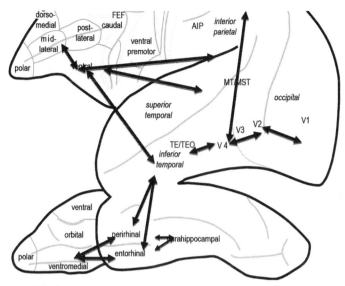

Fig. 6.4 Simplified diagram of the connections of the ventral system in a macaque brain. For references see text.

One of the special characteristics of the ventral system is that it contains clear examples of highly specialized cortical regions, such as the fusiform face area (FFA), parahippocampal place area (PPA), and extrastriate body area, which were identified by early fMRI studies (Downing et al., 2006). The identification of these areas has provided a valuable tool for studying the mechanisms of imagination. When subjects imagine seeing faces there is activation in the fusiform face area, and when they imagine seeing houses there is activation in the parahippocampal place area (Ishai et al., 2000). However, in addition there is activation in the ventral prefrontal cortex in both cases.

By using DCM, Mechelli et al. (2004) were able to show that during imagination there are top-down effects from the prefrontal cortex and parietal cortex. However, these effects differed. The influence from the prefrontal cortex led to enhancement in the category specific area that was appropriate, for example in the FFA but not the PPA when the subjects were imagining faces. This was not true for the influence from the parietal cortex which was non-selective.

The identification of body areas in the extrastriate and fusiform cortex has also provided a useful tool for studying the mechanisms that underlie repetition suppression. As already described in Chapter 5, if the same stimulus is repeated in a short space of time, the activation tends to decrease with repetition. It has usually been assumed that this is due to local effects. However, Ewbank et al. (2011) used DCM and compared models that incorporated feedback as well as feedforward effects between the two areas. If the size or view of the body was varied between repetitions, there was a feedback influence from the fusiform body area to the extrastriate body area.

These studies demonstrate interactions between areas but they do not tell us what information is transferred. To do this multivariate methods are helpful. There have been recent developments in these methods. For example, rather than simply using support vector machines, it is now possible to use supervised self-organizing maps (Hausfeld et al., 2014). These have been used successfully to distinguish who is speaking on the basis of the pattern of activation in cortical auditory areas (Hausfeld et al., 2014).

Furthermore, rather than analyzing data for individual subjects, there are now methods for analyzing multivariate data across a group of subjects. Haxby et al. (2014) have introduced the concept of a high-dimensional representational space, where each stimulus or response feature is represented by a vector of neural activations. The analysis calculates the distance between all such vectors as a matrix that can be mapped from one space to another.

It is an advantage of this method that matrices can be aligned across different brains. Conroy et al. (2013) have validated the method by presenting subjects with stimuli in different categories, such as faces, shoes, houses, and chairs. They have been able to discriminate what the subjects were viewing with a high level of accuracy. The results show that there is a progression through the ventral visual system in which the same categories are represented multiple times.

It remains to use imaging to compare the representations in different areas. We know from single-unit recording that cells in the inferotemporal cortex are more likely to code for visual features, whereas cells in the ventral prefrontal cortex are more likely to code for object categories (Freedman et al., 2003). Thus, imaging can be used to study the stages via which representations are transformed in the human brain.

Summary

The term "functional system" is properly applied to a group of areas that are anatomically well connected and that show a strong covariance in activity. This chapter has considered three such systems: the core system, the medial system, and the ventral system. Interactions within these systems can be studied by various methods. The chapter has briefly described three of these: psychophysiological interactions, structural equation modeling, and dynamic causal modeling. It has also illustrated the way in which they can be used to study the influence of one area on another within a system. Multivariate methods can be used to show what information is coded in each area and thus what information is transferred between areas within a system.

Chapter 7

Other methods

Abstract

Functional imaging is primarily a correlational technique. Although there are methods for analyzing the causal structure of systems, proof of causation requires methods that intervene in the workings of the system. If area A influences area B, preventing activity in A should diminish activity in B. The interference with activity in area A can be permanent, as after a brain lesion, or temporary, as with the application of transcranial magnetic stimulation. However, to understand the workings of the system we need to know not only that area A influences area B, but also how it does so. This involves the synchronization of activity in the two areas. To study this one needs methods such as electro-encephalography and magneto-encephalography that provide evidence of synchronized and dynamic oscillations at different frequencies.

Keywords

causal influences, brain lesions, compensation, transcranial magnetic brain stimulation, Granger causality, electro-encephalography, magneto-encephalography, oscillations, synchrony.

Introduction

The last two chapters have illustrated the use of fMRI to study functional specialization (Chapter 5) and functional systems (Chapter 6). Although fMRI has had a major influence on cognitive neuroscience over the last 20 years, it has its limitations. Like any other recording technique, it correlates changes in the state of the brain with events, tasks, or contexts. The problem is that only some of the observed brain changes may be critical for the task or performance. Brain lesions, whether permanent or temporary, can resolve the issue of whether a region is essential.

There is a further limitation, and that is the poor temporal resolution of fMRI. This arises both from the inherent smoothing of the signal from the hemodynamic response function (Chapter 2) and the acquisition of data every 1–2 seconds, the time taken to capture an image of the brain. The limited temporal resolution does not in any way prevent one from measuring responses to very brief stimuli. However, it does limit insights into the fine-grained detail of the physiological response itself, such as the delay in onset of the neural response to a stimulus, or whether the neural response is oscillatory. This constrains the degree to which fMRI can be used for physiological studies. It is here that EEG and MEG are most valuable because they provide the necessary temporal resolution, and they also provide information about the frequency of the signals. transcranial magnetic brain simulation (TMS) also has precise timing, so it too can be used to illuminate the sequence of physiological events.

There are two further reasons for considering methods other than fMRI. One is that conclusions based on the use of one method are most convincing when checked by using a different method. Because each method has its weaknesses, multi-modal cross-validation is good practice in all areas of science, and this includes imaging and the cognitive sciences.

A final and more general reason to consider other methods is that in science the questions asked should be driven by curiosity and importance, not skewed by particular methods, let alone the method with which you are most comfortable. You should first ask the question and then select the methods that are appropriate. It is easy to forget this principle when the methods are expensive, and it takes time and effort to become fully trained in using them. Investigators of the neuroscience of human cognition should not think of themselves as "imagers" but as neuroscientists, and this means that they should consider all the methods available.

We consider the use of other methods to study both functional specialization and functional integration. We describe first the methods that can be used to compare the functional contribution of different brain areas within a system. We then describe the methods that can be used to study the way in which areas communicate with each other when their activity synchronizes.

Co-activations

Within functional systems, areas tend to co-activate. For example, we saw in the last chapter that if fMRI is used to study the core system, co-activations occur in the parietal cortex, the dorsal prefrontal cortex, and the anterior cingulate cortex (Duncan, 2010). Indeed, spatiotemporal covariance is one of the defining features of a functional system. Methods are therefore needed to distinguish the contribution made by the different areas within a system. It is here that it can be of value to study the effects of lesions, whether temporary or permanent.

The way in which this can be done is best illustrated with an example from studies of macaque monkeys. There is enhanced activation in the cortex in the intraparietal sulcus, the caudal prefrontal area 8, and the anterior prefrontal area 46 when monkeys perform spatial working memory tasks (Inoue et al., 2004). These areas are linked not only by functional connectivity (spatiotemporal covariance between areas A and B), but also effective connectivity (causal influences from A to B). This can be shown by the use of temporary inactivation: cooling area 8 influences the delay related cell activity in the cortex in the intraparietal sulcus, and vice versa (Chafee and Goldman-Rakic, 2000).

Yet it is clear from lesion studies that the different areas in this system perform different functions. Lesions in prefrontal area 46 severely impair the ability of monkeys to learn (Goldman et al., 1971) and remember (Butters and Pandya, 1969) spatial delayed response tasks. But lesions of the lateral parietal cortex, including the cortex in the intraparietal sulcus, have no such effect, even if they are very large (Ettlinger et al., 1966). So, despite forming a functional system, the components are not interchangeable.

This can be explained when it is appreciated that the delayed response task could involve either retrospective or prospective memory. In other words, the monkeys could either remember the location that they saw or the location to which they are preparing to respond. The distinction can be made by comparing two versions of the task. This is most easily done with human subjects.

If the subjects are tested after the delay by presenting items for recognition, the task assesses retrospective memory; the reason is that they are unable to prepare their response during the delay. If the subjects are required to recall the items, the task may also probe prospective memory; the reason is that the subjects can prepare their response during the delay. It is a critical observation that patients with prefrontal lesions are not impaired if their memory is assessed via recognition but only if it is assessed via recall (Ferreira et al., 1998).

The explanation becomes clear when healthy subjects are scanned. Delay-period activations can be recorded in frontal area 8 and the cortex in the intraparietal sulcus on both versions of the task (Pochon et al., 2001). But delay-related activations can only be recorded in prefrontal area 46 on the recall version of the task. This suggests a distinctive role for this area in prospective memory.

The results in monkeys could thus be explained if we suppose that the delayed response task makes demands on prospective memory, and that the prefrontal area 46 is involved in maintaining goals in memory (Passingham and Wise, 2012). After a parietal lesion, the dorsal prefrontal area 46 remains intact. Furthermore, it can still receive visuospatial input, via connections with area 8 (Petrides and Pandya, 1999), and via the connections of area 8 with visual areas V2 and V3 (Stanton et al., 1995). Furthermore, prefrontal area 46 is also interconnected with the more caudal prefrontal area 9/46 (Petrides and Pandya, 1999), and area 9/46 receives a visuospatial projection from the medial parietal area 7m (Petrides and Pandya, 1999).

It remains to explain why the parietal cortex is unable to compensate for the loss of the prefrontal cortex given that there are delay-period activations in the parietal cortex. One possibility is that the parietal activations that reflect prospective memory derive from the prefrontal cortex. This hypothesis could be easily be tested by scanning patients who have prefrontal lesions. The prediction is that there would be delay-period activations on the recognition task, but not on the recall task.

The data from monkeys suggest that prefrontal and parietal lesions should also have different effects in human subjects. So Hamidi et al. (2008) tested subjects on a spatial delayed recognition task. Applying repetitive TMS (rTMS) over the parietal cortex disrupted performance, whereas applying it over the dorsal prefrontal cortex had no effect. In a subsequent experiment, the same authors (Hamidi et al., 2009) tested subjects on a spatial delayed recall task. In this case, applying rTMS over the prefrontal cortex had an effect, whereas applying it over the parietal cortex did not.

This is a double dissociation, often regarded as the gold standard for demonstrating functional specialization. The demonstration is impressive because it relates to two areas that lie within the same functional system. The areas are interconnected and share many connections (Selemon and Goldman-Rakic, 1988). However, they do not share all of them. The consequence is that after lesions of one area or the other, the connections that remain are not identical, and it is the remaining connections of the area that is intact that constrain its functional capacity (Chapter 4).

Structural brain lesions and focal TMS have also been important to understand the functional contributions of areas that co-activate within the language system. For example, Gough et al. (2005) compared semantic and phonological processing. They applied short trains of TMS at 10 Hz over two different areas in the left inferior frontal cortex, area 44, and area 12/47.

The subjects were tested on two tasks. One required phonological judgements, such as whether "jeans" and "genes" sound the same. The other required semantic judgements, such as whether "gift" and "present" have the same meaning. Applying rTMS over area 44 increased the response times for the phonological but not semantic judgements, whereas applying rTMS over area 12/47 increased the response times for the semantic but not phonological judgements. These results are as would be expected from the fMRI study of Hope et al. (2014)

described in Chapter 5. Figures 5.4a and 5.4b show parameter estimates from that study, and the estimates for the two areas are consistent with a dissociation between phonological and semantic processing.

It might be thought that such a dissociation is implausible, since the two areas are closely interconnected, but, as explained in Chapter 4, areas can contribute differently if they have a different *overall* pattern of connections. Tracing studies in the macaque monkeys show that area 44 receives an input from the anterior inferior parietal area PFG and the superior temporal area Tpt (Frey et al., 2014). These projections carry auditory and phonological information. By contrast, a study using DWI in the human brain shows that areas 45 and 47 receive an input from the middle temporal gyrus (Rilling et al., 2008). This communicates information that is relevant for semantic processing (Vandenberghe et al., 1996).

It could be objected that in the study by Gough et al. (2005), rTMS affected response times but not the accuracy of the judgements. But this is because the rTMS was applied *while* the subjects performed the tasks. As explained in Box 1.2, this procedure causes a temporary delay before the normal activity resumes and the judgement can be made. If rTMS is applied *before* testing it can affect accuracy because the activity is still disrupted at the time that the judgement must be made. Whitney et al. (2012) applied rTMS at 1 Hz to the inferior frontal area 45 before testing subjects on semantic judgements. This did affect accuracy: the subjects made errors, for example, when tested on whether "salt" goes with "grain."

At first sight the results of this study appear to contradict those of an earlier lesion study on semantic processing. Price et al. (1999) tested patient S.W. who had a large lesion that included the left inferior frontal cortex, and the lesion was confirmed by scanning him and showing that there was no activation in, or adjacent to, this area. Yet he was still able to judge, for example, whether "table" goes with "chair." So Price et al. argued that the left inferior frontal cortex is not "necessary" for performing the task. Since the scans showed that in S.W. the left middle and inferior temporal cortex *were* activated during the task, Price et al. argued that these areas are "sufficient" for performing the task.

In fact there is no contradiction. Whether the left inferior prefrontal cortex is involved depends on whether the association between the items is familiar or not. When patient S.W. was tested, the items were familiar, as in judging whether "oranges" go with "lemons." In the study by Whitney et al. (2012), rTMS had no effect if the items were familiar, as in when judging whether "salt" goes with "pepper." The conclusion from the two studies together is that the left inferior frontal cortex is indeed involved in controlled, but not automatic retrieval (Badre and Wagner, 2002).

Compensation

If the effects of lesions are to be studied, it is critical to understand the underlying logic. This is that the contribution of area A is assessed by testing what areas B, C, and D are unable to do in the absence of A. There are two problems here. One is that the conclusions are indirect. The other is that they could be unreliable if, after the lesion in area A, there are changes in areas B, C, and D, or changes in their connections. The reason is that these could allow areas B, C, and D to compensate for the loss of area A. In other words, one or more of these areas may have the capacity to function in the same way as A, even if they do not normally do so. Alternatively, they might be able to achieve the same end, but via a different strategy.

It is a common belief that compensation of this sort can occur. It is easy to see why because recovery can frequently be observed in the clinic after strokes, whether they affect movement or language. Furthermore, if the patients are scanned, activations can be often observed that are not present in subjects with no lesion.

This was true of an imaging study by Johansen-Berg et al. (2002). They studied patients who had a unilateral hemiparesis that resulted from a stroke in the internal capsule. When the patients made simple finger movements, there was activation in the premotor cortex ipsilateral to the affected hand. This is not normally seen in healthy adults when the movements are simple.

The finding could be taken to suggest that this new area had taken over the functional role of the damaged area on the other side. One way to confirm this is to block the function of the new area, for example, by applying rTMS to see whether this disturbs performance. In the study by Johansen-Berg et al. rTMS over the ipsilateral premotor cortex led to an increase in response times. But the surprising finding was that the effect was greater the *less* the patient had recovered. This is not consistent with the assumption that the ipsilateral premotor cortex was responsible for the recovery. It suggests instead that the patients who were least recovered were still attempting to relearn the simple movement.

That some of the patients had indeed recovered is not in dispute. However, there is an alternative explanation for that recovery. This is that capsular strokes rarely cut off *all* the fibers that descend from the motor cortex. Bosnell et al. (2011) used diffusion imaging in a study of patients with capsular strokes. The less the disruption of the fibers in the posterior limb of the internal capsule, the greater the improvement the patients showed with practice on a motor task.

The same points can be made in relation to recovery from aphasia. Many patients recover their speech after a left hemisphere stroke (Price et al., 2010), and one explanation that is commonly suggested is that this recovery depends on new activity in areas in the non-dominant hemisphere. It is a typical finding that if patients with a non-fluent aphasia are tested soon after the stroke, there is an abnormal degree of activation in the right inferior frontal gyrus (Winhuisen et al., 2005).

So Winhuisen et al. (2005) applied rTMS to the right inferior frontal gyrus. There were patients in whom this increased the reaction time for speaking, but these were again the patients who were *less* well recovered. Furthermore, as in the case of motor lesions, the degree of recovery depended on the completeness of the lesion. The patients who recovered best were those in whom it was possible to detect some residual left frontal activation (Winhuisen et al., 2005).

These were studies of patients who had suffered strokes, and it may be difficult for neuroplasticity in the brain to establish compensation following sudden severe lesions. However, it may be easier to develop compensation if the onset of the lesion is slow, either from a slow-growing tumor or focal neurodegeneration. Thiel et al. (2006) scanned patients with aphasia that resulted from a tumor and there was activation in the right inferior frontal gyrus while the patients performed a verb generation task.

However, the results of applying rTMS over this area depended on the speed with which the tumors had grown. It disrupted performance in patients with slow-growing but not fast-growing tumors. This suggests that the right inferior frontal cortex can indeed compensate, but only if the lesions increase slowly. This compensation is possible because homologous areas in the two hemispheres have a similar overall pattern of connections.

Causal influence

Once the contribution of the different areas within a system is established, the next step is to see how they influence each other. When fMRI is used to study interactions within systems, the inferences concerning causal influence are made on the basis of observational data alone. So the interpretations of the data, whether by SEM, DCM, or similar methods, cannot be taken to constitute certain proof of the presence and necessity of the influence. Methods like DCM can provide direct evidence in support of a given model of causality, but the conclusions only hold for the range of models tested.

To prove that A influences B, one can also intervene in the system. If the activation in area A causes the activation in area B, then enhancing the activation in A should enhance the activation in B. Alternately, reducing or eliminating the activation in area A should reduce or eliminate the activation in area B. The combination of imaging methods is especially helpful in this effort, using one method such as TMS for perturbing area A and a second method such as EEG, MEG, or fMRI as the "readout." This means that the effect or perturbation can be measured behaviorally and also related to activations in the target region B.

Single-pulse TMS can be used to induce transient activity in an area. As mentioned in Box 1.2, if it is applied over visual cortex, it can cause the perception of flashes of light or phosphenes; and if applied over motor cortex, it can cause muscle twitches (Stewart et al., 2001). Thus, TMS can also be used to see whether enhancing activity in area A leads to an enhancement in areas B or C with which it is connected.

So Morishima et al. (2009) applied single-pulse TMS to prefrontal area 8 and at the same time recorded the effect with EEG. The aim was to study the influence of top-down projections from the prefrontal cortex to early sensory areas. As mentioned in Chapter 6, a previous fMRI study had shown that activation in the prefrontal cortex correlated with activation in different areas depending on the task (Sakai and Passingham, 2006). The advantage of using TMS is that it can be used to directly stimulate the top-down connections from prefrontal cortex and so prove causal influence.

Morishima et al. presented their subjects with faces made up of moving dots. One task was to discriminate the gender of the face and the other to discriminate the direction in which the dots were moving. Localization of the EEG signals suggested sources in the fusiform gyrus and MT/V5 complex. This accords with fMRI studies showing that the FFA is specialized for face perception (Grill-Spector et al., 2004) and the MT/V5 complex for motion perception (Sunaert et al., 1999).

Morishima et al. applied a TMS pulse to prefrontal area 8 after the task instruction had been given. There was then a brief delay before the stimulus was presented. During that delay the TMS pulse induced an increase in the current source density in the fusiform gyrus if the task was to discriminate the gender of the face, and in the MT/V5 complex if the task was to discriminate the direction of motion. In other words, the task instruction had increased the strength of the connection between the prefrontal cortex and one of the target areas.

TMS can also be combined with concurrent fMRI to study the same issue. Heinen et al. (2014) used the identical task, presenting faces made up of moving dots. A short train of three TMS pulses was applied to the prefrontal area 8 after the instruction and before the stimuli were presented. The effect was an increase in the BOLD signal in the fusiform gyrus on gender trials and in the MT/V5 complex on motion trials.

These studies serve to confirm the principle, mentioned in Chapter 6, that interactions within the system are context dependent (Stephan and Friston, 2010). In context 1 area A influences area B, and in context 2 area A influences area C (Passingham et al., 2012).

If this principle holds, then removing area A should abolish the enhancement in areas B or C. So Gregoriou et al. (2014) removed the whole of the tissue on the lateral surface of the prefrontal cortex in one hemisphere of macaque monkeys. Both the corpus callosum and anterior commissure were also cut. This meant that a comparison could be made between the effects when visual stimuli were presented contralateral to the lesioned hemisphere and the effects when they were presented contralateral to the intact hemisphere. The effect of the lesion was measured by recording from cells in V4.

The task was to find a target grating amongst distractor gratings, and the identity of the target was indicated by the color of the fixation point. When stimuli were presented to the intact hemisphere, there was attentional enhancement when the target appeared in the receptive field of the cell in V4 from which the recording was taken. When stimuli were presented to the lesioned hemisphere, there was a significant reduction in this effect.

This suggests that the attentional enhancement of activity in V4 depends on a driving influence from the prefrontal cortex. It is true that the enhancement was not totally abolished. But this could be because the lesion did not include the orbital prefrontal cortex, which is interconnected with the ventral visual system and so indirectly with V4 (Saleem et al., 2008).

Whereas Gregoriou et al. recorded from single cells, Zanto et al. (2011) used EEG to measure enhancement in the visual system of human subjects. The subjects were tested on delayed recognition tasks for either color or motion. rTMS was applied to the prefrontal cortex before testing, so as to produce a period of altered prefrontal cortical function lasting several minutes. There was a significant reduction in the enhancement in sensory areas on color trials, but this did not reach significance on motion trials.

The reason for the lack of a significant effect on motion trials may relate to details of the anatomy. Zanto et al. applied rTMS to the inferior frontal junction, whereas the prefrontal connections with the MT/V5 complex come mainly from the dorsal part of area 8 (Petrides and Pandya, 1999). It would be possible to test this explanation by repeating the experiment, but applying rTMS over area 8 on motion trials.

Temporal precedence

If A influences B, it should occur before B, even if the difference in time is very small. One way to detect such a difference is to record from pairs of cells with electrodes. Zhou and Desimone (2011) recorded simultaneously from cell pairs in the frontal eye field and visual area V4 in macaque monkeys. The cells were chosen such that both cells in a pair were responsive to stimuli occurring in the same part of the visual field; that is, both cells had a similar receptive field. The task for the monkeys was to find a target in an array of distractors that was identical to a colored shape that had been presented earlier.

Zhou and Desimone were able to compare the relative times at which cells in the two areas changed their activity when a target was presented in the receptive field of the cell. The data were shown by plotting the cumulative distributions of the times at which the cells fired. There was a clear difference, with the change in activity occurring earlier in the frontal eye field than in area V4.

However, the fact that A occurs before B does not prove that it is causal. There must be something about A that is predictive of B. This is captured by the notion of "Granger causality." This is briefly explained in Box 7.1. We refer the interested reader to Stephan and Roebroeck (2012) and Friston et al. (2013) for a more detailed discussion. Box 7.1 also contrasts the use of Granger causality and dynamic causal modeling (DCM).

Moratti et al. (2011) used a Granger analysis for MEG data. The subjects were presented with pictures that were of pleasant, neutral, or highly disturbing scenes. There was an increase in the activity in the parietal cortex and dorsal prefrontal cortex for the pictures that were either pleasant or disturbing, and this reflects the effects of attention. However, these effects could be stimulus driven or goal directed (Corbetta and Shulman, 2002). A picture can capture attention because of its intrinsic properties or the subject can engage in a directed search. The distinction is between effects that are bottom-up and effects that are top-down.

These effects can be distinguished using Granger analysis. When the pictures were pleasant, there were significant unidirectional effects between the parietal and prefrontal cortex. The direction of this influence was from the parietal to the prefrontal cortex. By contrast, when the pictures were disturbing there were significant effects on connectivity in both directions.

As stressed in the previous chapter, it is one thing to demonstrate bottom-up or top-down processing, but another to be able follow the information that is transmitted. So King et al. (2014) used MEG to study the signals that occur when a novel sound was presented, as opposed to an habitual sound. Classifiers were used to decode these "mismatch" signals, based not on a simple evoked response or peak "activation," but on the information contained across voxels.

At a sequence of different locations, decoding accuracy was above chance from as early as 100 milliseconds and lasted until 400 milliseconds. King et al. then tested to what extent the classifier that succeeded at one time point also succeeded at a later time point. They found that generalization across time was generally poor. Thus, the richness of the MEG signal was able to show how the representation of the signal is transformed dynamically over time.

Box 7.1 Granger causality

This concept was introduced by Clive Granger, an economist. He suggested that if there are two time series, and time series A can be used to predict time series B more than recent events in B itself, it can be said to have "predictive causality." This has become known as "Granger causality."

Granger causality was introduced as a method for interpreting fMRI data by Goebel et al. (2003). However, its use has been limited by the relatively poor temporal resolution of fMRI and the fact that the hemodynamic response can differ between areas. If the inference is to be valid, it is necessary to control for the vascular difference. One way of doing this is to compare two experimental conditions that differ in their cognitive demands. If the Granger causality between two areas differs between the two conditions, it is less likely to be due to a vascular artifact (Roebroeck et al., 2005).

The use of Granger causality as a method for analyzing EEG and MEG data is not limited in the same way because the temporal resolution is in milliseconds and the signal is not dependent on the slow vascular response. However, there remains the limitation that it simply shows the direction of coupling between two time series. Like multivariate autoregressive modeling and phase difference in coherence between two regions, it can be useful to explore interactions and generate hypotheses about networks.

In many experiments, the hypothesis refers not just to the strength of a connection, but the architecture of a network as a whole, and this is better tested with generative models. For EEG and MEG, as for fMRI, it is possible to compare the evidence for several possible models so as to identify which is the most likely, given the data. This is the approach that is used by DCM. The advantage is that, unlike DCM for fMRI, DCM for EEG and MEG can include neural mass models with detailed specifications about cell populations, cortical laminae, and receptor dynamics (Moran et al., 2013). Note that, unlike Granger causality, DCM is not based on temporal lags or precedence, but on instantaneous dynamic interactions.

Synchrony

The results in the previous section have pointed to the advantage of using methods that have a fine temporal resolution. But Chapter 2 argued that the most important reason for having recourse to EEG and MEG is that they can be used to measure how the signals oscillate. Measures of the power of oscillations can be derived at different frequency bands; Table 7.1 describes these frequency bands.

Table 7.1 Oscillations

Band	Frequency	Association
Delta	(1–3 Hz)	Slow wave sleep
Theta	(4–8 Hz)	Inhibition of responses
Alpha	(9–12 Hz)	Awake and relaxed
Beta	(13–30 Hz)	Active thinking, motor preparation
Gamma	(31–100 Hz)	Task performance, information processing

The table gives a rough guide to the bands that characterize the frequencies at which the EEG and MEG signals oscillate. The bands are only approximate, in part because the values given in different accounts are not identical, and in part because they can differ from area to area.

The function of the different oscillations is not fully established. However, two potential principles have emerged. The first is that variation in the peak frequency of the oscillations may play a role in modulating the timing of action potentials (cell "firing") (Cohen, 2014). The second is that communication between neurons may occur optimally when there is phase synchronization between their rhythmic fluctuations (Fries, 2005); this is referred to as "communication through coherence."

This principle is supported by an experiment by Gregoriou et al. (2012). They recorded simultaneously from cells in the frontal eye field and visual area V4. Monkeys were trained to detect a change in the color of one of three sinusoidal gratings, and the color of the fixation spot told the animals which one was the target. The enhancement of activity with attention was associated with an increase in synchronization at the gamma frequency between cells in the frontal eye field and V4. This was confined to the cells in the frontal eye field that were classed as visual. Cells that were classed as motor or visuomotor did not synchronize with cells in V4 in this way.

If synchronization is involved in communication between cells, it should be possible to detect it in the human brain by using EEG and MEG. So Siegel et al. (2008) used MEG to study the frequency of synchronization during peripheral attention. The task was the Posner cueing task (Posner et al., 1984). The subjects had to discriminate the direction of movement in a display of moving dots, and the display was presented in the periphery either to the left or to the right of the fixation point.

MEG activity was measured during the delay before the target appeared, and during this delay the subjects attended covertly to the side that had been cued. In the hemisphere opposite to the target, there was an increase in the synchronization in the low gamma band between the MT/V5 complex and the cortex in the intraparietal sulcus, and in both the low and high gamma bands between the cortex in the intraparietal sulcus and the prefrontal area 8.

So as to study the direction of influence, rTMS can be applied to area A before testing. The subsequent effect can then be established by recording the degree of synchrony between activity in areas A and B. In an experiment mentioned earlier, Zanto et al. (2011) used EEG to record synchrony.

The subjects performed delayed recognition tasks for color or motion. Phase coherence was measured between the activity in the inferior prefrontal junction and posterior regions. When color was relevant as opposed to irrelevant, there was an increase in phase locking in the alpha band early after the presentation of the stimuli. But when rTMS was applied to the inferior prefrontal junction before testing, the effect was significantly attenuated. This suggests that the connectivity between these connections is dependent on phase locking of synchronization in the source and target regions.

Collaboration

This chapter has covered a variety of methods: studies of patients; TMS, EEG, MEG in human subjects; and lesions and single-unit recording in animals. Each method demands an expertise and there are not many laboratories that can include experts in all of them. However, this should not prevent cross-disciplinary research, since collaborations can be formed across laboratories.

We, therefore, end with three examples of such collaboration. In each case the scientists started out with a question that they addressed with imaging. They then followed up the results by collaborating with other scientists who had a different expertise. For clarity we number the three examples.

1. The first example concerns the "K.E." family. This is a family of four generations in which half the members suffer from a severe speech and language disorder. Their speech is very non-fluent and their grammatical comprehension impaired (Vargha-Khadem et al., 1998). The first move was to scan the affected and unaffected members with MRI, and several abnormalities were found, including a reduction in the size of the caudate nucleus (Watkins et al., 2002). As expected there was also a reduction in the activation of the caudate nucleus (Watkins et al., 1999).

   Given the proportions of affected and unaffected members, inheritance appeared to be via a dominant gene (Vargha-Khadem et al., 1998). Collaboration with a group of geneticists soon identified a mutation in the FoxP2 gene in the forkhead domain (Lai et al., 2001). It then turned out that mice with a mutated FoxP2 gene were very impaired at learning a task that required them to associate sounds with movements (Kurt et al., 2012). These results suggest that the fundamental impairment in the affected K.E. members is a disruption of the ability to learn to associate different sounds so as to produce the articulation patterns of speech (Watkins, 2011). So the collaborations have served to elucidate the mechanisms that are disrupted in the affected members of the K.E. family.

2. The next example concerns the effects of practice during the learning of a skill. One of the notable findings from brain imaging is that practice can lead to gross changes in the anatomy of the human brain (Maguire et al., 2000a; Woollett and Maguire, 2011). For example, Bengtsson et al. (2005) used diffusion imaging to show that the longer adults had practiced the piano since childhood, the greater the white-matter density in the pyramidal tract as it descends through the internal capsule. It is tempting to suppose that the practice had caused the changes in the white matter, although it could also have been that differences in white matter conferred an advantage that led to persistent piano playing.

   Because of such ambiguity, changes of this sort are best documented not by cross-sectional studies but by prospective studies. So Johansen-Berg and colleagues (Sampaio-Baptista et al., 2014) gave subjects six weeks of daily practice in juggling. There were increases in the gray-matter volume in the motor cortex and dorsal parietal cortex.

   But structural MRI does not have the spatial resolution to distinguish whether these changes are due to increases in spine formation, synapto-genesis, the number of glial cells, or the degree of myelinization. So Johansen-Berg collaborated with psychologists with an expertise in training rats, and with biologists with an expertise in analyzing myelin. Rats were first given 11 days of training on a skilled reaching task (Sampaio-Baptista et al., 2014).

   An immuno-histological analysis of the histological data then showed that there was an increase in the density of myelin staining in the white matter underlying the motor cortex. This was confined to the cortex contralateral to the trained limb. The significance of the finding is that the degree of myelinization may influence the timing of spikes and thus phase synchronization. It also suggests that in the DWI study on pianists by Bengtsson et al. (2005), the changes observed related to myelinization of the descending fibers.

3. The final example concerns the hypothesis that mirror neurons are involved in the ability of people to interpret the actions of others. Several groups have used the repetition suppression technique to try to identify the presence of such neurons, and the technique has been mentioned in previous chapters.

   In repetition suppression, the response to a repeated stimulus diminishes, and one explanation is that there is neuronal adaptation. So Kilner and colleagues

(Press et al., 2012) used fMRI to scan subjects either while they observed an action or while they executed that same action. There were two actions: opposing the forefinger to the thumb or a pulling with the index finger. If the subjects had just executed an action, there was a decrease in activation in Broca's area when the subjects observed that same action. Correspondingly, if they had just observed an action, there was a decrease in the same area when they executed that same action. The effect was specific in that it did not occur if the actions observed and executed did not match.

However, the same effect was not found in premotor cortex. This was surprising because mirror neurons were first described in area F5 of the premotor cortex in macaque monkeys (Gallese et al., 1996). So Kilner collaborated with a laboratory with long expertise in single-unit recording in the motor system of macaque monkeys. Recordings were taken from mirror neurons in premotor area F5 while monkeys observed a person picking up a small piece of food (Kilner et al., 2014). The finding was that there was no decrease in firing rate after the monkeys had observed just two repetitions. However, there were changes in both latency and firing after seven or more such repetitions. The significance of this finding is that a failure to find repetition suppression using fMRI could simply reflect the limited number of repetitions.

These three examples have been deliberately chosen to show how imaging findings can be followed up in different ways: in the first case the collaborations were with geneticists; in the second with cell biologists; and in the third with electrophysiologists. The research question was addressed initially by an imaging experiment but was then pursued through other branches of neuroscience.

The message is that studying the neuroscience of human cognition requires good scientists. The question comes first, the method second. So it is dangerous for those who use fMRI to regard themselves as "imagers." Instead they should look to a broad range of methodologies. And science is by its nature collaborative.

Summary

Like single-unit recording, fMRI is a correlational method. It measures activations and relates them to the performance of particular tasks or the presentation of particular conditions. As outlined at the beginning of the book, this is only one way to study a system. The advantage of intervention in the system is that it is easier to work out causal relations. If A causes B, then stimulating A should lead to an increase in B. Furthermore, removing A, or impairing A, should lead to the decrease in B. This chapter has explored the potential of permanent lesions, TMS and rTMS to study effects of this sort.

If A causes B it should occur before B, even if the time difference is slight. EEG and MEG offer a temporal resolution in milliseconds and are, therefore, appropriate methods for studying the order of neural events. However, they have the further advantage that they measure the oscillations between electrical (EEG) or magnetic signals (MEG) arising from neuronal populations. There is increasing evidence that cells in one area communicate optimally with cells in another when their oscillations are coherent. Thus, EEG and MEG are essential tools for studying the mechanisms via which cell populations communicate.

We end with a plea that those trained in fMRI should not just view themselves as "imagers". They are first and foremost neuroscientists, and scientists have recourse to whatever method is necessary to answer their question.

Chapter 8

The neuroscience of human cognition

Abstract

The motivation for an imaging study should be better than simply "little is known about the neural basis of X." As in other areas of science, interest should be in phenomena that are in need of explanation. These could concern normal cognition, for example that it is difficult to carry out two tasks at the same time; or abnormal cognition, for example that there are patients who hear voices. Answering questions such as these can require a combination of methods, which can be best achieved by collaboration between scientists who are experts in different methods. With the maturation of brain imaging, users should think of themselves not as "imagers" but as neuroscientists.

Keywords

brain states and mental states, psychology and imaging, cerebral dominance, the attentional bottleneck, economic decision-making, hearing voices, alien limb, rumination, neuroculture, neuroscience.

Introduction

In combination with other methods, brain imaging has made it possible to advance a true neuroscience of human cognition. The reason why this cannot be done by animal experimentation alone is that people have cognitive abilities that are unique. As a result, there are also disorders that are peculiar to the human condition.

As discussed in Chapter 1, prior to the advent of imaging, the main method available for studying the neural basis of human cognition was the neuropsychological study of the effects of lesions in patients. But this study was limited, because it relied either on the accidents of nature or on the clinical needs for surgery. Furthermore, it could not tell us about mechanisms, for example about how regions interact and influence each other. Functional imaging differs in that it studies the human brain in operation and does so across the whole brain; and this means that it can study functional systems and the interactions between areas within them.

The images are acquired while subjects are performing particular tasks or during a defined period of "rest." So imaging relates a brain state to a mental state. Thus, it is important to understand the relationship between neural functions and psychological processes.

Brain states and mental states

For every thought, perception, memory, or act there is a brain state. But this is not to claim that the same mental state is always associated with the same brain state. It is an empirical issue to what extent the brain is, or is not, in the same state when the same thought is repeated or indeed when others have the same thought. For example, Haxby et al. (2014) examined the issue using multivariate pattern analysis to "decode" the neural states; they were able to identify common patterns of activation throughout the neocortex when subjects viewed the same stimuli. And Zhang and Rowe (2015) used similar methods to examine the mental representations of task rules when the same task rule had been acquired by different means. Studies of this sort will inevitably become more common, as neuroscientists begin to look for common patterns of activation when subjects have particular thoughts or make particular decisions.

Whether or not the same mental state can arise from multiple neural states, it is clear that if there were no brain state, there would be no mental state. Imaging allows us to identify the brain state B while the person is in mental state M. However, this does not necessarily mean that the explanation for why the person is in that mental state is to be found by studying the brain. There are two possible answers as to why the person is in mental state M: the first is that there has been a change in the brain and that this change was not the result of external stimulation; the second is that the change in mental state occurred because of stimulation from the external environment. These options apply not only to momentary events as in the perception of stimuli, but also to chronic states of mood or appetite.

Consider depression as an example of such a state. If people are scanned while they are depressed, the brain image shows a difference in the degree of activation in the subgenual cingulate cortex, area 25 (Drevets et al., 1997). In some studies under-activation has been reported and in others over-activation. The difference is probably accounted for by the degree to which depression has led to a state of apathy or to a state of anxiety (Bench et al., 1993).

There is a temptation to believe that the imaging results show that depression is a "brain disorder." It is, of course, in the sense that any mental state is necessarily associated with a particular brain state. But the results need not be evidence of an abnormality of the brain. The same brain state can be produced simply by asking healthy subjects to think about sad events. This procedure also induces a change in the degree of activation of the subgenual cingulate cortex, even though the brain is normal (Kohn et al., 2014). The differences in activation observed in depressed subjects may therefore be the result of their negative thoughts, rather than the cause.

So the difference in activation in the subgenual cingulate cortex is agnostic as to why the brain state is present. It could reflect genetic inheritance: reduced activation has been found in this area in subjects with a particular genetic polymorphism (Wang et al., 2012). Or it could reflect life events: there is reduced activation in subjects with a history of childhood abuse (Banihashemi et al., 2015).

Furthermore, the fact that depression is related to a given brain state says nothing about whether physical, pharmacological, or psychological treatments will be effective in relieving the depression. Medication can be effective: in patients treated with the antidepressant venlafaxine, there is an increase in glucose metabolism in the subgenual area 25 (Kennedy et al., 2007). But psychological therapies can also be effective: in patients treated with cognitive behavior therapy, there is an increase in glucose metabolism in the pregenual area 32, just adjacent to area 25 (Kennedy et al., 2007).

So brain-based explanations do not necessarily trump psychological or social explanations. This is not some mystery that necessitates belief in dualism. It is the simple consequence of the fact that people are not simply brains: they also have eyes, ears, and bodies. It is people who see, remember, decide, learn, and interact, not their brains, even if the brain is essential to do so (Bennett and Hacker, 2003).

Psychology and brain imaging

The study of cognition has traditionally been the province of psychology. There is a long history of psychologists trying to explain the phenomena of perception and learning (Hebb, 1949). The explanations could be mathematical: for example, a model involving a delta learning rule was devised to account for classical conditioning (Rescorla, 1976). Or the explanations could be models of information flow: models of this sort (Broadbent, 1958) were called "black box models" because at the time that these models were popular there were no means of visualizing what actually occurred in the brain itself.

Current explanations are more likely to involve computational (Dayan, 2005) or connectionist models (McLeod et al., 1998). So now that imaging is available, it is important to be clear about the relation between these models and the accounts that can be provided by imaging. Here it is helpful to invoke the three levels of explanation that were proposed by David Marr (1982).

He suggested that it was important to distinguish the computational, algorithmic, and implementational levels. The first says what a process does, for example, what vision is for. The second suggests the input–output transformations that are required to do this. And the third gives an account of the ways in which these are implemented in the brain itself in terms of cell populations and their connections. The essential insight is that there could be many different ways in which computational and algorithmic theories could be implemented. They could as well be implemented in a computer or robot as in the brain.

Nonetheless, people have brains with neuronal functions that underlie psychological processes. So it should be possible to use the way in which their behavior is actually implemented to test a psychological theory. However, Coltheart (2006) has argued that imaging is unable to do this because psychological theories make no statement about the location of the relevant neuronal functions within the brain.

There are three weaknesses in this argument. The first is that it is not true that location is uninformative. It can show, for example, that two processes are dissociable. Behavioral measures can show that there are distinct modules (Sternberg, 2011), but as Henson (2011) has argued, this can also be shown if there are two measures in imaging data that are not monotonically related.

The second weakness with Coltheart's argument is that it assumes that imaging can only be used for brain mapping or localization. But as this book has argued throughout, imaging can also be also used to study mechanisms. The mechanisms for the voluntary direction of attention serve as a good example. Goal-directed attention depends on the enhancement of cell activity (Gee et al., 2008), and that enhancement can be detected with fMRI (Buchel et al., 1998).

Psychologists have long discussed whether unattended stimuli are filtered out completely or continue for further processing. However, Lavie (1995) proposed a resolution: that the degree of processing of the unattended channel depends on the perceptual load in the attended channel. So Rees et al. (1997) carried out an imaging experiment in which they manipulated load; and, as predicted, the activation in the unattended channel was less than the greater the load in the attended channel. So imaging can indeed be informative about mechanism.

There is a third weakness in the argument: it aims to show that fMRI is unable to test psychological theories without considering whether fMRI can do so when combined with other methods. When evaluating what imaging has shown, Coltheart and colleagues (Tressoldi et al., 2012) deliberately restricted their review to studies that use fMRI alone. But we have not claimed that fMRI is sufficient for studying the human brain on its own. The message of Chapter 7 is exactly that fMRI needs to be used in combination with other imaging methods.

The example of task switching illustrates the point. Psychologists have long been interested in why responses take longer after switching between tasks that have different rules than they do when switching between tasks that have the same rules. The extra time is called the switch cost. One possibility is that there is inertia from the old task set (Wylie and Allport, 2000), but it has been difficult to demonstrate this on the basis of behavioral data alone.

So Akaishi et al. (2010) applied single TMS pulses to the prefrontal cortex while the subjects prepared to perform the second task. They measured the influence of the TMS pulse by recording from other cortical regions with EEG. Regardless of the upcoming task, there was an effect of the TMS pulse on posterior areas that depended on the previous task. Thus, the combination of task, TMS, and EEG provided direct evidence for the persistence of the previous task set.

The neuroscience of human cognition

Previous chapters have shown how imaging can be used to visualize the state of the brain while subjects perform particular tasks. The procedure has been to scan subjects while they were in different mental states. It remains to show how well the knowledge acquired by this and related methods can be used to explain human cognition and its disorders.

In this section, we provide worked examples of how either the work or the methods that were described in earlier chapters can be relevant to answering three questions concerning normal human cognition. In the next section we provide three examples that are relevant to disordered cognition. In each case we explain why the experiments require human subjects.

Cerebral dominance

The first question is how we can account for cerebral dominance for language. Here it is clear that the experiments can only be performed with human subjects. It is true that great apes can learn a protolanguage (Savage-Rumbaugh and Lewin, 1994) and also that the understanding of words depends on mechanisms for the perception of calls that can found in other primates (Wilson and Petkov, 2011). However, neither macaque monkeys nor chimpanzees can be taught a fully developed language.

The reason is that they lack specializations that are unique to the human brain. Diffusion weighted imaging has been used to chart the paths that run between the parietal and Broca's area and between the temporal lobe and Broca's area. In the human brain there is an asymmetry such that these paths are more extensive and more clearly defined in a diffusion image in the left hemisphere. This has been shown both for the arcuate fasciculus that runs between the superior and middle temporal gyrus and Broca's area (Rilling et al., 2008), and for the path that runs between the inferior parietal cortex and Broca's area (Caspers et al., 2011). These asymmetries do not exist in the brains of chimpanzees or macaque monkeys (Rilling et al., 2008).

It has long been known that in right-handers the left hemisphere is dominant for language. However, imaging studies have shown that the left hemisphere is also dominant for the control of action. Schluter et al. (2001) used PET to scan subjects while they performed simple or choice reaction time tasks with either the right or left hand. The motor cortical activation was lateralized according to the hand that was used, but there was activation in the left premotor cortex for the choice reaction time task irrespective of the hand used. This was also true for activations in the inferior frontal cortex and the cortex in the intraparietal sulcus.

Biagi et al. (2010) also scanned subjects with fMRI while they observed a video of a hand playing notes on piano keys. The movements were performed with either the right or left hand. There was an activation in the cortex in the left, but not right, intraparietal sulcus, and again it occurred irrespective of the hand used.

As already mentioned in Chapter 5, there is activation in the inferior parietal cortex when subjects observe motion (Fig. 5.5) (Passingham et al., 2014). But what we did not stress there is that the activation is much more extensive in the left than in the right hemisphere (Fig. 8.1). And, surprisingly, there is also an asymmetry in the activations in areas processing biological motion in the superior temporal sulcus (Fig. 8.1). The reason why this asymmetry is surprising is that, as can be seen in Fig. 8.1, there is no such asymmetry in earlier visual areas such as the human MT complex (hMT+). The asymmetry is almost certainly explained by top-down projections, since the activations in frontal areas are also strongly asymmetrical (Fig. 8.1) (Passingham et al., 2014). The operation of top-down projections from the frontal cortex was described in Chapter 6.

One way of explaining the link between dominance for language and handedness for actions is to suppose that in hominid evolution, manual gestures were used to point and communicate requests (Arbib, 2005). There is evidence that this would involve Broca's area. If rTMS is applied to Broca's area at the

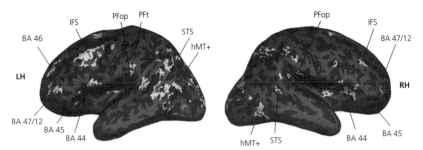

Fig. 8.1 Activations in the left and right hemisphere while subjects observe actions. hMT + = human motion complex, STS = superior temporal sulcus.

Reprinted from Brain Research, 1582, R.E. Passingham, A. Chung, B. Goparaju, A. Cowey, and L.M. Vaina, Using action understanding to understand the left inferior parietal cortex in the human brain, pp. 64–76. doi: 10.1016/j.brainres.2014.07.035, Copyright (2014), with permission from Elsevier.

theta frequency, it interferes with the production of gestures (Bohlhalter et al., 2011). But Broca's area is only part of the system. Chapter 2 mentioned an experiment by Rumiati et al. (2004) in which subjects were scanned while they used gestures to show how objects can be used. There were activations not only in Broca's area, but also in the left anterior inferior parietal cortex with which it is connected.

If we suppose that communication was indeed first via manual gestures, there is a ready explanation for cerebral dominance. The use of one hand for skilled and rapid movements probably evolved because of the demands for toolmaking (Passingham, 2008). If so, handedness for one set of tasks would transfer to handedness for making gestures. The consequence is that the left hemisphere would already be dominant for gestures before the elaboration of the vocal articulatory system that was necessary to say protowords.

If this account is correct, the initial anatomical asymmetry was for the connections between the inferior parietal cortex and Broca's area. It would follow that when the hominids developed speech, the asymmetry in the connections between the temporal lobe and Broca's area would favor the same hemisphere.

Dual-task costs

The second question is why it is difficult to carry out two demanding tasks at the same time. There is no reason to believe that the explanation for this phenomenon is peculiar to the human brain. However, it is not easy to set up experiments to study dual-task costs in macaque monkeys, though it can be done (Watanabe and Funahashi, 2014). It is an advantage of using human subjects that they can be instructed what to do and they can rapidly acquire multiple new tasks to perform. The analysis in this section depends on evidence from the use of eight different tasks.

Baddeley et al. (1998) instructed subjects to produce random sequences of key presses, and subjects could indeed produce sequences that were highly variable. However, the sequences became stereotyped if the subjects were also required to generate a random series of numbers at the same time. Yet, this was not true if the secondary task was counting. So the impact of the secondary task on the primary task depended on the complexity of the secondary task.

Pashler (1994) suggested that dual-task costs of this sort are due to the convergence of different streams into a bottleneck. It should, therefore, be possible to use imaging to visualize *where* that bottleneck occurs. However, we have argued that imaging should not simply be used to establish localization. The aim should also be to reveal *why* there is a bottleneck.

The location of the bottleneck becomes clear when subjects are scanned while doing the tasks used by Baddeley et al. (1998). If subjects are required to generate a series of finger presses (Rowe et al., 2005) or random numbers (Jahanshahi et al., 2000), there is activation in the dorsal prefrontal cortex for both tasks individually. Chapter 3 has already mentioned that the activation only occurs if a series of movements are required; it is not present on the first movement (Rowe et al., 2010). Thus the activation reflects the need to take previous moves into account when deciding which one to select on the next trial (Zhang and Rowe, 2015).

We are not suggesting that the bottleneck is confined to the dorsal prefrontal cortex. Two related fMRI studies (Dux et al., 2006; Tombu et al., 2011) used a behavioral method that was introduced by Pashler (1994) to identify a bottleneck. This is to present two tasks, but to vary the delay between the start of one task and the start of the other. If the delay is long, there is no dual-task cost; but if the delay is short, there is a measurable cost. The assumption is that, if the delay is long, the first response will have been selected by the time that the selection of the second response has been started. In the two imaging studies, activations that were greater with short than with long delays were found in the ventral prefrontal cortex, dorsal prefrontal cortex, and the anterior cingulate sulcus.

The next question is why counting does not interfere when used as a secondary task. If subjects are scanned while they count from one to ten, there is no activation in either the ventral or the dorsal prefrontal cortex (Vanlancker-Sidtis et al., 2003). The activations are limited to Broca's area, the supplementary speech area, and the posterior putamen. The reason is that for adult subjects counting is a highly overlearned task. Chapter 6 mentioned that there is no activation in the prefrontal cortex if subjects move their fingers in a repetitive sequence (using fingers1–4, in that order), and that the dorsal prefrontal cortex is only activated in such repetitive sequences when the subjects are asked to mentally prepare for or attend to each move (Rowe et al., 2002).

Taken together, all the above findings suggest that two tasks only interfere behaviorally if they both make demands on a single region. There are other results that are consistent with this proposal. For example, Baddeley et al. (1998) have demonstrated behavioral interference if subjects are required to generate a random sequence at the same time as trying to solve IQ problems. As already mentioned, there is activation in the dorsal prefrontal cortex for random generation (Frith, 2000). And, as one would predict on the basis of the proposal, there is also activation in the same area when subjects are required to take tests of general intelligence (Duncan et al., 2000).

These results point to the location of a bottleneck, but they do not tell us why it should exist. After all, there could be parallel streams *within* the prefrontal cortex, and if so, two tasks could be performed concurrently, with activation for the tasks being in different streams.

There is, however, a hidden advantage in convergence of processing streams. This can be illustrated by considering the ventral prefrontal cortex. There is activation in the ventral prefrontal cortex both when subjects press keys according to visual cues and when they repeat words that they hear (Stelzel et al., 2006). However, the important observation is that there is also activation in the same area when the subjects perform the cross-over tasks, pressing keys according to auditory cues and saying words according to visual cues. The fact that the same area is involved, whatever the combination of cue and response, suggests that within that area there are dense interconnections so as to allow any input to influence any output. Thus, the suggested advantage of the bottleneck is the gain in flexibility.

Economic decisions

The third question is why people can be bad at making economic decisions. Chapter 5 described an experiment in which subjects were scanned while they considered counterfactual choices; that is, with alternatives that they later rejected. People are able to evaluate different alternatives before making their decision. It is not clear whether other animals are capable of mentally evaluating alternatives in turn, but it is clear that people are (Passingham and Wise, 2012).

Chau et al. (2014) adapted a model of how decisions are made that suggests that the evidence for alternatives accumulates in a competitive race. Accumulation-to-threshold models of this sort were discussed in Chapter 5. They were produced to explain data from single-cell recording studies (Gold and Shadlen, 2007). The difference is that the model used by Chau et al. incorporated inhibitory connections (Wang, 2002). Chau et al. realized that the model made a counter-intuitive prediction: that deciding between two alternatives would be difficult if there was a third very poor alternative as opposed to a good one.

So Chau et al. scanned subjects while they made decisions between alternatives that differed in their expected value. As predicted, decision-making was indeed suboptimal in the critical condition. And, critically, there was an activation in the ventromedial prefrontal cortex that related to the difference in value between the two main alternatives, and this signal decreased when there was a third very poor alternative.

Thus, the work used a model to make a novel prediction about the decision process and then tested that prediction using neuroimaging. It did so by first looking for a signal that relates to the difference in value. It then showed that that signal is indeed influenced by the presence of a third, but poor, alternative. Finally, the results served as a test of the model: if the signal had not been influenced in this way, this would have shown that the model could not explain the phenomenon.

A critic might object that the model made a behavioral prediction, and all that the imaging contributed was to show a neural correlate of that prediction. But the objection is invalid. The reason is that the model only made the prediction because it posited an intermediary process, and it was the imaging that tested whether that process actually occurs.

The neuroscience of abnormal mental states

The same methods that are used to understand normal cognition can also be used to understand disorders of cognition. As in medicine in general, the results of basic research can be applied to explain disorders in the clinic. Again we suggest how three questions could be answered.

Hearing voices

The first question is why some patients with schizophrenia hear voices. There is no satisfactory animal model of schizophrenia, despite candidate genetic models in rodents that are based on genetic risk factors for schizophrenia (Lipina and Roder, 2014). Paradigms for the disruption of language and for complex psychotic beliefs cannot be developed in non-human primates, let alone lower order species. It would, in principle, be possible to investigate auditory hallucinations in monkeys, but this has not yet been done.

If patients are scanned while they hear voices, there is activation in the superior temporal gyrus (Rapin et al., 2012). There could be two explanations of how activation in this area of auditory association cortex is related to the subjective reports given by the patients that they are "hearing voices."

One is that the patients are mistaking their own silent thoughts for overt speech coming from outside. Since there is activation in the inferior frontal cortex during silent speech (Petrovich et al., 2005), the origin could therefore be in the frontal cortex. It has been suggested that in healthy subjects, the subjective perception is canceled because thoughts are fully predicted (Frith 1992). This would involve the operation of a re-afferent signal.

There are results that could be taken to be consistent with this suggestion. In healthy subjects the superior temporal cortex is less activated when they are just thinking, rather than when they actually hear words. This effect is less marked in patients who hear voices (Simons et al., 2010). And this could indicate an impairment in the re-afferent signal.

But there is a second possibility: that the hallucinations arise from an abnormality in the superior temporal cortex itself. Hubl et al. (2007) used EEG to record the N1 evoked potential to tones. The advantage is that this potential is thought to reflect activity in the primary and second auditory cortex. The finding was that the N1 response to tones was reduced if the patients were hearing voices at the same time. This could be explained if we suppose that ongoing activity, reflecting the voices, inhibited local activity that was evoked by the tones.

It is clear that there is a need to resolve the issue of whether the hallucinations arise in auditory areas or speech areas. Recording activations alone with fMRI cannot do this. The reason is that activation in the superior temporal cortex could result in activation in the inferior frontal gyrus with which it is connected, and vice versa.

There are three ways in which the issue could be resolved. One would be to compare anatomically constrained models and to use DCM to compare the evidence for feedforward and feedback connections. This is the approach described in Chapter 6.

The second method would be to use time-resolved MEG and to measure temporal precedence or Granger causality. Van Lutterveld et al. (2012) scanned with MEG and found changes during auditory verbal hallucinations in the superior temporal gyrus and inferior frontal gyrus. Unfortunately, the authors do not report whether, at the onset of the voices, the neural changes occurred earlier in the temporal or the frontal lobe.

The final method would be to apply rTMS to either the superior temporal cortex or the inferior frontal cortex while the patients are hearing voices. rTMS has been applied to the superior temporal cortex or temporal parietal area Tpt as a treatment for auditory hallucinations, and a meta-analysis of ten studies has reported that it has some success (Otani et al., 2014) So rTMS could now be applied to either the superior temporal or inferior frontal cortex while the patients hear voices. If stimulating the temporal cortex interferes with the subjective perception, but stimulating the frontal cortex does not, the experiment would show that the primary dysfunction is in the auditory system.

Unwanted actions

The second question is how there can be patients who complain that their arm is carrying out actions that they had not themselves chosen (Rowe and Wolpe, 2014). This has been called the "alien hand syndrome" when the hand does not feel as if it belongs to the person; it is also sometimes called the "anarchic hand syndrome" given that the sense of ownership is not always absent (Blakemore et al., 2002). When the limb moves, the patients may be aware of the movement, but they are not aware of intending the movement. While it could be that the same phenomenon occurs in animals, there is no way of knowing, since we are unable assess what they had intended.

One way of studying the sense of agency in human subjects is to use the method introduced by Libet et al. (1983b) to estimate the time at which people become aware of their intention to move. The method has already been described in Chapter 6. In the study described there, Lau et al. (2004) reported an enhancement in the activation of the Pre-SMA when subjects attended to their intention to move.

In a further development of the method, Haggard and his colleagues (2008) measured the interval between the time at which subjects reported movement and the time at which they reported the outcome of that movement. They found that if the movement was voluntary, there was "temporal binding," that is, the subjective interval was shorter than the actual interval. So Moore et al. (2010) applied theta burst TMS to the Pre-SMA, and found that, as predicted, it disrupted this temporal binding.

These results led Wolpe et al. (2014) to assess temporal binding in ten patients with corticobasal degeneration and varying degrees of alien limb syndrome. The more severe the syndrome, the shorter the interval that subjects reported between a movement and the outcome. The effect was specific to the patients. Furthermore, the distortion only occurred when they moved the limb for which they reported alien movements, not when they moved the unaffected limb.

The patients were also scanned and this perceptual distortion correlated with several measures. One was the volume of the gray matter in the Pre-SMA. Another was the extent of the white-matter tracts connecting the Pre-SMA with the prefrontal and premotor cortex.

However, there was a third finding, which is very significant in the light of the results of the study of Lau et al. (2004). As described in Chapter 6, these authors found that when the subjects attended to action, there was a significant psycho-physiological interaction between the dorsal prefrontal cortex and the Pre-SMA. In the study of patients by Wolpe et al. (2014), the change in temporal binding could be related to the degree of functional connectivity between the dorsal prefrontal cortex and the Pre-SMA while the subjects were at rest.

This shows how a study of healthy subjects can inform a study of patients. The results suggest that the patients may be inaccurate at timing movements in relation to their outcomes because they lack a reliable internal model of their intentions.

Rumination

The final question is why anxiety and depression can be so prolonged in patients. Macaque monkeys can also become depressed when separated from their mothers, but the state does not last (Spencer-Booth and Hinde, 1971). One possible reason why it lasts in people is that they have mechanisms that allow them to reason, to retrieve episodic memories from the past, and to imagine the distant future. These thoughts can be maladaptive when the content is emotional. The result can be the temporal extension of an aversive state and thus the risk of a longer period of depression.

Freton et al. (2014) compared subjects who tend to brood with subjects who do not. The subjects were asked to focus either on the causes of particular experiences or on what they felt like. Focusing on the causes led to activation in the medial system in the subjects who tended to brood but not in those who did not: there were strong activations in the retrosplenial and posterior cingulate cortex.

Chapter 6 pointed out that these areas are activated when subjects retrieve episodes in their life or imagine future ones (Hassabis et al., 2007). However, this does not prove that the activation in the study by Freton et al. reflects the same thought processes. The reason is that, as explained in Chapter 3, this interpretation involves a reverse inference.

So as to have experimental control over the thoughts, Berman et al. (2014) studied patients with major depressive disorder and instructed them to think about particular negative events. They were specifically told to recall what had happened and re-experience the events. The results for the patients were compared with the results for healthy subjects. The difference was that, when the patients concentrated on their negative thoughts, there was increased functional connectivity of the posterior cingulate cortex with other areas in the medial system.

These activations and interactions reflect the continuous recall of emotionally charged events. But people with depression also tend to have negative views about the world and about themselves as persons (Kovacs and Beck, 1978). Hamilton et al. (2015) therefore scanned depressed patients while they considered criticisms of themselves or of others. The dorsal paracingulate cortex (area 32 in the medial system) was especially activated in the patients compared with controls when they considered criticism of themselves.

The study could be extended by using a paradigm that was developed by Bengtsson et al. (2009). One group of healthy subjects was primed that errors on a task mattered, and the control group was not. There was enhanced activation in the dorsal paracingulate cortex, area 32, on error trials for the subjects that were primed; and this was true whether the priming was explicit (Bengtsson et al., 2009) or implicit (Bengtsson et al., 2011). The peak for this activation is shown in Fig. 5.6 (peak 7). The prediction is that, even if they are not primed, the same enhancement will be seen in the dorsal paracingulate cortex when the results for depressed patients are compared with those for healthy subjects.

But these results would only show a correlation between subjective thoughts and depression. Chapter 7 suggested the use of rTMS to prove a causal link. So Kreuzer et al. (2015) applied rTMS to either the dorsal or ventral anterior cingulate cortex. They were able to do so because of the development of a double cone coil that is designed to impose magnetic pulses at a greater depth from the midline than is possible with the normal butterfly coil. There was an effect on relieving the depression, but only after treatment with the double cone coil.

This study only measured depression, not rumination per se. The next step is to see whether stimulation aimed at either the dorsal paracingulate cortex or the subgenual cortex produces effects that differ. We already know that electrical stimulation of the subgenual cortex relieves the depressive state (Holtzheimer et al., 2012). The question of interest is whether targeting the dorsal paracingulate cortex has a specific effect on rumination.

This section has highlighted the problems of depending on reverse inference or correlations. By combining imaging with other methods, it is possible to establish causality in clinical conditions.

Neuroscience

We had three aims in choosing the worked examples in this chapter. One was that they should show how experimental results mentioned earlier in the book can be used to address new questions. For instance, the elucidation of the core system is helpful in identifying the bottleneck in attentional processing.

Another was that the examples should illustrate the use of the wide range of methods that are available. Thus, two studies used PET (Schluter et al., 2001;

Rumiati et al., 2004) and there were many that used fMRI, as in the case of the attentional bottleneck (Dux et al., 2006; Tombu et al., 2011). Two studies used diffusion weight imaging (Rilling et al., 2008; Wolpe et al., 2014) and others measured resting state connectivity and connectivity during a task (Berman et al., 2014; Wolpe et al., 2014). Chau et al. (2014) related activations to a term in a computational model. Bohlhalter et al. (2011) used theta burst rTMS to disrupt performance. Finally, Hubl et al. (2007) recorded the N1 potential with EEG while patients with schizophrenia heard voices, and van Lutterveld et al. (2012) used MEG to scan during auditory verbal hallucinations.

However, there was a final aim in the choice of examples in this chapter: that they should persuade the reader that in neuroscience, as in any other branch of science, the question comes first and the methods follow. And the questions should be genuine questions. Too many papers start with a weak statement of the sort "we do not know how the brain supports mental operation X." The subjects are scanned and the conclusion turns out to be that the brain is in state B during mental state X.

But this is not how the best science proceeds. The scientist starts with a puzzle, suggests an explanation, and designs an experiment to test it. It has become common to add the prefix "neuro-" to a discipline, as in "neuro-economics," "neuro-ethics," "neuro-esthetics," "neuro-philosophy," or "neuro-culture" (Rolls, 2012). And there are indeed questions in each of the original disciplines that are in need of an answer. But the danger is that all that is achieved by adding "neuro" is to present brain correlates, without actually providing an *explanation*. To take a trivial example, "neuro-magic" (Blakeslee et al., 2011) does not tell us *why* the observers are fooled. It has to be true that there are changes in the brain when the gaze of the audience is misdirected, but imaging the brain tells us nothing that the conjuror does not already know.

So a true neuroscience of human cognition must provide answers, and it is our hope that this book has equipped the reader to evaluate those answers. Does the imaging study actually support the claims made? Are there alternative explanations of the imaging results? Are the claims dependent on reverse inference? Does the imaging study tell us anything that we did not already know from the behavior? Does the imaging study add anything to what we already knew from studies of animals? And so on. It is only with such a critical approach that the vivid images can enlighten rather than mislead.

There is no doubt that there have been extraordinary advances in neuroimaging over the last 25 years. It was not our purpose to review all of those advances. Instead we have tried to encourage the user to see imaging in the context of anatomy and physiology. This is the way to achieve a true "neuro-science" of human cognition.

Summary

Previous chapters have shown how imaging and related methods can be used to study human cognition. This chapter provides six worked examples of how questions can be answered. The first three examples relate to normal cognition: these concern cerebral dominance, dual-task costs, and decision-making. The other three examples relate to abnormal cognition: these concern hearing voices, unwanted movements, and rumination.

The examples were also chosen because they illustrate the fact that a variety of methods are needed when answering questions of this sort. We called the book *A Short Guide to Brain Imaging*. This chapter has illustrated what is needed to justify the subtitle *The Neuroscience of Human Cognition*.

References

Addis DR, Wong AT, Schacter DL (2007) Remembering the past and imagining the future: common and distinct neural substrates during event construction and elaboration. Neuropsychol **45**:1363–1377.

Akaishi R, Morishima Y, Rajeswaren VP, Aoki S, Sakai K (2010) Stimulation of the frontal eye field reveals persistent effective connectivity after controlled behavior. J Neurosci **30**:4295–4305.

Alexander GE, Crutcher MD, DeLong MR (1991) Basal ganglia-thalamocortical circuits: parallel substrates for motor, oculomotor, 'prefrontal' and 'limbic' functions. Progr Brain Res **85**:119–146.

Allport A (1986) Selection for action: some behavioral and neurophysiological considerations of attention and action. In: Perspectives on Perception and Action (Heuer, H. and Sanders, A. F., eds), pp 395–417 Hillsdale: Erlbaum.

Amaro E, Jr., Barker GJ (2006) Study design in fMRI: basic principles. Brain Cogn **60**:220–232.

Amiez C, Joseph JP, Procyk E (2006) Reward encoding in the monkey anterior cingulate cortex. Cereb Cortex **16**:1040–1055.

Amodio DM, Frith CD (2006) Meeting of minds: the medial frontal cortex and social cognition. Nat Rev Neurosci **7**:268–277.

Amunts K, Schleicher A, Zilles K (2007) Cytoarchitecture of the cerebral cortex-More than localization. Neuroimage **37**:1061–1065.

Andrews-Hanna JR, Reidler JS, Sepulcre J, Poulin R, Buckner RL (2010) Functional-anatomic fractionation of the brain's default network. Neuron **65**:550–562.

Arbib MA (2005) From monkey-like action recognition to human language: an evolutionary framework for neurolinguistics. Behav Brain Sci **28**:105–124; discussion 125–167.

Asaad WF, Rainer G, Miller EK (1998) Neural activity in the primate prefrontal cortex during associative learning. Neuron **21**:1399–1407.

Ashburner J (2007) A fast diffeomorphic image registration algorithm. Neuroimage **38**:95–113.

Astafiev SV, Shulman GL, Stanley CM, Snyder AZ, Van Essen DC, Corbetta M (2003) Functional organization of human intraparietal and frontal cortex for attending, looking, and pointing. J Neurosci **23**:4689–4699.

Attal Y, Bhattacharjee M, Yelnik J, Cottereau B, Lefevre J, Okada Y, Bardinet E, Chupin M, Baillet S (2007) Modeling and detecting deep brain activity with MEG & EEG. Conf Proc IEEE Eng Med Biol Soc **2007**:4937–4940.

Averbeck BB, Lehman J, Jacobson M, Haber SN (2014) Estimates of projection overlap and zones of convergence within frontal-striatal circuits. J Neurosci **34**:9497–9505.

Avillac M, Deneve S, Olivier E, Pouget A, Duhamel JR (2005) Reference frames for representing visual and tactile locations in parietal cortex. Nat Neurosci **8**:941–949.

Baddeley A, Emslie H, Kolodny J, Duncan J (1998) Random generation and the executive control of working memory. Q J Exp Psychol A **51**:819–852.

Badre D, Wagner AD (2002) Semantic retrieval, mnemonic control, and prefrontal cortex. Behav Cogn Neurosci Rev **1**:206–218.

Balsters JH, Cussans E, Diedrichsen J, Phillips KA, Preuss TM, Rilling JK, Ramnani N (2010) Evolution of the cerebellar cortex: the selective expansion of prefrontal-projecting cerebellar lobules. Neuroimage **49**:2045–2052.

Banihashemi L, Sheu LK, Midei AJ, Gianaros PJ (2015) Childhood physical abuse predicts stressor-evoked activity within central visceral control regions. Soc Cogn Affect Neurosci. **10**:474–485.

Barbas H (2000) Connections underlying the synthesis of cognition, memory, and emotion in primate prefrontal cortices. Brain Res Bull **52**:319–330.

Bargh JA (2006) What have we been priming all these years? On the development, mechanisms, and ecology of nonconscious social behavior. Eur J Soc Psychol **36**:147–168.

Barkley GL (2004) Controversies in neurophysiology. MEG is superior to EEG in localization of interictal epileptiform activity: Pro. Clin Neurophysiol **115**:1001–1009.

Barry RL, Williams JM, Klassen LM, Gallivan JP, Culham JC, Menon RS (2010) Evaluation of preprocessing steps to compensate for magnetic field distortions due to body movements in BOLD fMRI. Magn Reson Imaging **28**:235–244.

Bastos AM, Usrey WM, Adams RA, Mangun GR, Fries P, Friston KJ (2012) Canonical microcircuits for predictive coding. Neuron **76**:695–711.

Baylis GC, Rolls ET (1987) Responses of neurons in the inferior temporal cortex in short term and serial recognition memory tasks. Exp Brain Res **65**:614–622.

Becker-Bense S, Buchholz HG, Zu Eulenburg P, Best C, Bartenstein P, Schreckenberger M, Dieterich M (2012) Ventral and dorsal streams processing visual motion perception (FDG-PET study). BMC Neurosci **13**:81.

Beckmann M, Johansen-Berg H, Rushworth MF (2009) Connectivity-based parcellation of human cingulate cortex and its relation to functional specialization. J Neurosci **29**:1175–1190.

Behrens TE, Sporns O (2012) Human connectomics. Curr Opin Neurobiol **22**:144–153.

Behrens TE, Woolrich MW, Walton ME, Rushworth MF (2007) Learning the value of information in an uncertain world. Nat Neurosci **10**:1214–1221.

Bench CJ, Friston KJ, Brown RG, Frackowiak RSJ, Dolan RJ (1993) Regional cerebral blood flow in depression measured by positron emission tomography: the relationship with clinical dimensions. Psychol Med **23**:579–590.

Bengtsson SL, Nagy Z, Skare S, Forsman L, Forssberg H, Ullen F (2005) Extensive piano practicing has regionally specific effects on white matter development. Nat Neurosci **8**:1148–1150.

Bengtsson SL, Lau HC, Passingham RE (2009) Motivation to do well enhances responses to errors and self-monitoring. Cereb Cortex **19**:797–804.

Bengtsson SL, Dolan RJ, Passingham RE (2011) Priming for self-esteem influences the monitoring of one's own performance. Soc Cogn Affect Neurosci. **6**:417–425.

Benjamini Y, Hochberg Y (1995) Controlling the false discovery rate: a practical and powerful approach to multiple testing. J Stat Soc B **57**:289–300.

Bennett MR, Hacker PMS (2003) Philosophical Foundations of Neuroscience. Oxford: Blackwells.

Bennett CM, Wolford GL, Miller MB (2009) The principled control of false positives in neuroimaging. Soc Cogn Affect Neurosci **4**:417–422.

Berman MG, Misic B, Buschkuehl M, Kross E, Deldin PJ, Peltier S, Churchill NW, Jaeggi SM, Vakorin V, McIntosh AR, Jonides J (2014) Does resting-state connectivity reflect depressive rumination? A tale of two analyses. Neuroimage **103C**:267–279.

Biagi L, Cioni G, Fogassi L, Guzzetta A, Tosetti M (2010) Anterior intraparietal cortex codes complexity of observed hand movements. Brain Res Bull **81**:434–440.

Biswal BB, Mennes M, Zuo XN, Gohel S, Kelly C, Smith SM, Beckmann CF, Adelstein JS, Buckner RL, Colcombe S, Dogonowski AM, Ernst M, Fair D, Hampson M, Hoptman MJ, Hyde JS, Kiviniemi VJ, Kotter R, Li SJ, Lin CP, Lowe MJ, Mackay C, Madden DJ, Madsen KH, Margulies DS, Mayberg HS, McMahon K, Monk CS, Mostofsky SH, Nagel BJ, Pekar JJ, Peltier SJ, Petersen SE, Riedl V, Rombouts SA, Rypma B, Schlaggar BL, Schmidt S, Seidler RD, Siegle GJ, Sorg C, Teng GJ, Veijola J, Villringer A, Walter M, Wang L, Weng XC, Whitfield-Gabrieli S, Williamson P, Windischberger C, Zang YF, Zhang HY, Castellanos FX, Milham MP (2010) Toward discovery science of human brain function. Proc Natl Acad Sci U S A **107**:4734–4739.

Blakemore SJ, Wolpert DM, Frith CD (2002) Abnormalities in the awareness of action. Trends Cogn Sci **6**:237–242.

Blakeslee S, Macknik SL, Martinez -C, S. (2011) Sleights of Mind: Profile Books.

Blumenfeld RS, Bliss DP, Perez F, D'Esposito M (2014) CoCoTools: open-source software for building connectomes using the CoCoMac anatomical database. J Cogn Neurosci **26**:722–745.

Blumensath T, Behrens TE, Smith SM (2012) Resting-state FMRI single subject cortical parcellation based on region growing. Med Image Comput Comput Assist Interv **15**:188–195.

Boekel W, Wagenmakers EJ, Belay L, Verhagen J, Brown S, Forstmann BU (2015) A purely confirmatory replication study of structural brain-behavior correlations. Cortex **66**:115–133.

Bohlhalter S, Vanbellingen T, Bertschi M, Wurtz P, Cazzoli D, Nyffeler T, Hess CW, Muri R (2011) Interference with gesture production by theta burst stimulation over left inferior frontal cortex. Clin Neurophysiol **122**:1197–1202.

Bonini L, Rozzi S, Serventi FU, Simone L, Ferrari PF, Fogassi L (2010) Ventral premotor and inferior parietal cortices make distinct contribution to action organization and intention understanding. Cereb Cortex **20**:1372–1385.

Bonnici HM, Chadwick MJ, Lutti A, Hassabis D, Weiskopf N, Maguire EA (2012) Detecting representations of recent and remote autobiographical memories in vmPFC and hippocampus. J Neurosci **32**:16982–16991.

Boorman ED, Behrens TE, Rushworth MF (2011) Counterfactual choice and learning in a neural network centered on human lateral frontopolar cortex. PLoS Biol **9**:e1001093.

Borra E, Belmalih A, Calzavara R, Gerbella M, Murata A, Rozzi S, Luppino G (2008) Cortical connections of the macaque anterior intraparietal (AIP) area. Cereb Cortex **18**:1094–1111.

Borra E, Gerbella M, Rozzi S, Luppino G (2011) Anatomical evidence for the involvement of the macaque ventrolateral prefrontal area 12r in controlling goal-directed actions. J Neurosci **31**:12351–12363.

Bosnell RA, Kincses T, Stagg CJ, Tomassini V, Kischka U, Jbabdi S, Woolrich MW, Andersson J, Matthews PM, Johansen-Berg H (2011) Motor practice promotes increased activity in brain regions structurally disconnected after subcortical stroke. Neurorehabil Neural Repair 25:607–616.

Boudrias MH, Goncalves CS, Penny WD, Park CH, Rossiter HE, Talelli P, Ward NS (2012) Age-related changes in causal interactions between cortical motor regions during hand grip. Neuroimage 59:3398–3405.

Bregadze N, Lavric A (2006) ERP differences with vs. without concurrent fMRI. Int J Psychophysiol 62:54–59.

Bremmer F, Schlack A, Shah NJ, Zafiris O, Kubischik M, Hoffmann K, Zilles K, Fink GR (2001) Polymodal motion processing in posterior parietal and premotor cortex: a human fMRI study strongly implies equivalencies between humans and monkeys. Neuron 29:287–296.

Broadbent D (1958) Perception and Communication. Oxford: Oxford University Press.

Brodmann K (1909) Vergleichende Lokalisationlehre der Grosshirnrinde. Leipzig: Barth.

Brooks DJ, Pavese N (2011) Imaging biomarkers in Parkinson's disease. Prog Neurobiol 95:614–628.

Browning PG, Gaffan D (2008) Impairment in object-in-place scene learning after uncinate fascicle section in macaque monkeys. Behav Neurosci 122:477–482.

Bruce C, Desimone R, Gross CG (1981) Visual properties of neurons in a polysensory area in superior temporal sulcus of the macaque. J Neurophysiol 46:369–384.

Buchel C, Friston KJ (1997) Modulation of connectivity in visual pathways by attention: cortical interactions evaluated with structural equation modelling and fMRI. Cereb Cortex 7:768–778.

Buchel C, Wise RJ, Mummery CJ, Poline JB, Friston KJ (1996) Nonlinear regression in parametric activation studies. Neuroimage 4:60–66.

Buchel C, Josephs O, Rees G, Turner R, Frith CD, Friston KJ (1998) The functional anatomy of attention to visual motion. A functional MRI study. Brain 121:1281–1294.

Buckner RL, Andrews-Hanna JR, Schacter DL (2008) The brain's default network: anatomy, function, and relevance to disease. Ann N Y Acad Sci 1124:1–38.

Bullmore E, Sporns O (2009) Complex brain networks: graph theoretical analysis of structural and functional systems. Nat Rev Neurosci 10:186–198.

Bunge SA, Wendelken C, Badre D, Wagner AD (2005) Analogical reasoning and prefrontal cortex: evidence for separable retrieval and integration mechanisms. Cereb Cortex 15:239–249.

Burgess N, Cacucci F, Lever C, O'Keefe J (2005) Characterizing multiple independent behavioral correlates of cell firing in freely moving animals. Hippocampus 15:149–153.

Bussey TJ, Saksida LM, Murray EA (2005) The perceptual-mnemonic/feature conjunction model of perirhinal cortex function. Q J Exp Psychol B 58:269–282.

Buszaki G (2006) Rhythms of the Brain. Oxford: Oxford University Press.

Butters N, Pandya D. 1969. Retention of delayed-alternation: effects of selective lesions of sulcus principalis. Science 165:1271–1273.

Button KS, Ioannidis JP, Mokrysz C, Nosek BA, Flint J, Robinson ES, Munafo MR (2013) Power failure: why small sample size undermines the reliability of neuroscience. Nat Rev Neurosci 14:365–376.

Bzdok D, Langner R, Schilbach L, Jakobs O, Roski C, Caspers S, Laird AR, Fox PT, Zilles K, Eickhoff SB (2013) Characterization of the temporo-parietal junction by combining data-driven parcellation, complementary connectivity analyses, and functional decoding. Neuroimage **81**:381–392.

Cadieu C, Kouh M, Pasupathy A, Connor CE, Riesenhuber M, Poggio T (2007) A model of V4 shape selectivity and invariance. J Neurophysiol **98**:1733–1750.

Carlin JD, Calder AJ, Kriegeskorte N, Nili H, Rowe JB (2011) A head-view invariant representation of gaze direction in anterior superior temporal sulcus. Curr Biol **21**:1817–1821.

Carlin JD, Rowe JB, Kriegeskorte N, Thompson R, Calder AJ (2012) Direction-sensitive codes for observed head turns in human superior temporal sulcus. Cereb Cortex **22**:735–744.

Carmichael DW, Thomas DL, De Vita E, Fernandez-Seara MA, Chhina N, Cooper M, Sunderland C, Randell C, Turner R, Ordidge RJ (2006) Improving whole brain structural MRI at 4.7 Tesla using 4 irregularly shaped receiver coils. Neuroimage **32**:1176–1184.

Caspers S, Geyer S, Schleicher A, Mohlberg H, Amunts K, Zilles K (2006) The human inferior parietal cortex: cytoarchitectonic parcellation and interindividual variability. Neuroimage **33**:430–448.

Caspers S, Eickhoff SB, Rick T, von Kapri A, Kuhlen T, Huang R, Shah NJ, Zilles K (2011) Probabilistic fibre tract analysis of cytoarchitectonically defined human inferior parietal lobule areas reveals similarities to macaques. Neuroimage **58**:362–380.

Chadwick MJ, Hassabis D, Weiskopf N, Maguire EA (2010) Decoding individual episodic memory traces in the human hippocampus. Curr Biol **20**:544–547.

Chafee MV, Goldman-Rakic PS (2000) Inactivation of parietal and prefrontal cortex reveals interdependence of neural activity during memory-guided saccades. J Neurophysiol **83**:1550–1566.

Chau BK, Kolling N, Hunt LT, Walton ME, Rushworth MF (2014) A neural mechanism underlying failure of optimal choice with multiple alternatives. Nat Neurosci **17**:463–470.

Chiarelli PA, Bulte DP, Gallichan D, Piechnik SK, Wise R, Jezzard P (2007) Flow-metabolism coupling in human visual, motor, and supplementary motor areas assessed by magnetic resonance imaging. Magn Reson Med **57**:538–547.

Choi EY, Yeo BT, Buckner RL (2012) The organization of the human striatum estimated by intrinsic functional connectivity. J Neurophysiol **108**:2242–2263.

Chong TT, Cunnington R, Williams MA, Kanwisher N, Mattingley JB (2008) fMRI adaptation reveals mirror neurons in human inferior parietal cortex. Curr Biol **18**:1576–1580.

Chumbley J, Worsley K, Flandin G, Friston K (2010) Topological FDR for neuroimaging. Neuroimage **49**:3057–3064.

Churchland AK, Kiani R, Shadlen MN (2008) Decision-making with multiple alternatives. Nat Neurosci **11**:693–702.

Cieslik EC, Zilles K, Caspers S, Roski C, Kellermann TS, Jakobs O, Langner R, Laird AR, Fox PT, Eickhoff SB (2013) Is there 'one' DLPFC in cognitive action control? Evidence for heterogeneity from co-activation-based parcellation. Cereb Cortex **23**:2677–2689.

Cohen MX (2014) Fluctuations in oscillation frequency control spike timing and coordinate neural networks. J Neurosci **34**:8988–8998.

Cohen Kadosh K, Johnson MH, Henson RN, Dick F, Blakemore SJ (2013) Differential face-network adaptation in children, adolescents and adults. Neuroimage **69**:11–20.

Coltheart M (2006) What has functional neuroimaging told us about the mind (so far)? Cortex **42**:323–331.

Conrad R (1972) Short-term memory in the deaf: a test for speech coding. Br J Psychol **63**:173–180.

Conroy BR, Singer BD, Guntupalli JS, Ramadge PJ, Haxby JV (2013) Inter-subject alignment of human cortical anatomy using functional connectivity. Neuroimage **81**:400–411.

Constantinidis C, Franowicz MN, Goldman-Rakic P (2001) Coding specificity in cortical microcircuits: a multiple-electrode analysis of primate prefrontal cortex. J Neurosci **21**:3646–3655.

Corbetta M, Shulman GL (2002) Control of goal-directed and stimulus-driven attention in the brain. Nat Neurosci Rev **3**:201–215.

Corbetta M, Akbudak E, Conturo TE, Snyder AZ, Ollinger JM, Drury HA, Linenweber MR, Petersen SE, Raichle ME, Van Essen DC, Shulman GL (1998) A common network of functional areas for attention and eye movements. Neuron **21**:761–773.

Craddock RC, James GA, Holtzheimer PE, 3rd, Hu XP, Mayberg HS (2012) A whole brain fMRI atlas generated via spatially constrained spectral clustering. Hum Brain Mapp **33**:1914–1928.

Crick F, Jones E (1993) Backwardness of human neuroanatomy. Nature **361**:109–110.

Crittenden BM, Duncan J (2014) Task difficulty manipulation reveals multiple demand activity but no frontal lobe hierarchy. Cereb Cortex **24**:532–540.

Crone EA, Wendelken C, van Leijenhorst L, R.D. H, Christoff K, Bunge SA (2009) Neuro-cognitive development of relational reasoning. Dev Sci **12**:55–66.

Crowe DA, Chafee MV, Averbeck BB, Georgopoulos AP (2004) Neural activity in primate parietal area 7a related to spatial analysis of visual mazes. Cereb Cortex **14**:23–34.

Croxson PL, Johansen-Berg H, Behrens TE, Robson MD, Pinsk MA, Gross CG, Richter W, Richter MC, Kastner S, Rushworth MF (2005) Quantitative investigation of connections of the prefrontal cortex in the human and macaque using probabilistic diffusion tractography. J Neurosci **25**:8854–8866.

da Costa NM, Martin KA (2010) Whose cortical column would that be? Front Neuroanat **4**:16.

Dale A, Sereno M (1993) Improved localization of cortical activity by combining EEG and MEG with MRI cortical surface reconstruction. J Cogn Neurosci **5**:162–176.

Dale AM, Liu AK, Fischl BR, Buckner RL, Belliveau JW, Lewine JD, Halgren E (2000) Dynamic statistical parametric mapping: combining fMRI and MEG for high-resolution imaging of cortical activity. Neuron **26**:55–67.

David O, Guillemain I, Saillet S, Reyt S, Deransart C, Segebarth C, Depaulis A (2008) Identifying neural drivers with functional MRI: an electrophysiological validation. PLoS Biol **6**:2683–2697.

Dayan P (2005) Theoretical Neuroscience. Cambridge: MIT Press.

de Araujo MF, Hori E, Maior RS, Tomaz C, Ono T, Nishijo H (2012) Neuronal activity of the anterior cingulate cortex during an observation-based decision making task in monkeys. Behav Brain Res **230**:48–61.

Deco G, Jirsa VK, McIntosh AR (2011) Emerging concepts for the dynamical organization of resting-state activity in the brain. Nat Rev Neurosci **12**:43–56.

Desimone R, Schein SJ, Moran J, Ungerleider LG (1985) Contour, color and shape analysis beyond the striate cortex. Vision Res **25**:441–452.

Desimone R, Ungerleider L (1989) Neural mechanisms of visual processing in monkeys. In: Handbook of Neuropsychology, **vol. 2** (Boller, F. and Graffman, J., eds), pp 267–300. New York: Elsevier.

D'Esposito M, Ballard D, Aguirre GK, Zarahn E (1998) Human prefrontal cortex is not specific for working memory: a functional MRI study. Neuroimage **8**:274–282.

Di Lazzaro V, Pilato F, Dileone M, Profice P, Oliviero A, Mazzone P, Insola A, Ranieri F, Tonali PA, Rothwell JC (2008) Low-frequency repetitive transcranial magnetic stimulation suppresses specific excitatory circuits in the human motor cortex. J Physiol **586**:4481–4487.

Diedrichsen J, Balsters JH, Flavell J, Cussans E, Ramnani N (2009) A probabilistic MR atlas of the human cerebellum. Neuroimage **46**:39–46.

Dilks DD, Julian JB, Paunov AM, Kanwisher N (2013) The occipital place area is causally and selectively involved in scene perception. J Neurosci **33**:1331–1336a.

di Pellegrino G, Wise SP (1991) A neurophysiological comparison of three distinct regions of the primate frontal lobe. Brain **114**:951–978.

Donders FC (1969) On the speed of mental processes. Acta Psychol (Amst) **30**:412–431.

Dosenbach NU, Visscher KM, Palmer ED, Miezin FM, Wenger KK, Kang HC, Burgund ED, Grimes AL, Schlaggar BL, Petersen SE (2006) A core system for the implementation of task sets. Neuron **50**:799–812.

Dosenbach NU, Fair DA, Miezin FM, Cohen AL, Wenger KK, Dosenbach RA, Fox MD, Snyder AZ, Vincent JL, Raichle ME, Schlaggar BL, Petersen SE (2007) Distinct brain networks for adaptive and stable task control in humans. Proc Natl Acad Sci U S A **104**:11073–11078.

Downing PE, Chan AW, Peelen MV, Dodds CM, Kanwisher N (2006) Domain specificity in visual cortex. Cereb Cortex **16**:1453–1461.

Drevets WC, Price JL, Simpson JR, Todd RD, Reich T, Vannier M, Raichle ME (1997) Subgenual prefrontal cortex abnormalities in mood disorders. Nature **386**:824–827.

Dronkers NF (1996) A new brain region for coordinating speech articulation. Nature **384**:159–161.

Dum RP, Strick PL (2005) Frontal lobe inputs to the digit representations of the motor areas on the lateral surface of the hemisphere. J Neurosci **25**:1375–1386.

Duncan J (2010) The multiple-demand (MD) system of the primate brain: mental programs for intelligent behaviour. Trends Cogn Sci **14**:172–179.

Duncan J (2013) The structure of cognition: attentional episodes in mind and brain. Neuron **80**:35–50.

Duncan J, Owen AM (2000) Common regions of the frontal lobe recruited by diverse cognitive demands. TINS **23**:475–482.

Duncan J, Seitz RJ, Kolodny J, Bor D, Herzog H, Ahmed A, Newell FN, Emslie H (2000) A neural basis for general intelligence. Science **289**:457–460.

Duvernoy HM (1991) The Human Brain: surface, blood supply and three dimensional surface anatomy. New York: Springer.

Dux PE, Ivanoff J, Asplund CL, Marois R (2006) Isolation of a central bottleneck of information processing with time-resolved FMRI. Neuron **52**:1109–1120.

Eickhoff SB, Stephan KE, Mohlberg H, Grefkes C, Fink GR, Amunts K, Zilles K (2005) A new SPM toolbox for combining probabilistic cytoarchitectonic maps and functional imaging data. Neuroimage **25**:1325–1335.

Elston GN (2007) Specialization of the neocortical pyramidal cell during primate evolution. In: Evolution of Nervous Systems: a comprehensive reference, **vol. 4** (Kaas, J. and Preuss, T. M., eds), pp 191–242 New York: Elsevier.

Engel AK, Moll CK, Fried I, Ojemann GA (2005) Invasive recordings from the human brain: clinical insights and beyond. Nat Rev Neurosci **6**:35–47.

Ettlinger G, Morton HB, Moffett AM (1966) Tactile disrimination in the monkey: the effect of bilateral posterior parietal and lateral frontal ablations, and of callosal section. Cortex **2**:30–49.

Ewbank MP, Lawson RP, Henson RN, Rowe JB, Passamonti L, Calder AJ (2011) Changes in 'top-down' connectivity underlie repetition suppression in the ventral visual pathway. J Neurosci **31**:5635–5642.

Fedorenko E, Duncan J, Kanwisher N (2013) Broad domain generality in focal regions of frontal and parietal cortex. Proc Natl Acad Sci U S A **110**:16616–16621.

Ferreira CT, Verin M, Pillon B, Levy R, Dubois B, Agid Y (1998) Spatio-temporal working memory and frontal lesions in man. Cortex **34**:83–98.

Fischl B, Dale AM (2000) Measuring the thickness of the human cerebral cortex from magnetic resonance images. Proc Natl Acad Sci U S A **97**:11050–11055.

Fischl B, Rajendran N, Busa E, Augustinack J, Hinds O, Yeo BT, Mohlberg H, Amunts K, Zilles K (2008) Cortical folding patterns and predicting cytoarchitecture. Cereb Cortex **18**:1973–1980.

Fletcher PC, Happe F, Frith U, Baker SC, Dolan RJ, Frackowiak RSJ, Frith CD (1995) Other minds in the brain: a functional imaging study of 'theory of mind' in story comprehension. Cognition **57**:109–128.

Floyer-Lea A, Matthews PM (2004) Changing brain networks for visuomotor control with increased movement automaticity. J Neurophysiol **92**:2405–2412.

Fox PT, Raichle ME (1986) Focal physiological uncoupling of cerebral blood flow and oxidative metabolism during somatosensory stimulation in human subjects. Proc Natl Acad Sci U S A **83**:1140–1144.

Freedman DJ, Riesenhuber M, Poggio T, Miller EK (2003) A comparison of primate prefrontal and inferior temporal cortices during visual categorization. J Neurosci **23**:5235–5246.

Freton M, Lemogne C, Delaveau P, Guionnet S, Wright E, Wiernik E, Bertasi E, Fossati P (2014) The dark side of self-focus: brain activity during self-focus in low and high brooders. Soc Cogn Affect Neurosci **9**:1808–1813.

Frey S, Mackey S, Petrides M (2014) Cortico-cortical connections of areas 44 and 45B in the macaque monkey. Brain Lang. **131**:36–55.

Fried I, Mukamel R, Kreiman G (2011) Internally generated preactivation of single neurons in human medial frontal cortex predicts volition. Neuron **69**:548–562.

Fries W (1984) Cortical projections to the superior colliculus in the macaque monkey: a retrograde study using horseradish peroxidase. J Comp Neurol **230**:55–76.

Fries P (2005) A mechanism for cognitive dynamics: neuronal communication through neuronal coherence. Trends Cogn Sci **9**:474–480.

Fries P (2009) Neuronal gamma-band synchronization as a fundamental process in cortical computation. Annu Rev Neurosci **32**:209–224.

Friston K (2002) Beyond phrenology: what can neuroimaging tell us about distributed circuitry? Annu Rev Neurosci **25**:221–250.

Friston K (2012) Ten ironic rules for non-statistical reviewers. Neuroimage **61**:1300–1310.

Friston KJ, Price CJ, Fletcher P, Moore C, Frackowiak RSJ, Dolan RJ (1996) The trouble with cognitive subtraction. Neuroimage 4:97–104.

Friston KJ, Buechel C, Fink GR, Morris J, Rolls E, Dolan RJ (1997) Psychophysiological and modulatory interactions in neuroimaging. Neuroimage 7:218–229.

Friston KJ, Fletcher P, Josephs O, Holmes A, Rugg MD, Turner R (1998) Event-related fMRI: characterizing differential responses. Neuroimage 7:30–40.

Friston K, Harrison L, Penny W (2003) Dynamic causal modelling. Neuroimage **19**:1273–1302.

Friston KJ, Penny WD, Glaser DE (2005) Conjunction revisited. Neuroimage **25**:661–667.

Friston K, Moran R, Seth AK (2013) Analysing connectivity with Granger causality and dynamic causal modelling. Curr Opin Neurobiol **23**:172–178.

Frith CD (1997) The Cognitive Neuropsychology of Schizophrenia. East Sussex: Psychology Press.

Frith CD (2000) The role of dorsolateral prefrontal cortex in the selection of action. In: Control of Cognitive Processes: attention and performance XVIII (Monsell, S. and Driver, J., eds), pp 549–565 Cambridge: MIT Press.

Frith CD, Frith U (2006) The neural basis of mentalizing. Neuron **50**:531–534.

Frith C, Friston KJ, Liddle PF, Frackowiak RSJ (1991) A PET study of word finding. Neuropsychol **29**:1137–1148.

Funahashi S, Bruce CJ, Goldman-Rakic PS (1989) Mnemonic coding of visual space in monkey dorsolateral prefrontal cortex. J Neurophysiol **61**:331–349.

Gaertner FC, Souvatzoglou M, Brix G, Beer AJ (2012) Imaging of hypoxia using PET and MRI. Curr Pharm Biotechnol **13**:552–570.

Galaburda AM, Sanides F, Geschwind N (1978) Human brain. Cytoarchitectonic left-right asymmetries in the temporal speech region. Arch Neurol **35**:812–817.

Gallese V, Fadiga L, Fogassi L, Rizzolatti G (1996) Action recognition in the premotor cortex. Brain **119**:593–610.

Garey LJ (2006) Translation of The Principles of Comparative Localisation in the Cerebral Cortex based on Cytoarchitectonics. Berlin: Springer.

Gee AL, Ipata AE, Gottlieb J, Bisley JW, Goldberg ME (2008) Neural enhancement and pre-emptive perception: the genesis of attention and the attentional maintenance of the cortical salience map. Perception **37**:389–400.

Genovesio A, Wise SP, Passingham RE (2014) Prefrontal-parietal function: from foraging to foresight. Trends Cogn Sci **18**:72–81.

Georgopoulos AP, Schwartz AB, Kettner RE (1986) Neuronal population coding of movement direction. Science **233**:1416–1419.

Gerardin A, Sirigu A, Lehericy S, Poline J-B, Gaymard B, Marsault C, Agid Y, Le Bihan D (2000) Partially overlapping neural networks for real and imagined hand movements. Cereb Cortex **10**:1093–1104.

Goebel R, Roebroeck A, Kim DS, Formisano E (2003) Investigating directed cortical interactions in time-resolved fMRI data using vector autoregressive modeling and Granger causality mapping. Magn Reson Imaging **21**:1251–1261.

Goense JB, Ku SP, Merkle H, Tolias AS, Logothetis NK (2008) fMRI of the temporal lobe of the awake monkey at 7 T. Neuroimage **39**:1081–1093.

Gold JI, Shadlen MN (2007) The neural basis of decision making. Annu Rev Neurosci **30**:535–574.

Goldman PS, Rosvold HE (1970) Localization of function within the dorsolateral prefrontal cortex of the rhesus monkey. Exp Neurol **27**:291–304.

Goldman PS, Rosvold HE, Vest B, Galkin TW. 1971. Analysis of the delayed alternation deficit produced by dorsolateral prefrontal lesions in the rhesus monkey. J Comp Physiol Psychol **77**:212–220.

Goldman-Rakic PS, Selemon LD, Schwartz MR (1984) Dual pathway connecting the dorsolateral prefrontal cortex with the hippocampal formation and the perihippocampal cortex in the rhesus monkey. Neurosci **12**:719–749.

Gopinath K, Crosson B, McGregor K, Peck K, Chang YL, Moore A, Sherod M, Cavanagh C, Wabnitz A, Wierenga C, White K, Cheshkov S, Krishnamurthy V, Briggs RW (2009) Selective detrending method for reducing task-correlated motion artifact during speech in event-related FMRI. Hum Brain Mapp **30**:1105–1119.

Gough PM, Nobre AC, Devlin JT (2005) Dissociating linguistic processes in the left inferior frontal cortex with transcranial magnetic stimulation. J Neurosci **25**:8010–8016.

Grefkes C, Weiss PH, Zilles K, Fink GR (2002) Crossmodal processing of object features in human anterior intraparietal cortex: an fMRI study implies equivalencies between humans and monkeys. Neuron **35**:173–184.

Gregoriou GG, Gotts SJ, Desimone R (2012) Cell-type-specific synchronization of neural activity in FEF with V4 during attention. Neuron **73**:581–594.

Gregoriou GG, Rossi AF, Ungerleider LG, Desimone R (2014) Lesions of prefrontal cortex reduce attentional modulation of neuronal responses and synchrony in V4. Nat Neurosci **17**:1003–1011.

Grezes J, Fonlupt P, Bertenthal B, Delon-Martin C, Segebarth C, Decety J (2001) Does perception of biological motion rely on specific brain regions? Neuroimage **13**:794–800.

Grezes J, Frith C, Passingham RE (2004a) Brain mechanisms for inferring deceit in the actions of others. J Neurosci **24**:5500–5505.

Grezes J, Frith CD, Passingham RE (2004b) Inferring false beliefs from the actions of oneself and others: an fMRI study. Neuroimage **21**:744–750.

Grill-Spector K, Kushnir T, Hendler T, Edelman S, Itzchak Y, Malach R (1998) A sequence of object-processing stages revealed by fMRI in the human occipital lobe. HumBrain Map **6**:316–328.

Grill-Spector K, Knouf N, Kanwisher N (2004) The fusiform face area subserves face perception, not generic within-category identification. Nat Neurosci **7**:555–562.

Haggard P. 2008. Human volition: towards a neuroscience of will. Nat Rev Neurosci. **9**:934–946.

Hamidi M, Tononi G, Postle BR (2008) Evaluating frontal and parietal contributions to spatial working memory with repetitive transcranial magnetic stimulation. Brain Res **1230**:202–210.

Hamidi M, Tononi G, Postle BR (2009) Evaluating the role of prefrontal and parietal cortices in memory-guided response with repetitive transcranial magnetic stimulation. Neuropsych **47**:296–302.

Hamilton JP, Chen MC, Waugh CE, Joormann J, Gotlib IH (2015) Distinctive and common neural underpinnings of major depression, social anxiety, and their comorbidity. Soc Cogn Affect Neurosci **10**: 552–560.

Handwerker DA, Ollinger JM, D'Esposito M (2004) Variation of BOLD hemodynamic responses across subjects and brain regions and their effects on statistical analyses. Neuroimage **21**:1639–1651.

Hari R, Parkkonen L, Nangini C (2010) The brain in time: insights from neuromagnetic recordings. Ann N Y Acad Sci **1191**:89–109.

Harriger L, van den Heuvel MP, Sporns O (2012) Rich club organization of macaqu cortex and its role in network communication. Plos one **7**:e46497.

Hassabis D, Kumaran D, Maguire EA (2007) Using imagination to understand the neural basis of episodic memory. J Neurosci **27**:14365–14374.

Hausfeld L, Valente G, Formisano E (2014) Multiclass fMRI data decoding and visualization using supervised self-organizing maps. Neuroimage **96**:54–66.

Haxby JV, Connolly AC, Guntupalli JS (2014) Decoding neural representational spaces using multivariate pattern analysis. Annu Rev Neurosci **37**:435–456.

Haynes JD, Rees G (2006) Decoding mental states from brain activity in humans. Nat Rev Neurosci **7**:523–534.

Haynes JD, Sakai K, Rees G, Gilbert S, Frith C, Passingham RE (2007) Reading hidden intentions in the human brain. Curr Biol **17**:323–328.

He S-Q, Dum RP, Strick PL (1993) Topographnic organization of corticospinal projections from the frontal lobe: motor areas on the lateral surface of the hemisphere. J Neurosci **13**:952–980.

Hebb DO (1949) The Organization of Behavior. New York: Wiley.

Heinen K, Feredoes E, Weiskopf N, Ruff CC, Driver J (2014) Direct Evidence for Attention-Dependent Influences of the Frontal Eye-Fields on Feature-Responsive Visual Cortex. Cereb Cortex **24**:2815–2821.

Henson RN (2011) How to discover modules in mind and brain: the curse of nonlinearity, and blessing of neuroimaging. A comment on Sternberg (2011). Cogn Neuropsychol **28**:209–223.

Henson R, Friston K (2006) Convolution models for fMRI. In: Statistical Parametric Mapping: the analysis of functional brain images (Friston, K. et al., eds), pp 178–192 London: Academic Press.

Henson RN, Wakeman DG, Litvak V, Friston KJ (2011) A parametric empirical Bayesian framework for the EEG/MEG inverse problem: generative models for multi-subject and multi-modal integration. Front Hum Neurosci **5**:76.

Hocking J, McMahon KL, de Zubicaray GI (2009) Semantic context and visual feature effects in object naming: an fMRI study using arterial spin labeling. J Cogn Neurosci **21**:1571–1583.

Holtzheimer PE, Kelley ME, Gross RE, Filkowski MM, Garlow SJ, Barrocas A, Wint D, Craighead MC, Kozarsky J, Chismar R, Moreines JL, Mewes K, Posse PR, Gutman DA, Mayberg HS (2012) Subcallosal cingulate deep brain stimulation for treatment-resistant unipolar and bipolar depression. Arch Gen Psychiatry **69**:150–158.

Hope TM, Prejawa S, Parker J, Oberhuber M, Seghier ML, Green DW, Price CJ (2014) Dissecting the functional anatomy of auditory word repetition. Front Hum Neurosci **8**:246.

Horwitz B, Tagamets MA, McIntosh AR (1999) Neural modeling, functional brain imaging, and cognition. Trends Cogn Sci 3:91–98.

Huber L, Goense J, Kennerley AJ, Ivanov D, Krieger SN, Lepsien J, Trampel R, Turner R, Moller HE (2014) Investigation of the neurovascular coupling in positive and negative BOLD responses in human brain at 7 T. Neuroimage 97:349–362.

Hubl D, Koenig T, Strik WK, Garcia LM, Dierks T (2007) Competition for neuronal resources: how hallucinations make themselves heard. Br J Psychiatry 190:57–62.

Huettel SA, Song AW, McCarthy G (2009) Functional Magnetic Resonance Imaging. Sunderland: Sinauer.

Huk AC, Shadlen MN (2005) Neural activity in macaque parietal cortex reflects temporal integration of visual motion signals during perceptual decision making. J Neurosci 25:10420–10436.

Huppert TJ, Hoge RD, Diamond SG, Franceschini MA, Boas DA (2006) A temporal comparison of BOLD, ASL, and NIRS hemodynamic responses to motor stimuli in adult humans. Neuroimage 29:368–382.

Hurlemann R, Matusch A, Kuhn KU, Berning J, Elmenhorst D, Winz O, Kolsch H, Zilles K, Wagner M, Maier W, Bauer A (2008) 5-HT2A receptor density is decreased in the at-risk mental state. Psychopharmacology (Berl) 195:579–590.

Huster RJ, Debener S, Eichele T, Herrmann CS (2012) Methods for simultaneous EEG-fMRI: an introductory review. J Neurosci 32:6053–6060.

Inoue M, Mikami A, Ando I, Tsukada H (2004) Functional brain mapping of the macaque related to spatial working memory as revealed by PET. Cereb Cortex 14:106–119.

Ishai A, Ungerleider LG, Haxby JV (2000) Distributed neural systems for the generation of visual images. Neuron 28:979–990.

Ishai A, Yago E (2006) Recognition memory of newly learned faces. Brain Res Bull 71:167–173.

Jahanshahi M, Dirnberger G, Fuller R, Frith CD (2000) The role of the dorsolateral prefrontal cortex in random number generation: a study with positron emission tomography. Neuroimage 12:713–725.

Jastorff J, Orban GA (2009) Human functional magnetic resonance imaging reveals separation and integration of shape and motion cues in biological motion processing. J Neurosci 29:7315–7329.

Jellema T, Perrett DI (2003) Cells in monkey STS responsive to articulated body motions and consequent static posture: a case of implied motion? Neuropsychol 41:1728–1737.

Jerde TA, Lewis SM, Goerke U, Gourtzelidis P, Tzagarakis C, Lynch J, Moeller S, Van de Moortele PF, Adriany G, Trangle J, Ugurbil K, Georgopoulos AP (2008) Ultra-high field parallel imaging of the superior parietal lobule during mental maze solving. Exp Brain Res 187:551–561.

Jiang J, Zhu W, Shi F, Liu Y, Li J, Qin W, Li K, Yu C, Jiang T (2009) Thick visual cortex in the early blind. J Neurosci 29:2205–2211.

Johansen-Berg H, Behrens T (eds) (2014) Diffusion Imaging. Oxford: Academic Press.

Johansen-Berg H, Behrens TE, Robson MD, Drobnjak I, Rushworth MF, Brady JM, Smith SM, Higham DJ, Matthews PM (2004) Changes in connectivity profiles define functionally distinct regions in human medial frontal cortex. Proc Natl Acad Sci U S A 101:13335–13340.

Johnson PB, Ferraina S, Caminiti R (1993) Cortical networks for visual reaching. Exp Brain Res **97**:361–365.

Johnston JM, Vaishnavi SN, Smyth MD, Zhang D, He BJ, Zempel JM, Shimony JS, Snyder AZ, Raichle ME (2008) Loss of resting interhemispheric functional connectivity after complete section of the corpus callosum. J Neurosci **28**:6453–6458.

Joyce KE, Hayasaka S (2012) Development of PowerMap: a software package for statistical power calculation in neuroimaging studies. Neuroinformatics **10**:351–365.

Kaas J (2007) The evolution of sensory and motor systems in primates. In: Evolution of Nervous Systems: a comprehensive reference, **vol. 4** (Kaas, J. and Preuss, T. M., eds), pp 34–57 New York: Elsevier.

Kamitani Y, Tong F (2005) Decoding the visual and subjective contents of the human brain. Nat Neurosci **8**:679–685.

Kelly AM, Hester R, Murphy K, Javitt DC, Foxe JJ, Garavan H (2004) Prefrontal-subcortical dissociations underlying inhibitory control revealed by event-related fMRI. Eur J Neurosci **19**:3105–3112.

Kennedy C, des Rosiers M, Reivich M, Sokoloff L (1974) Mapping of functional pathways in brain by autoradiographic survey of local cerebral metabolism. Trans Amer Neurol Assoc **99**:143–147.

Kennedy SH Konarski JZ, Segal ZV, Lau MA, Bieling, P.J., McIntyre RS, Mayberg HS (2007) Differences in brain glucose metabolism between responders to CBT and venlafaxine in a 16-week randomized controlled trial. Am J Psychiatr **164**:778–788.

Kiebel SJ, Poline JB, Friston KJ, Holmes AP, Worsley KJ (1999) Robust smoothness estimation in statistical parametric maps using standardized residuals from the general linear model. Neuroimage **10**:756–766.

Kilner JM, Kraskov A, Lemon RN (2014) Do monkey F5 mirror neurons show changes in firing rate during repeated observation of natural actions? J Neurophysiol **111**:1214–1226.

King JR, Gramfort A, Schurger A, Naccache L, Dehaene S (2014) Two distinct dynamic modes subtend the detection of unexpected sounds. PLoS One **9**:e85791.

Kivisaari SL, Tyler LK, Monsch AU, Taylor KI (2012) Medial perirhinal cortex disambiguates confusable objects. Brain **135**:3757–3769.

Klapwijk ET, Goddings AL, Burnett Heyes S, Bird G, Viner RM, Blakemore SJ (2013) Increased functional connectivity with puberty in the mentalising network involved in social emotion processing. Horm Behav **64**:314–322.

Klein JC, Behrens TE, Robson MD, Mackay CE, Higham DJ, Johansen-Berg H (2007) Connectivity-based parcellation of human cortex using diffusion MRI: establishing reproducibility, validity and observer independence in BA 44/45 and SMA/Pre-SMA. Neuroimage **34**:204–211.

Klein A, Andersson J, Ardekani BA, Ashburner J, Avants B, Chiang MC, Christensen GE, Collins DL, Gee J, Hellier P, Song JH, Jenkinson M, Lepage C, Rueckert D, Thompson P, Vercauteren T, Woods RP, Mann JJ, Parsey RV (2009) Evaluation of 14 nonlinear deformation algorithms applied to human brain MRI registration. Neuroimage **46**:786–802.

Kobayashi Y, Amaral DG (2003) Macaque monkey retrosplenial cortex: II. Cortical afferents. J Comp Neurol **466**:48–79.

Kohn N, Eickhoff SB, Scheller M, Laird AR, Fox PT, Habel U (2014) Neural network of cognitive emotion regulation—an ALE meta-analysis and MACM analysis. Neuroimage **87**:345–355.

Koski L, Paus T (2000) Functional connectivity of the anterior cingulate cortex within the human frontal lobe: a brain-mapping meta-analysis. Exper Brain Res **133**:55–65.

Kovacs M, Beck AT (1978) Maladaptive cognitive structures in depression. Am J Psychiatry **135**:525–533.

Kreuzer PM, Schecklmann M, Lehner A, Wetter TC, Poeppl TB, Rupprecht R, de Ridder D, Landgrebe M, Langguth B (2015) The ACDC pilot trial: targeting the anterior cingulate by double cone coil rTMS for the treatment of depression. Brain Stimulation **8**:240–246.

Kriegeskorte N, Goebel R, Bandettini P (2006) Information-based functional brain mapping. Proc Natl Acad Sci U S A **103**:3863–3868.

Kriegeskorte N, Simmons WK, Bellgowan PS, Baker CI (2009) Circular analysis in systems neuroscience: the dangers of double dipping. Nat Neurosci **12**:535–540.

Kritzer MF, Goldman-Rakic PS (1995) Intrinsic circuit organization of the major layers and sublayers of the dorsolateral prefrontal cortex in the rhesus monkey. J Comp Neurol **359**:131–143.

Krubitzer L, Huffman KJ (2000) Arealization of the neocortex in mammals: genetic and epigenetic contributions to the phenotype. Brain Behav Evol **55**:322–335.

Kurt S, Fisher SE, Ehret G (2012) Foxp2 mutations impair auditory-motor association learning. PLoS One **7**:e33130.

Lachaux JP, Axmacher N, Mormann F, Halgren E, Crone NE (2012) High-frequency neural activity and human cognition: past, present and possible future of intracranial EEG research. Prog Neurobiol **98**:279–301.

Lai CS, Fisher SE, Hurst JA, Vargha-Khadem F, Monaco AP (2001) A forkhead-domain gene is mutated in a severe speech and language disorder. Nature **413**:519–523.

Lancaster JL, Rainey LH, Summerlin JL, Freitas CS, Fox PT, Evans AC, Toga AW, Mazziotta JC (1997) Automated labeling of the human brain: a preliminary report on the development and evaluation of a forward-transform method. Hum Brain Mapp **5**:238–242.

Lancaster JL, Laird AR, Eickhoff SB, Martinez MJ, Fox PM, Fox PT (2012) Automated regional behavioral analysis for human brain images. Front Neuroinform **6**:23.

Lau H, Rosenthal D (2011) Empirical support for higher-order theories of conscious awareness. Trends Cogn Sci **15**:365–373.

Lau HC, Rogers RD, Haggard P, Passingham RE (2004) Attention to intention. Science **303**:1208–1210.

Lauwereyns J, Sakagami M, Tsutsui K, Kobayashi S, Koizumi M, Hikosaka O (2001) Responses to task-irrelevant visual features by primate prefrontal neurons. J Neurophysiol **86**:2001–2010.

Lavie N (1995) Perceptual load as a necessary condition for selective attention. J Exp Psychol Hum Percept Perform **21**:451–468.

Lebedev MA, Messinger A, Kralik JD, Wise SP (2004) Representation of attended versus remembered locations in prefrontal cortex. PLoS Biol **2**:e365.

Lewis-Peacock JA, Postle BR (2008) Temporary activation of long-term memory supports working memory. J Neurosci **28**:8765–8771.

Libet B, Gleason CA, Wright EW, Pearl DK (1983a) Time of conscious intention to act in relation to onset of cerebral activity (readiness-potential). The unconscious initiation of a freely voluntary act. Brain **106**:623–642.

Libet B, Wright EW, Jr., Gleason CA (1983b) Preparation- or intention-to-act, in relation to pre-event potentials recorded at the vertex. Electroencephalogr Clin Neurophysiol **56**:367–372.

Lipina TV, Roder JC (2014) Disrupted-In-Schizophrenia-1 (DISC1) interactome and mental disorders: impact of mouse models. Neurosci Biobehav Rev **45**:271–294.

Logothetis NK (2008) What we can do and what we cannot do with fMRI. Nature **453**:869–878.

Logothetis NK, Wandell BA (2004) Interpreting the BOLD signal. Ann Rev Physiol **66**:735–769.

Lu M-T, Preston JB, Strick PL (1994) Interconnections between the prefrontal cortex and the premotor areas in the frontal lobe. J Comp Neurol **341**:375–392.

Maass A, Schutze H, Speck O, Yonelinas A, Tempelmann C, Heinze HJ, Berron D, Cardenas-Blanco A, Brodersen KH, Enno Stephan K, Duzel E (2014) Laminar activity in the hippocampus and entorhinal cortex related to novelty and episodic encoding. Nature Communications **5**:5547.

Magri C, Schridde U, Murayama Y, Panzeri S, Logothetis NK (2012) The amplitude and timing of the BOLD signal reflects the relationship between local field potential power at different frequencies. J Neurosci **32**:1395–1407.

Maguire EA (2012) Studying the freely-behaving brain with fMRI. Neuroimage **62**:1170–1176.

Maguire EA, Gadian DG, Johnstrude IS, Good CD, Ashburner J, Frackowiak RSJ, Frith CD (2000a) Nativation-related structural change in the hippocampi of taxi drivers. Proc Nat Acad Sci **97**:4398–4403.

Maguire EA, Mummery CJ, Buchel C (2000b) Patterns of hippocampal-cortical interaction dissociate temporal lobe memory subsystems. Hippocampus **10**:475–482.

Maguire EA, Kumaran D, Hassabis D, Kopelman MD (2010) Autobiographical memory in semantic dementia: a longitudinal fMRI study. Neuropsychol **48**:123–136.

Mai JK, Paxinos G, Voss T (2011) Atlas of the Human Brain. New York: Elsevier.

Maier A, Wilke M, Aura C, Zhu C, Ye FQ, Leopold DA (2008) Divergence of fMRI and neural signals in V1 during perceptual suppression in the awake monkey. Nat Neurosci **11**:1193–1200.

Mantini D, Vanduffel W (2013) Emerging roles of the brain's default network. Neuroscientist **19**:76–87.

Maris E, Womelsdorf T, Desimone R, Fries P (2013) Rhythmic neuronal synchronization in visual cortex entails spatial phase relation diversity that is modulated by stimulation and attention. Neuroimage **74**:99–116.

Markov NT, Kennedy H (2013) The importance of being hierarchical. Curr Opin Neurobiol **23**:187–194.

Markov NT, Misery P, Falchier A, Lamy C, Vezoli J, Quilodran R, Gariel MA, Giroud P, Ercsey-Ravasz M, Pilaz LJ, Huissoud C, Barone P, Dehay C, Toroczkai Z, Van Essen DC, Kennedy H, Knoblauch K (2011) Weight consistency specifies regularities of macaque cortical networks. Cereb Cortex **21**:1254–1272.

Markov NT, Ercsey-Ravasz MM, Ribeiro Gomes AR, Lamy C, Magrou L, Vezoli J, Misery P, Falchier A, Quilodran R, Gariel MA, Sallet J, Gamanut R, Huissoud C, Clavagnier

S, Giroud P, Sappey-Marinier D, Barone P, Dehay C, Toroczkai Z, Knoblauch K, Van Essen DC, Kennedy H (2014) A Weighted and Directed Interareal Connectivity Matrix for Macaque Cerebral Cortex. Cereb Cortex. **24**:17–36.

Markov NT, Ercsey-Ravasz M, Van Essen DC, Knoblauch K, Toroczkai Z, Kennedy H (2013) Cortical high-density counterstream architectures. Science **342**:1238406.

Marr D (1982) Vision. Cambridge: MIT Press.

Mars RB, Sallet J, Neubert FX, Rushworth MF (2013) Connectivity profiles reveal the relationship between brain areas for social cognition in human and monkey temporoparietal cortex. Proc Natl Acad Sci U S A **110**:10806–10811.

Marshall PJ, Saby JN, Meltzoff AN (2013) Imitation and the developing social brain: infants' somatotopic EEG patterns for acts of self and other. Int J Psychol Res **6**:22–29.

Mason MF, Norton MI, Van Horn JD, Wegner DM, Grafton ST, Macrae CN (2007) Wandering minds: the default network and stimulus-independent thought. Science **315**:393–395.

McIntosh AR (2000) Towards a network theory of cognition. Neural Netw **13**:861–870.

McIntosh AR, Gonzalez-Lima F (1994) Network interactions among limbic cortices, basal forebrain, and cerebellum differentiate a tone conditioned as a Pavlovian excitor or inhibitor: fluorodeoxyglucose mapping and covariance structural modeling. J Neurophysiol **72**:1717–1733.

McLaren DG, Ries ML, Xu G, Johnson SC (2012) A generalized form of context-dependent psychophysiological interactions (gPPI): a comparison to standard approaches. Neuroimage **61**:1277–1286.

McLeod P, Plunkett PK, Rolls E (1998) Introduction to Connectionist Modelling of Cognitive Processes. Oxford: Oxford University Press.

Mechelli A, Price CJ, Friston KJ (2001) Nonlinear coupling between evoked rCBF and BOLD signals: a simulation study of hemodynamic responses. Neuroimage **14**:862–872.

Mechelli A, Price CJ, Henson RN, Friston KJ (2003) Estimating efficiency a priori: a comparison of blocked and randomized designs. Neuroimage **18**:798–805.

Mechelli A, Price CJ, Friston KJ, Ishai A (2004) Where bottom-up meets top-down: neuronal interactions during perception and imagery. Cereb Cortex **14**:1256–1265.

Medland SE, Jahanshad N, Neale BM, Thompson PM (2014) Whole-genome analyses of whole-brain data: working within an expanded search space. Nat Neurosci **17**:791–800.

Mesulam M-M, Mufson EJ (1985) The insula of Reil in man and monkey: architectonics, connectivity, and function. In: Association and Asuditory Cortices (Jones, E. G., ed.), pp 179–226 New York: Plenum.

Middleton FA, Strick PL (2001) Cerebellar projections to the prefrontal cortex of the primate. J Neurosci **21**:700–712.

Miller EK, Li L, Desimone R (1991) A neural mechanism for working and recognition memory in inferior temporal cortex. Science **254**:1377–1379.

Mishkin M (1964) Perseveration of central sets after frontal lesions in monkeys. In: The Frontal Granular Cortex (Warren, J. M. and Akert, K., eds), pp 219–241 New York: McGraw-Hill.

Miyashita Y (1990) Associative representation of the visual long-term memory in the neurons of the primate temporal cortex. In: Vision, Memory and the Temporal Lobe (Iwai E, Mishkin M. eds), pp 75–87 New York: Elsevier.

Monchi O, Petrides M, Petre V, Worsley K, Dagher A (2001) Wisconsin Card Sorting revisited: distinct neural circuits participating in different stages of the task identified by event-related fMRI. J Neurosci 21:7733–7741.

Moore JW, Ruge D, Wenke D, Rothwell J, Haggard P (2010) Disrupting the experience of control in the human brain: pre-supplementary motor area contributes to the sense of agency. Proc Biol Sci 277:2503–2509.

Moran R, Pinotsis DA, Friston K (2013) Neural masses and fields in dynamic causal modeling. Front Comput Neurosci 7:57.

Moratti S, Saugar C, Strange BA (2011) Prefrontal-occipitoparietal coupling underlies late latency human neuronal responses to emotion. J Neurosci 31:17278–17286.

Morecraft RJ, Stilwell-Morecraft KS, Cipolloni PB, Ge J, McNeal DW, Pandya DN (2012) Cytoarchitecture and cortical connections of the anterior cingulate and adjacent somatomotor fields in the rhesus monkey. Brain Res Bull 87:457–497.

Morishima Y, Akaishi R, Yamada Y, Okuda J, Toma K, Sakai K (2009) Task-specific signal transmission from prefrontal cortex in visual selective attention. Nat Neurosci 12:85–91.

Morris R, Pandya DN, Petrides M (1999) Fiber system linking the mid-dorsolateral frontal cortex with the retrosplenial/presubicular region in the rhesus monkey. J Comp Neurol 407:183–192.

Muakkassa KF, Strick PL (1979) Frontal lobe inputs to primate motor cortex: evidence for four somatotopically organized 'premotor areas'. Brain Res 177:176–182.

Mukamel R, Ekstrom AD, Kaplan J, Iacoboni M, Fried I (2010) Single-neuron responses in humans during execution and observation of actions. Curr Biol 20:750–756.

Mukamel R, Fried I (2012) Human intracranial recordings and cognitive neuroscience. Annu Rev Psychol 63:511–537.

Mumford JA, Nichols TE (2008) Power calculation for group fMRI studies accounting for arbitrary design and temporal autocorrelation. Neuroimage 39:261–268.

Munafo MR, Clark TG, Moore LR, Payne E, Walton R, Flint J (2003) Genetic polymorphisms and personality in healthy adults: a systematic review and meta-analysis. Mol Psychiatry 8:471–484.

Munafo MR, Flint J (2004) Meta-analysis of genetic association studies. Trends Genet 20:439–444.

Murayama Y, Weber B, Saleem KS, Augath M, Logothetis NK (2006) Tracing neural circuits in vivo with Mn-enhanced MRI. Magn Reson Imaging 24:349–358.

Murphy K, Garavan H (2004) An empirical investigation into the number of subjects required for an event-related fMRI study. Neuroimage 22:879–885.

Mushiake H, Inase M, Tanji J (1991) Neuronal activity in the primate premotor, supplementary, and precentral motor cortex during visually guided and internally determined sequential movements. JNeurophysiol 66:705–718.

Naidich TP, Duvernoy HM, Delman BN (2009) Duvernoy's Atlas of the Human Brain Stem and Cerebellum. New York: Springer.

Nelissen K, Borra E, Gerbella M, Rozzi S, Luppino G, Vanduffel W, Rizzolatti G, Orban GA (2011) Action observation circuits in the macaque monkey cortex. J Neurosci 31:3743–3756.

Neubert FX, Mars RB, Buch ER, Olivier E, Rushworth MF (2010) Cortical and subcortical interactions during action reprogramming and their related white matter pathways. Proc Natl Acad Sci U S A 107:13240–13245.

Neubert FX, Mars RB, Thomas AG, Sallet J, Rushworth MF (2014) Comparison of human ventral frontal cortex areas for cognitive control and language with areas in monkey frontal cortex. Neuron 81:700–713.

Nieder A, Freedman DJ, Miller EK (2002) Representation of the quantity of visual items in the primate prefrontal cortex. Science 297:1708–1711.

Nikolic D, Fries P, Singer W (2013) Gamma oscillations: precise temporal coordination without a metronome. Trends Cogn Sci 17:54–55.

Norman KA, Polyn SM, Detre GJ, Haxby JV (2006) Beyond mind-reading: multi-voxel pattern analysis of fMRI data. Trends Cogn Sci 10:424–430.

O'Doherty JP, Dayan P, Friston K, Critchley H, Dolan RJ (2003) Temporal difference models and reward-related learning in the human brain. Neuron 38:329–337.

O'Reilly JX, Croxson PL, Jbabdi S, Sallet J, Noonan MP, Mars RB, Browning PG, Wilson CR, Mitchell AS, Miller KL, Rushworth MF, Baxter MG (2013) Causal effect of disconnection lesions on interhemispheric functional connectivity in rhesus monkeys. Proc Natl Acad Sci U S A 110:13982–13987.

Ogawa S, Menon RS, Tank DW, Kim SG, Merkle H, Ellermann JM, Ugurbil K (1993) Functional brain mapping by blood oxygenation level-dependent contrast magnetic resonance imaging. A comparison of signal characteristics with a biophysical model. Biophys J 64:803–812.

Otani VH, Uchida RR, Junior QC, Shiozawa P (2014) A systematic review and meta-analysis of the use of repetitive transcranial magnetic stimulation for auditory hallucinations treatment in refractory schizophrenic patients. Intern J Psychiatr Clin Pract epub.

Padoa-Schioppa C, Assad JA (2006) Neurons in the orbitofrontal cortex encode economic value. Nature 441:223–226.

Pashler H (1994) Dual-task interference in simple tasks: data and theory. Psychol Bull 116:220–244.

Passingham RE (2008) What is Special about the Human Brain. Oxford: Oxford University Press.

Passingham R (2009) How good is the macaque monkey model of the human brain? Curr Opin Neurobiol 19:6–11.

Passingham RE, Wise SP (2012) The Neurobiology of Prefrontal Cortex. Oxford: Oxford University Press.

Passingham RE, Stephan KE, Kotter R (2002) The anatomical basis of functional localization in the cortex. Nat Rev Neurosci 3:606–616.

Passingham RE, Bengtsson SL, Lau HC (2010) Medial frontal cortex: from self-generated action to reflection on one's own performance. Trends Cogn Sci 14:16–21.

Passingham RE, Rowe JB, Sakai K (2012) Has brain imaging discovered anything new about how the brain works? Neuroimage 66C:142–150.

Passingham RE, Chung A, Goparaju B, Cowey A, Vaina LM (2014) Using action understanding to understand the left inferior parietal cortex in the human brain. Brain Res 1582:64–74.

Penny WD, Stephan KE, Mechelli A, Friston KJ (2004) Modelling functional integration: a comparison of structural equation and dynamic causal models. Neuroimage 23 Suppl 1:S264–274.

Penny WD, Zeidman P, Burgess N (2013) Forward and backward inference in spatial cognition. PLoS Comput Biol 9:e1003383.

Petersen SE, Fox PT, Posner MI, Mintun M, Raichle ME (1988) Positron emission tomographic studies of the cortical anatomy of single-word processing. Nature **331**:585–589.

Petrides M (2000) Dissociable roles of mid-dorsolateral prefrontal and anterior inferotemporal cortex in visual working memory. J Neurosci **20**:7496–7503.

Petrides M, Pandya DN (1999) Dorsolateral prefrontal cortex: comparative cytoarchitectonic analysis in the human and the macaque brain and corticocortical connection patterns. Eur J Neurosci **11**:1011–1036.

Petrides M, Pandya DN (2007) Efferent association pathways from the rostral prefrontal cortex in the macaque monkey. J Neurosci **27**:11573–11586.

Petrides M, Cadoret G, Mackey S (2005) Orofacial somatomotor responses in the macaque monkey homologue of Broca's area. Nature **435**:1235–1238.

Petrovich N, Holodny AI, Tabar V, Correa DD, Hirsch J, Gutin PH, Brennan CW (2005) Discordance between functional magnetic resonance imaging during silent speech tasks and intraoperative speech arrest. J Neurosurg **103**:267–274.

Phelps ME, Hoffman EJ, Coleman RE, Welch MJ, Raichle ME, Weiss ES, Sobel BE, Ter-Pogossian MM (1976) Tomographic images of blood pool and perfusion in brain and heart. J Nucl Med **17**:603–612.

Plichta MM, Schwarz AJ, Grimm O, Morgen K, Mier D, Haddad L, Gerdes AB, Sauer C, Tost H, Esslinger C, Colman P, Wilson F, Kirsch P, Meyer-Lindenberg A (2012) Test-retest reliability of evoked BOLD signals from a cognitive-emotive fMRI test battery. Neuroimage **60**:1746–1758.

Pochon J-B, Levy R, Poline J-B, Crozier S, Lehericy S, Pillon B, Deweer B, Bihan DL, Dubois B (2001) The role of dorsolateral prefrontal cortex in the preparation of forthcoming actions: an fMRI study. Cereb Cortex **11**:260–266.

Poldrack RA (2006) Can cognitive processes be inferred from neuroimaging data? Trends Cogn Sci **10**:59–63.

Poldrack RA, Mumford JA (2009) Independence in ROI analysis: where is the voodoo? Soc Cogn Affect Neurosci **4**:208–213.

Poldrack RA, Mumford JA, Nichols TE (2011) Handbook of Functional MRI Data Analysis. Cambridge: Cambridge.

Posner MI, Walker JA, Friedrich FJ, Rafal RD (1984) Effects of parietal injury on covert orienting of attention. J Neurosci **4**:1863–1874.

Power JD, Barnes KA, Snyder AZ, Schlaggar BL, Petersen SE (2012) Spurious but systematic correlations in functional connectivity MRI networks arise from subject motion. Neuroimage **59**:2142–2154.

Press C, Weiskopf N, Kilner JM (2012) Dissociable roles of human inferior frontal gyrus during action execution and observation. Neuroimage **60**:1671–1677.

Pribram KH, Mishkin M, Rosvold HE, Kaplan SJ (1952) Effects on delayed-response performance of lesions of dorsolateral and ventromedial frontal cortex of baboons. J Comp Physiol Psychol **45**:565–575.

Price CJ, Wise RJS, Watson JDG, Patterson K, Howard D, Frackowiak RSJ (1994) Brain activity during reading: the effects of exposure duration and task. Brain **117**:1255–1269.

Price CJ, Mummery CJ, Moore CJ, Frakowiak RS, Friston KJ (1999) Delineating necessary and sufficient neural systems with functional imaging studies of neuropsychological patients. J Cogn Neurosci **11**:371–382.

Price CJ, Seghier ML, Leff AP (2010) Predicting language outcome and recovery after stroke: the PLORAS system. Nat Rev Neurol 6:202–210.

Procyk E, Tanaka YL, Joseph JP (2000) Anterior cingulate activity during routine and non-routine sequential behaviors in macaques. Nat Neurosci 3:502–509.

Rae CL, Hughes LE, Anderson MC, Rowe JB (2015) The prefrontal cortex achieves inhibitory control by facilitating subcortical motor pathway connectivity. J Neurosci 35:786–794.

Raichle ME, Snyder AZ (2007) A default mode of brain function: a brief history of an evolving idea. Neuroimage 37:1083–1090; discussion 1097–1089.

Raichle ME, MacLeod AM, Snyder AZ, Powers WJ, Gusnard DA, Shulman GL (2001) A default mode of brain function. Proc Natl Acad Sci U S A 98:676–682.

Rainer G, Miller EK (2000) Effects of visual experience on the representation of objects in the prefrontal cortex. Neuron 27:179–189.

Rainer G, Rao SC, Miller EK (1999) Prospective coding for objects in primate prefrontal cortex. J Neurosci 19:5493–5505.

Raos V, Umilta MA, Murata A, Fogassi L, Gallese V (2006) Functional properties of grasping-related neurons in the ventral premotor area F5 of the macaque monkey. J Neurophysiol 95:709–729.

Rapin LA, Dohen M, Loevenbruck H, Whitman JC, Metzak PD, Woodward TS (2012) Hyperintensity of functional networks involving voice-selective cortical regions during silent thought in schizophrenia. Psychiatry Res 202:110–117.

Ratcliff R, Cherian A, Segraves M (2003) A comparison of macaque behavior and superior colliculus neuronal activity to predictions from models of two-choice decisions. J Neurophysiol 90:1392–1407.

Rauch A, Rainer G, Logothetis NK (2008) The effect of a serotonin-induced dissociation between spiking and perisynaptic activity on BOLD functional MRI. Proc Natl Acad Sci U S A 105:6759–6764.

Rees G, Frith CD, Lavie N (1997) Modulating irrelevant motion perception by varying attentional load in an unrelated task. Science 278:1616–1619.

Rescorla RA (1976) Stimulus generalization: some predictions from a model of Pavlovian conditioning. J Exp Psychol Anim Behav Process 2:88–96.

Richter W, Andersen PM, Georgopoulos AP, Kim S-G (1997) Sequential activity in human motor areas during a delayed cued finger movement task studied by time-resolved fMRI. Neurorep 8:1257–1261.

Richter W, Somorjai R, Summers R, Jarmasz M, Menon RS, Gati JS, Georgopoulos AP, Tegeler C, Ugurbil K, Kim SG (2000) Motor area activity during mental rotation studied by time-resolved single-trial fMRI. J Cogn Neurosci 12:310–320.

Rilling JK (2014) Comparative primate neuroimaging: insights into human brain evolution. Trends Cogn Sci 18:45–55.

Rilling JK, Glasser MF, Preuss TM, Ma X, Zhao T, Hu X, Behrens TE (2008) The evolution of the arcuate fasciculus revealed with comparative DWI. Nat Neurosci 11:426–428.

Roberts MJ, Lowet E, Brunet NM, Ter Wal M, Tiesinga P, Fries P, De Weerd P (2013) Robust gamma coherence between macaque V1 and V2 by dynamic frequency matching. Neuron 78:523–536.

Roebroeck A, Formisano E, Goebel R (2005) Mapping directed influence over the brain using Granger causality and fMRI. Neuroimage 25:230–242.

Rolls ET (2012) Neuroculture. Oxford: Oxford University Press.

Romo R, Schultz W (1987) Neuronal activity preceding self-initiated or externally timed arm movements in area 6 of monkey cortex. Exp Brain Res **67**:656–662.

Rowe JB, Wolpe N (eds) (2014) Altered Action Awareness in Neurological Conditions. Oxford: Oxford University Press.

Rowe J, Friston K, Frackowiak R, Passingham R (2002) Attention to action: specific modulation of corticocortical interactions in humans. Neuroimage **17**:988–998.

Rowe JB, Stephan KE, Friston K, Frackowiak RS, Passingham RE (2005) The prefrontal cortex shows context-specific changes in effective connectivity to motor or visual cortex during the selection of action or colour. Cereb Cortex **15**:85–95.

Rowe JB, Hughes L, Nimmo-Smith I (2010) Action selection: a race model for selected and non-selected actions distinguishes the contribution of premotor and prefrontal areas. Neuroimage **51**:888–896.

Rozzi S, Calzavara R, Belmalih A, Borra E, Gregoriou GG, Matelli M, Luppino G (2006) Cortical connections of the inferior parietal cortical convexity of the macaque monkey. Cereb Cortex **16**:1389–1417.

Rozzi S, Ferrari PF, Bonini L, Rizzolatti G, Fogassi L (2008) Functional organization of inferior parietal lobule convexity in the macaque monkey: electrophysiological characterization of motor, sensory and mirror responses and their correlation with cytoarchitectonic areas. Eur J Neurosci **28**:1569–1588.

Rudebeck PH, Buckley MJ, Walton ME, Rushworth MF (2006) A role for the macaque anterior cingulate gyrus in social valuation. Science **313**:1310–1312.

Rumiati RI, Weiss PH, Shallice T, Ottoboni G, Noth J, Zilles K, Fink GR (2004) Neural basis of pantomiming the use of visually presented objects. Neuroimage **21**: 1224–1231.

Rushworth MF, Behrens TE, Johansen-Berg H (2005) Connection patterns distinguish 3 regions of human parietal cortex. Cereb Cortex **16**:1418–1430.

Rushworth MF, Buckley MJ, Behrens TE, Walton ME, Bannerman DM (2007) Functional organization of the medial frontal cortex. Curr Opin Neurobiol **17**:220–227.

Rushworth MF, Mars RB, Sallet J (2013) Are there specialized circuits for social cognition and are they unique to humans? Curr Opin Neurobiol **23**:436–442.

Sakai K, Miyashita Y (1991) Neural organization for the long-term memory of paired associates. Nature **354**:152–155.

Sakai K, Passingham RE (2006) Prefrontal set activity predicts rule-specific neural processing during subsequent cognitive performance. J Neurosci **26**:1211–1218.

Saleem KS, Kondo H, Price JL (2008) Complementary circuits connecting the orbital and medial prefrontal networks with the temporal, insular, and opercular cortex in the macaque monkey. J Comp Neurol **506**:659–693.

Sallet J, Mars RB, Andersson J, O'Reilly JX, Jhabdi S, Croxson PL, Miller KL, Jenkinson M, Rushworth MF (2011) Social network size affects neural circuits in macaques. Science **334**:698–700.

Sallet J, Mars RB, Noonan MP, Neubert FX, Jbabdi S, O'Reilly JX, Filippini N, Thomas AG, Rushworth MF (2013) The organization of dorsal frontal cortex in humans and macaques. J Neurosci **33**:12255–12274.

Sampaio-Baptista C, Khrapitchev AA, Foxley S, Schlagheck T, Scholz J, Jbabdi S, DeLuca GC, Miller KL, Taylor A, Thomas N, Kleim J, Sibson NR, Bannerman D,

Johansen-Berg H (2013) Motor skill learning induces changes in white matter micro-structure and myelination. J Neurosci **33**:19499–19503.

Sampaio-BaptistaC, Scholz J, Jenkinson M, Thomas AG, Filippini N, Smit G, Douaud G, Johansen-Berg H (2014) Gray matter volume is associated with rate of subsequent skill learning after a long term training intervention. Neuroimage **96**:158–166.

Sanei S (2013) Adaptive Processing of Brain Signals. New York: Wiley.

Savage-Rumbaugh ES, Lewin R (1994) Kanzi: the Ape on the Brink of the Human Mind. London: Doubleday.

Saygin ZM, Osher DE, Koldewyn K, Reynolds G, Gabrieli JD, Saxe RR (2011) Anatomical connectivity patterns predict face selectivity in the fusiform gyrus. Nat Neurosci **15**:321–327.

Scheeringa R, Fries P, Petersson KM, Oostenveld R, Grothe I, Norris DG, Hagoort P, Bastiaansen MC (2011) Neuronal dynamics underlying high- and low-frequency EEG oscillations contribute independently to the human BOLD signal. Neuron **69**:572–583.

Scheperjans F, Hermann K, Eickhoff SB, Amunts K, Schleicher A, Zilles K (2008) Observer-independent cytoarchitectonic mapping of the human superior parietal cortex. Cereb Cortex **18**:846–867.

Schleicher A, Amunts K, Geyer S, Morosan P, Zilles K (1999) Observer-independent method for microstructural parcellation of cerebral cortex: a quantitative approach to cytoarchitecture. Neuroimage **9**:165–177.

Schluter ND, Krams M, Rushworth MF, Passingham RE (2001) Cerebral dominance for action in the human brain: the selection of actions. Neuropsychol **39**:105–113.

Schmahmann JD, Doyon JD, McDonald D, Holmes C, Lavgoie K, Hurwitz AS, Kabani N, Toga A, Evans A, Petrides M (1999) Three-dimensional MRI atlas of the human cerebellum in proportional stereotaxic space. Neuroimage **10**:233–260.

Schmahmann JD, Pandya DN, Wang R, Dai G, D'Arceuil HE, de Crespigny AJ, Wedeen VJ (2007) Association fibre pathways of the brain: parallel observations from diffusion spectrum imaging and autoradiography. Brain **130**:630–653.

Schultz W (1998) Predictive reward signal of dopamine neurons. J Neurophysiol **80**:1–27.

Schultz W, Dickinson A (2000) Neuronal coding of prediction errors. Annu Rev Neurosci **23**:473–500.

Schultz W, Dayan P, Montague PR (1997) A neural substrate of prediction and reward. Science **275**:1593–1599.

Schultz W, Tremblay L, Hollerman JR (2000) Reward processing in primate orbitofrontal cortex and basal ganglia. Cereb Cortex **10**:272–284.

Segraves MA (1992) Activity of monkey frontal eye field neurons projecting to oculomotor regions of the pons. J Neurophysiol **68**:1967–1985.

Selemon LD, Goldman-Rakic PS (1988) Common cortical and subcortical targets of the dorsolateral prefrontal and parietal cortices in the rhesus monkey: evidence for a distributed neural network subserving spatially guided behavior. J Neurosci **8**:4049–4068.

Seymour B, O'Doherty JP, Dayan P, Koltzenburg M, Jones AK, Dolan RJ, Friston KJ, Frackowiak RS (2004) Temporal difference models describe higher-order learning in humans. Nature **429**:664–667.

Shadmehr R, Wise S (2005) The Computational Neurobiology of Reaching and Pointing. Cambridge: MIT press.

Shafto MA, Tyler LK, Dixon M, Taylor JR, Rowe JB, Cusack R, Calder AJ, Marslen-Wilson WD, Duncan J, Dalgleish T, Henson RN, Brayne C, Matthews FE (2014) The Cambridge Centre for Ageing and Neuroscience (Cam-CAN) study protocol: a cross-sectional, lifespan, multidisciplinary examination of healthy cognitive ageing. BMC Neurol 14:204.

Shen L, Alexander GE (1997) Preferential representation of instructed target location versus limb trajectory in dorsal premotor cortex. J Neurophysiol 77:1195–1212.

Shen Q, Ren H, Duong TQ (2008) CBF, BOLD, CBV, and CMRO(2) fMRI signal temporal dynamics at 500-msec resolution. J Magn Reson Imaging 27:599–606.

Shipp S (2005) The importance of being agranular: a comparative account of visual and motor cortex. Philos Trans R Soc Lond B Biol Sci 360:797–814.

Shmuel A, Chaimow D, Raddatz G, Ugurbil K, Yacoub E (2010) Mechanisms underlying decoding at 7 T: ocular dominance columns, broad structures, and macroscopic blood vessels in V1 convey information on the stimulated eye. Neuroimage 49:1957–1964.

Siebner HR, Strafella AP, Rowe JB (2014) The white elephant revived: a new marriage between PET and MRI: comment to Cumming: 'PET neuroimaging: the white elephant packs his trunk?'. Neuroimage 84:1104–1106.

Siegel M, Donner TH, Oostenveld R, Fries P, Engel AK (2008) Neuronal synchronization along the dorsal visual pathway reflects the focus of spatial attention. Neuron 60:709–719.

Siero JC, Hendrikse J, Hoogduin H, Petridou N, Luijten P, Donahue MJ (2014a) Cortical depth dependence of the BOLD initial dip and poststimulus undershoot in human visual cortex at 7 Tesla. Magn Reson Med 73:2283–2295.

Siero JC, Hermes D, Hoogduin H, Luijten PR, Ramsey NF, Petridou N (2014b) BOLD matches neuronal activity at the mm scale: A combined 7T fMRI and ECoG study in human sensorimotor cortex. Neuroimage 101C:177–184.

Silva AC, Lee SP, Iadecola C, Kim SG (2000) Early temporal characteristics of cerebral blood flow and deoxyhemoglobin changes during somatosensory stimulation. J Cereb Blood Flow Metab 20:201–206.

Simons CJ, Tracy DK, Sanghera KK, O'Daly O, Gilleen J, Dominguez MD, Krabbendam L, Shergill SS (2010) Functional magnetic resonance imaging of inner speech in schizophrenia. Biol Psychiatry 67:232–237.

Sirigu A, Daprati E, Ciancia S, Giraux P, Nighoghossian N, Posada A, Haggard P (2004) Altered awareness of voluntary action after damage to the parietal cortex. Nat Neurosci 7:80–84.

Sloan HL, Austin VC, Blamire AM, Schnupp JW, Lowe AS, Allers KA, Matthews PM, Sibson NR (2010) Regional differences in neurovascular coupling in rat brain as determined by fMRI and electrophysiology. Neuroimage 53:399–411.

Song AW, Chang HC, Petty C, Guidon A, Chen NK (2014) Improved delineation of short cortical association fibers and gray/white matter boundary using whole-brain 3D DWI at sub-millimeter spatial resolution. Brain Connectivity 4:636–640.

Spencer-Booth Y, Hinde RA (1971) Effects of brief separations from mothers during infancy on behaviour of rhesus monkeys 6–24 months later. J Child Psychol Psychiatry 12:157–172.

Sporns O (2014) Contributions and challenges for network models in cognitive neuroscience. Nat Neurosci 17:652–660.

Sporns O, Tononi G, Edelman GM (2000) Connectivity and complexity: the relationship between neuroanatomy and brain dynamics. Neural Netw **13**:909–922.

Sporns O, Tononi G, Kotter R (2005) The human connectome: A structural description of the human brain. PLoS Comput Biol **1**:e42.

Sreenivasan KK, Vytlacil J, D'Esposito M (2014) Distributed and dynamic storage of working memory stimulus information in extrastriate cortex. J Cogn Neurosci **26**:1141–1153.

Stanton GB, Goldberg ME, Bruce CJ (1988) Frontal eye field efferents in the macaque monkey: II Topography of terminal fields in midbrain and pons. J Comp Neurol **271**:493–506.

Stanton GB, Bruce CJ, Goldberg ME (1995) Topography of projections to posterior cortical areas from the macaque frontal eye fields. J Comp Neurol **353**:291–305.

Stelzel C, Schumacher EH, Schubert T, D'Esposito M (2006) The neural effect of stimulus-response modality compatibility on dual-task performance: an fMRI study. Psychol Res **70**:514–525.

Stephan KE (2013) The history of CoCoMac. Neuroimage **80**:46–52.

Stephan KE, Friston KJ (2010) Analyzing effective connectivity with fMRI. Wiley Interdiscip Rev Cogn Sci **1**:446–459.

Stephan KE, Roebroeck A (2012) A short history of causal modeling of fMRI data. Neuroimage **62**:856–863.

Stephan KE, Penny WD, Moran RJ, den Ouden HE, Daunizeau J, Friston KJ (2010) Ten simple rules for dynamic causal modeling. Neuroimage **49**:3099–3109.

Sternberg S (2011) Modular processes in mind and brain. Cogn Neuropsychol **28**:156–208.

Stewart LM, Walsh V, Rothwell JC (2001) Motor and phosphene thresholds: a transcranial magnetic stimulation correlation study. Neuropsychol **39**:415–419.

Stoewer S, Ku SP, Goense J, Steudel T, Logothetis NK, Duncan J, Sigala N (2010) Frontoparietal activity with minimal decision and control in the awake macaque at 7 T. Magn Reson Imaging **28**:1120–1128.

Summerfield JJ, Hassabis D, Maguire EA (2009) Cortical midline involvement in autobiographical memory. Neuroimage **44**:1188–1200.

Sunaert S, Van Hecke P, Marchal G, Orban GA (1999) Motion-responsive regions of the human brain. Exp Brain Res **127**:355–370.

Sveinsdottir E, Torlof P, Risberg J, Ingvar DH, Lassen NA (1971) Monitoring regional cerebral blood flow in normal man with a computer-controlled 32-dector system. Eur Neurol **6**:228–233.

Takeda K, Funahashi S (2004) Population vector analysis of primate prefrontal activity during spatial working memory. Cereb Cortex **14**:1328–1339.

Talairach J, Tournoux P (1988) Co-Planar Stereotaxic Atlas of the Human Brain. Stuttgart: Thieme.

Tanaka K (1997) Mechanisms of visual object recognition. Curr Opin Neurobiol **7**:523–529.

Taylor PC, Rushworth MF, Nobre AC (2008) Choosing where to attend and the medial frontal cortex: an FMRI study. J Neurophysiol **100**:1397–1406.

Thiel A, Habedank B, Herholz K, Kessler J, Winhuisen L, Haupt WF, Heiss WD (2006) From the left to the right: how the brain compensates progressive loss of language function. Brain Lang **98**:57–65.

Thomsen K, Piilgaard H, Gjedde A, Bonvento G, Lauritzen M (2009) Principal cell spiking, postsynaptic excitation, and oxygen consumption in the rat cerebellar cortex. J Neurophysiol **102**:1503–1512.

Tomassini V, Jbabdi S, Klein JC, Behrens TE, Pozzilli C, Matthews PM, Rushworth MF, Johansen-Berg H (2007) Diffusion-weighted imaging tractography-based parcellation of the human lateral premotor cortex identifies dorsal and ventral subregions with anatomical and functional specializations. J Neurosci **27**:10259–10269.

Tomassini V, Matthews PM, Thompson AJ, Fuglo D, Geurts JJ, Johansen-Berg H, Jones DK, Rocca MA, Wise RG, Barkhof F, Palace J (2012) Neuroplasticity and functional recovery in multiple sclerosis. Nat Rev Neurol **8**:635–646.

Tombu MN, Asplund CL, Dux PE, Godwin D, Martin JW, Marois R (2011) A Unified attentional bottleneck in the human brain. Proc Natl Acad Sci U S A **108**: 13426–13431.

Toni I, Schluter ND, Josephs O, Friston K, Passingham RE (1999) Signal-, set- and movement-related activity in the human brain: an event-related fMRI study. Cereb Cortex **9**:35–49.

Towlson EK, Vertes PE, Ahnert SE, Schafer WR, Bullmore ET (2013) The rich club of the C. elegans neuronal connectome. J Neurosci **33**:6380–6387.

Tressoldi PE, Sella F, Coltheart M, Umilta C (2012) Using functional neuroimaging to test theories of cognition: a selective survey of studies from 2007 to 2011 as a contribution to the Decade of the Mind Initiative. Cortex **48**:1247–1250.

Tressoldi PE, Giofre D, Sella F, Cumming G (2013) High impact = high statistical standards? Not necessarily so. PLoS One **8**:e56180.

Tsukiura T, Fujii T, Fukatsu R, Otsuki T, Okuda J, Umetsu A, Suzuki K, Tabuchi M, Yanagawa I, Nagasaka T, Kawashima R, Fukuda H, Takahashi S, Yamadori A (2002) Neural basis of the retrieval of people's names: evidence from brain-damaged patients and fMRI. J Cogn Neurosci **14**:922–937.

Tzourio-Mazoyer N, Landeau B, Papathanassiou D, Crivello F, Etard O, Delcroix N, Mazoyer B, Joliot M (2002) Automated anatomical labeling of activations in SPM using a macroscopic anatomical parcellation of the MNI MRI single-subject brain. Neuroimage **15**:273–289.

Ugurbil K, Hu X, Wei C, Zhu X-H, Kim S-G, Georgopoulos A (1999) Functional mapping in the human brain using high magnetic fields, Philosophical Transactions of the Royal Society B: Biological Sciences **354**:1195–1213.

Ungerleider G, Desimone R (1986) Cortical connections of visual area MT in the macaque. J Comp Neurol **248**:190–222.

Ungerleider LG, Galkin TW, Desimone R, Gattass R (2008) Cortical connections of area V4 in the macaque. Cereb Cortex **18**:477–499.

Van den Heuvel MP, Sporns O (2011) Rich-club organization of the human connectome. J Neurosci **31**:15775–15786.

Van Essen DC, Ugurbil K, Auerbach E, Barch D, Behrens TE, Bucholz R, Chang A, Chen L, Corbetta M, Curtiss SW, Della Penna S, Feinberg D, Glasser MF, Harel N, Heath AC, Larson-Prior L, Marcus D, Michalareas G, Moeller S, Oostenveld R, Petersen SE, Prior F, Schlaggar BL, Smith SM, Snyder AZ, Xu J, Yacoub E (2012) The Human Connectome Project: a data acquisition perspective. Neuroimage **62**:2222–2231.

Vandenberghe R, Price C, Wise R, Josephs O, Frackowiak RSJ (1996) Functional anatomy of a common semantic system for words and pictures. Nature **383**:254–256.

Vanlancker-Sidtis D, McIntosh AR, Grafton S (2003) PET activation studies comparing two speech tasks widely used in surgical mapping. Brain Lang **85**:245–261.

Van Lutterveld R, Hillebrand A, Diederen KM, Daalman K, Kahn RS, Stam CJ, Sommer IE (2012) Oscillatory cortical network involved in auditory verbal hallucinations in schizophrenia. PLoS One 7:e41149.

Vargha-Khadem F, Watkins KE, Price CJ, Ashburner J, Alcock KJ, Connelly A, Frackowiak RS, Friston KJ, Pembrey ME, Mishkin M, Gadian DG, Passingham RE (1998) Neural basis of an inherited speech and language disorder. Proc Natl Acad Sci U S A **95**:12695–12700.

Vincent JL, Kahn I, Snyder AZ, Raichle ME, Buckner RL (2008) Evidence for a frontoparietal control system revealed by intrinsic functional connectivity. J Neurophysiol **100**:3328–3342.

Vincent JL, Patel GH, Fox MD, Snyder AZ, Baker JT, Van Essen DC, Zempel JM, Snyder LH, Corbetta M, Raichle ME (2007) Intrinsic functional architecture in the anaesthetized monkey brain. Nature **447**:83–86.

Vogt BA, Pandya DN (1987) Cingulate cortex of the rhesus monkey: II Cortical afferents. J Comp Neurol **262**:271–289.

Von Bonin G, Bailey P (1947) The Neocortex of Macaca mulatta. Urbana: University of Illinois.

Von Economo C (1929) The Cytoarchitectonics of the Human Cerebral Cortex. London: Oxford University Press.

Vossel S, Weidner R, Driver J, Friston KJ, Fink GR (2012) Deconstructing the architecture of dorsal and ventral attention systems with dynamic causal modeling. J Neurosci **32**:10637–10648.

Wahl RL, Beanlands RSB (eds) (2008) Principles and Practice of PET and PET/CT. Philadelphia: Lippincott, Williams and Wilkins.

Wallis JD, Miller EK (2003) Neuronal activity in primate dorsolateral and orbital prefrontal cortex during performance of a reward preference task. Eur J Neurosci **18**:2069–2081.

Wang G, Tanifuji M, Tanaka K (1998) Functional architecture in monkey inferotemporal cortex revealed by in vivo optical imaging. Neurosci Res **32**:33–46.

Wang XJ (2002) Probabilistic decision making by slow reverberation in cortical circuits. Neuron **36**:955–968.

Wang Y, Shima K, Osoda M, Sawamura H, Tanji J (2002) Spatial distribution and density of prefrontal cortical cells projecting to three sectors of the premotor cortex. Neurorep **13**:1341–1344.

Wang L, Ashley-Koch A, Steffens DC, Krishnan KR, Taylor WD (2012) Impact of BDNF Val66Met and 5-HTTLPR polymorphism variants on neural substrates related to sadness and executive function. Genes Brain and Behav **11**:352–359.

Wassermann EM, Epstein CM, Ziemann U (eds) (2008) Oxford Handbook of Transcranial Magnetic Brain Stimulation. Oxford: Oxford University Press.

Watanabe K, Funahashi S (2014) Neural mechanisms of dual-task interference and cognitive capacity limitation in the prefrontal cortex. Nat Neurosci **17**:601–611.

Watkins K (2011) Developmental disorders of speech and language: from genes to brain structure and function. Prog Brain Res **189**:225–238.

Watkins KE, Gadian DG, Vargha-Khadem F (1999) Functional and structural brain abnormalities associated with a genetic disorder of speech and language. Am J Hum Genet **65**:1215–1221.

Watkins KE, Vargha-Khadem F, Ashburner J, Passingham RE, Connelly A, Friston KJ, Frackowiak RS, Mishkin M, Gadian DG (2002) MRI analysis of an inherited speech and language disorder: structural brain abnormalities. Brain **125**:465–478.

Watkins KE, Smith SM, Davis S, Howell P (2008) Structural and functional abnormalities of the motor system in developmental stuttering. Brain **131**:50–59.

Weber M, Thompson-Schill SL, Osherson D, Haxby J, Parsons L (2009) Predicting judged similarity of natural categories from their neural representations. Neuropsychol **47**:859–868.

Webster MJ, Bachevalier J, Ungerleider LG (1994) Connections of inferior temporal areas TEO and TE with parietal and frontal cortex in macaque monkeys. Cereb Cortex **4**:471–483.

Wedeen VJ, Wang RP, Schmahmann JD, Benner T, Tseng WY, Dai G, Pandya DN, Hagmann P, D'Arceuil H, de Crespigny AJ (2008) Diffusion spectrum magnetic resonance imaging (DSI) tractography of crossing fibers. Neuroimage **41**:1267–1277.

Weilke F, Spiegel S, Boecker H, von Einsiedel HG, Conrad B, Schwaiger M, Erhard P (2001) Time-resolved fMRI of activation patterns in MI and SMA during complex voluntary movement. J Neurophysiol **85**:1858–1863.

Weinrich M, Wise SP, Mauritz K-H (1984) A neurophysiological study of the premotor cortex in the rhesus monkey. Brain **107**:385–414.

White CM, Pope WB, Zaw T, Qiao J, Naeini KM, Lai A, Nghiemphu PL, Wang JJ, Cloughesy TF, Ellingson BM (2014) Regional and voxel-wise comparisons of blood flow measurements between dynamic susceptibility contrast magnetic resonance imaging (DSC-MRI) and arterial spin labeling (ASL) in brain tumors. J Neuroimaging **24**:23–30.

Whitney C, Kirk M, O'Sullivan J, Lambon Ralph MA, Jefferies E (2012) Executive semantic processing is underpinned by a large-scale neural network: revealing the contribution of left prefrontal, posterior temporal, and parietal cortex to controlled retrieval and selection using TMS. J Cogn Neurosci **24**:133–147.

Whittingstall K, Logothetis NK (2009) Frequency-band coupling in surface EEG reflects spiking activity in monkey visual cortex. Neuron **64**:281–289.

Wilson B, Petkov CI (2011) Communication and the primate brain: insights from neuroimaging studies in humans, chimpanzees and macaques. Human Biol **83**:175–189.

Winhuisen L, Thiel A, Schumacher B, Kessler J, Rudolf J, Haupt WF, Heiss WD (2005) Role of the contralateral inferior frontal gyrus in recovery of language function in post-stroke aphasia: a combined repetitive transcranial magnetic stimulation and positron emission tomography study. Stroke **36**:1759–1763.

Wolpe N, Moore JW, Rae CL, Rittman T, Altena E, Haggard P, Rowe JB (2014) The medial frontal-prefrontal network for altered awareness and control of action in corticobasal syndrome. Brain **137**:208–220.

Wong KF, Huk AC, Shadlen MN, Wang XJ (2007) Neural circuit dynamics underlying accumulation of time-varying evidence during perceptual decision making. Front Comp Neurosci **1**:6.

Woolgar A, Thompson R, Bor D, Duncan J (2011) Multi-voxel coding of stimuli, rules, and responses in human frontoparietal cortex. Neuroimage **56**:744–752.

Woollett K, Maguire EA (2011) Acquiring 'the Knowledge' of London's layout drives structural brain changes. Curr Biol **21**:2109–2114.

Wylie G, Allport A (2000) Task switching and the measurement of 'switch costs'. Psychol Res **63**:212–233.

Yamagata T, Nakayama Y, Tanji J, Hoshi E (2012) Distinct information representation and processing for goal-directed behavior in the dorsolateral and ventrolateral prefrontal cortex and the dorsal premotor cortex. J Neurosci **32**:12934–12949.

Yeterian EH, Pandya DN (2010) Fiber pathways and cortical connections of preoccipital areas in rhesus monkeys. J Comp Neurol **518**:3725–3751.

Young RM (1990) Mind, Brain and Adaptation. New York: Oxford University Press.

Young MP (1993) The organization of neural systems in the primate cerebral cortex. Proc Roy Soc Lond B **252**:13–18.

Young MP, Hilgetag CC, Scannell JW (2000) On imputing function to structure from the behavioural effects of brain lesions. Philos Trans R Soc Lond B Biol Sci **355**:147–161.

Zanto TP, Rubens MT, Thangavel A, Gazzaley A (2011) Causal role of the prefrontal cortex in top-down modulation of visual processing and working memory. Nat Neurosci **14**:656–661.

Zeidman P, Mullally SL, Maguire EA (2014) Constructing, Perceiving, and Maintaining Scenes: Hippocampal Activity and Connectivity. Cereb Cortex, Epub.

Zhang J, Rowe JB (2014) The neural signature of information regularity in temporally extended event sequences. Neuroimage **107C**:266–276.

Zhang J, Rowe JB (2015) The neural signature of information regularity in temporally extended event sequences. Neuroimage **107**:266–276.

Zhang J, Hughes LE, Rowe JB (2012) Selection and inhibition mechanisms for human voluntary action decisions. Neuroimage **63**:392–402.

Zhang J, Kriegeskorte N, Carlin JD, Rowe JB (2013) Choosing the rules: distinct and overlapping frontoparietal representations of task rules for perceptual decisions. J Neurosci **33**:11852–11862.

Zhou H, Desimone R (2011) Feature-based attention in the frontal eye field and area V4 during visual search. Neuron **70**:1205–1217.

Zilles K, Palomero-Gallagher N (2001) Cyto-, myelo-, and receptor architectonics of the human parietal cortex. Neuroimage **14**:S8–20.

Zwanenburg JJ, Hendrikse J, Visser F, Takahara T, Luijten PR (2010) Fluid attenuated inversion recovery (FLAIR) MRI at 7.0 Tesla: comparison with 1.5 and 3.0 Tesla. Eur Radiol **20**:915–922.

Index

Notes: Abbreviations used in the index are the same as in the List of Abbreviations.
Page numbers suffixed with 'b' refer to material in boxes, 'f' in figures and 't' in tables.

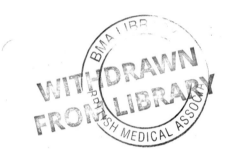